THIS TRANSFORMING
CYCLE A WORD

Commentary on the Readings for Sundays and Feast Days
of Cycle A of the Lectionary through 2020,
including full Scripture passages from
The Message: Catholic/Ecumenical Edition
by Eugene Peterson and William Griffin

ALICE CAMILLE

acta
PUBLICATIONS

THIS TRANSFORMING WORD, Cycle A
Commentary on the Readings for Sundays and Feast Days of Cycle A of the Lectionary through 2020, including full Scripture passages from *The Message: Catholic/Ecumenical Edition* by Eugene Peterson and William Griffin

Copyright © 2013 by Alice Camille

Edited by Gregory F. Augustine Pierce
Designed and typeset by Patricia Lynch, Harvest Graphics
Cover art © A Gleam of Glory, by Fr. Bob Gilroy, S.J. Courtesy of Trinity Stores, www.trinitystores.com, 800.699.4482

Published in association with the literary agency of Alive Communications, Inc., 7680 Goddard Street, Suite 200, Colorado Springs, CO 80920, www.alivecom.com.

ISBN: 978-0-87946-520-9
Library of Congress Number: 2013951605
Printed in the United States of America by United Graphics, Inc.
Year: 25 24 23 22 21 20 19 18 17 16 15 14 13
Printing: 15 14 13 12 11 10 9 8 7 6 5 4 3 2 First

CONTENTS

DEDICATION

In grateful memory of those who spoke a transforming word to me: Rev. Thomas F. Langan, Rev. Thomas R. Haney, Rev. Albert P. Vucinovich, and Francis Baur, OFM

ACKNOWLEDGMENTS

Most of this commentary breathed its first life as *Exploring the Sunday Readings* (Twenty-Third Publications) through the assistance of my long-time editors, Mary Carol Kendzia and Daniel Connors. This book achieved its present form, however, with a lot of help from my friends. Erin J. Boulton assembled the liturgical calendar projections and identified any future missing weeks amid the original reflections; when you find the stray moveable feast you're looking for, you can thank Erin for spotting it first! Evelyn Mautner inserted the complete Scripture passages from *The Message: Catholic/Ecumenical Edition* by Eugene Peterson and William Griffin (ACTA Publications) for your convenience, considerably livening up the readings with a fresh voice. Evelyn also did a great deal of editing you don't want to know about: just be grateful she did! My once-and-future collaborator, Paul Boudreau, handled the organization and final clean-up of the whole text as only a skilled liturgist and veteran preacher can. I thank God every day I have friends like these, and please consider them your friends too as you reap the benefits of their labor on these pages.

A NOTE FROM THE PUBLISHER

Alice Camille is a true treasure of the Catholic Church in the United States: a woman who can make the Scriptures come alive in new and exciting ways; a serious student of the Bible who understands how to use it effectively in catechesis and religious education; a lay person who tries to live out the kingdom of God in her daily life. Camille has been reflecting on the meaning of the Bible for committed Catholics for many years and was instrumental in reviewing the translation of the additional writings for *The Message: Catholic/Ecumenical Edition*. So, when ACTA Publications wanted to produce a new series of three books containing reflections on the readings for each of the Sundays and Feast Days of Cycles A, B, and C and include the translation of those readings from *The Message*, Alice Camille was our first (and only) choice.

First, a word about *The Message* by Eugene Peterson. Many Catholics and others have never heard of it, even though it has sold over 16 million copies in various editions. It is a compelling, fresh, challenging, and faith-filled translation of the Bible from the original languages into contemporary, idiomatic American English. Eugene Peterson is a Presbyterian minister, pastor, writer, speaker, poet, Bible scholar and translator. He specializes in what is called "paraphrasal" translation, which tries to reproduce the spirit of the original text rather than provide a literal translation of the words. Rev. Peterson did not include the additional writings of what some Jews and Protestants call the Apocrypha and Catholics and others call the Deuterocanonical books in the original version of *The Message*. Instead he recruited his friend and colleague, William Griffin, to translate these works in his same style. Griffin, a Catholic layman, writer, and translator, took his text from the *Nova Vulgata*, the revised and expanded version of the original Latin Vulgate that was approved for use by Catholics by Pope John Paul II in 1998. These additions were added to *The Message* in the biblical order expected by Catholics and published in 2013 as *The Message: Catholic/Ecumenical Edition*.

You may find the Scripture passages in this book jarring at first. Certainly, you will not hear this translation read at Mass. But they might provide new insights into overly familiar texts and help you think again about what they might have to say to people today—especially when accompanied by Camille's accessible yet erudite reflections.

We encourage you to try *This Transforming Word* for your own prayer and spiritual discernment as you prepare to preach (if you are the homilist) or listen (if you are a congregant) or discuss (if you belong to a small intentional group or community). Included in this book for Cycle A are the Sunday and Feast Day readings for the years 2014, 2017, and 2020. Separate books are available for Cycle B in 2015, 2018, and 2021 and for Cycle C in 2016, 2019, and 2022. If you would like to receive the complete readings for each Sunday from *The Message* at no charge, simply go to www.CatholicEcumenicalMessage.com and sign up to receive them by email.

To purchase a copy of *The Message: Catholic/Ecumenical Edition* by Eugene Peterson and William Griffin or books by Alice Camille, including *Invitation to Catholicism*, *Invitation to the Old and New Testament*, *Isaiah and the Kingdom of God*, *The Forgiveness Book*, *The Rosary*, and *Seven Last Words*, go to any seller of books or visit www.actapublications.com. If you have any questions or comments, please contact me at gpierce@actapublications.com.

Gregory F. Augustine Pierce
President and Co-Publisher
ACTA Publications
Chicago, Illinois

INTRODUCTION

"Use words truly and well. Don't stoop to cheap whining.
Then, but only then, you'll speak for me.
Let your words change them.
Don't change your words to suit them."
Jeremiah 15:19

Words, words, words. The world is choked with them, as Hamlet wearily lamented. But most of them don't amount to much. Thomas Merton agreed. After a short trip beyond the silence of his cloister at Gethsemani Abbey, Merton observed: "There is so much talking that goes on that is utterly useless."

We talk, text, and e-mail. Media shouts from every corner of the room and each bend in the road. Yet in the barrage of advertising and so-called reporting, little is actually communicated. "The world will little note, nor long remember what we say here." That sentence, from Abraham Lincoln, is a rare exception in a sea of forgettable phrases. What you and I say today will not only quickly disappear. It's a wonder if anyone hears us in the first place.

There is a cure for the endless, mindless, meaningless rant. Out of the silence, up from the deep, down from the heavens comes a transforming word that changes hearts—and *that* changes everything. This word transfigures because of its own remarkable metamorphosis: from cosmic eternal word to earthbound mortal flesh. This word shatters the barriers of time and needed to be spoken only once. Now it lives and moves and has being in those who hear it and reply.

This book is for those who are listening and hope to respond. Each Sunday and feast of the church year, the transforming word echoes its challenge. We hear it through stories of patriarchs and matriarchs who dare to embark in new directions trailing an untested divinity. It shouts in the oracles of wild prophets madly in love with an unlikely future. It sings in psalms and canticles. It beckons in Lady Wisdom. It invites us to come and see in gospels, and to repent and believe in letters of instruction. Creation testifies to it. Apocalypse mystically reveals it. And all the while this longing word is calling through the centuries, eternity waits in hushed silence for the freely rendered human response. Yours. Mine. Everybody's.

ADVENT

FIRST SUNDAY OF ADVENT

FIRST READING » ISAIAH 2:1-5

The Message Isaiah got regarding Judah and Jerusalem:
There's a day coming
    when the mountain of God's House
Will be The Mountain—
    solid, towering over all mountains.
All nations will river toward it,
    people from all over set out for it.
They'll say, "Come,
    let's climb God's Mountain,
    go to the House of the God of Jacob.
He'll show us the way he works
    so we can live the way we're made."
Zion's the source of the revelation.
    God's Message comes from Jerusalem.
He'll settle things fairly between nations.
    He'll make things right between many peoples.
They'll turn their swords into shovels,
    their spears into hoes.
No more will nation fight nation;
    they won't play war anymore.
Come, family of Jacob,
    let's live in the light of God.

A Church year ends; another begins. And we begin on a peaceful note, with the prophet's vision of a world without war. Oh, for a world in which the last bomb's metal had been melted down for peacetime purposes!

Instead, we live in a world in which our bombs can hardly be safely contained, even when they are not being hurled at an enemy. We live at a time when minefields sown from wars long ended continue the horror of war indefinitely. We live in an age where children cannot forget, and their parents do not dare to remember. War has seeped into the structure of our world, and it flows in our veins, poisoning any hope of peace. We believe in war. We believe it is necessary. And because we put our faith in war, there will be more of it.

In a corner of our warrior hearts, Isaiah's vision of a world beyond war waits up for us. Isaiah leaves the light on, and hopes for company.

Under what conditions do you think war is "necessary"?

SECOND READING » ROMANS 13:11-14

But make sure that you don't get so absorbed and exhausted in taking care of all your day-by-day obligations that you lose track of the time and doze off, oblivious to God. The night is about over, dawn is about to break. Be up and awake to what God is doing! God is putting the finishing touches on the salvation work he began when we first believed. We can't afford to waste a minute, must not squander these precious daylight hours in frivolity and indulgence, in sleeping around and dissipation, in bickering and grabbing everything in sight. Get out of bed and get dressed! Don't loiter and linger, waiting until the very last minute. Dress yourselves in Christ, and be up and about!

Okay, for the sake of argument, say that you're willing to make an ADVENT resolution this year, just to be novel. For a mere four weeks — thank God, Advent is shorter than Lent! — you are willing to cast off deeds of darkness and put on the armor of light. So you run down the checklist of Paul's "deeds of darkness" (carousing, drunkenness, sexual excess, quarreling, jealousy) and you find you can go the distance on at least four of these easily enough. It's nobody's business which one has you biting your nails.

But even after you sign off on the deeds of darkness, there is still this business about putting on the light. That may be an even greater challenge, and it has no list (at least in this short passage) to go by. So be creative. Get together with a close friend or two and put on some Christmas lights that require no juice from the electric company. Check out parish or community efforts to assist those in need. Sing in a choir. Give freely. Laugh often. Love children. Invite someone to church. Forgive an enemy.

> **What deeds of darkness are you being invited to surrender?**
> **What armor of light might you take on at this time?**

GOSPEL » MATTHEW 24:37-44

"The Arrival of the Son of Man will take place in times like Noah's. Before the great flood everyone was carrying on as usual, having a good time right up to the day Noah boarded the ark. They knew nothing—until the flood hit and swept everything away.

"The Son of Man's Arrival will be like that: Two men will be working in the field—one will be taken, one left behind; two women will be grinding at the mill—one will be taken, one left behind. So stay awake, alert. You have no idea what day your Master will show up. But you do know this: You know that if the homeowner had known what time of night the burglar would arrive, he would have been there with his dogs to prevent the break-in. Be vigilant just like that. You have no idea when the Son of Man is going to show up.

We know for sure that Santa Claus is coming to town; and so is Snoopy, Frosty, the Grinch, Rudolph, and more seasonal visitors than we may care to name. We also know that Jesus is coming, but he doesn't advertise his arrival as relentlessly as these others so we aren't sure quite when. Will he arrive in time for the holidays? too late to stop the next war? too soon for me to acquire all the things I'd like to have in this world?

This is the Advent from which the season takes it name. Jesus is coming, and his advent is the one all these modern myths seek to recreate. Will Charlie Brown find the real meaning of Christmas? Only with a Scripture-quoting friend like Linus. Will the Grinch get a life? Only if he learns to share. Will Jimmy Stewart learn that it's a wonderful life? Only if he opens his eyes to the world he's always had. Jesus is coming all the time, but we won't know it if we refuse to change. That is the purpose of Advent, to give us fair notice that it's time to take time seriously.

For whom or what are you waiting?

WE RESPOND

Be a friend like Linus to someone who has not heard the message of the story of Bethlehem. Share your faith with someone who is still waiting for love to come.

The night is about over,
dawn is about to break.
Be up and awake to what God is doing!

SECOND SUNDAY OF ADVENT

.... The Wolf and the Lamb

FIRST READING » ISAIAH 11:1-10

A green Shoot will sprout from Jesse's stump,
*   from his roots a budding Branch.*
The life-giving Spirit of GOD will hover over him,
*   the Spirit that brings wisdom and understanding,*
The Spirit that gives direction and builds strength,
*   the Spirit that instills knowledge and Fear-of-GOD.*
Fear-of-GOD
*   will be all his joy and delight.*
He won't judge by appearances,
*   won't decide on the basis of hearsay.*
He'll judge the needy by what is right,
*   render decisions on earth's poor with justice.*
His words will bring everyone to awed attention.
*   A mere breath from his lips will topple the wicked.*
Each morning he'll pull on sturdy work clothes and boots,
*   and build righteousness and faithfulness in the land.*
The wolf will romp with the lamb,
*   the leopard sleep with the kid.*
Calf and lion will eat from the same trough,
*   and a little child will tend them.*
Cow and bear will graze the same pasture,
*   their calves and cubs grow up together,*
*   and the lion eat straw like the ox.*
The nursing child will crawl over rattlesnake dens,
*   the toddler stick his hand down the hole of a serpent.*
Neither animal nor human will hurt or kill
*   on my holy mountain.*
The whole earth will be brimming with knowing God-Alive,
*   a living knowledge of God ocean-deep, ocean-wide.*
On that day, Jesse's Root will be raised high, posted as a rallying banner for the
peoples. The nations will all come to him. His headquarters will be glorious.

Jesus is coming, the recent joke warns; everybody look busy! The punch line reveals our confusion about the Second Coming. What does it really mean to say "Jesus is coming?"

Prophecy tells us that the son of justice is the one we are expecting. He is inspired with what we have come to call the gifts of the Spirit: wisdom, understanding, counsel, strength, knowledge and fear of the Lord. (Piety is added in some transla-

THIS TRANSFORMING WORD

tions.) He brings justice for the poor, and judgment for the wicked. A time of peace attends his arrival. In that time, the powerful and the vulnerable will learn to live together in harmony.

Whenever prophets talk like this, about a world so different from the one we live in, a great many people just sigh and pray for kingdom come. Meanwhile, however, it's business as usual. The poor are ignored, or blamed, while the wicked get on quite well. Wars are fought for profit, and the powerful take advantage of the weak. Someday, it is believed, when Jesus blows the whistle, things will change....

This, however, is not what prophecy means or what the church holds true. If Jesus is coming, everybody ought to get busy, in earnest, being children of justice. We need to seek liberty for the poor and challenge the wicked. We need to be people of peace who protect the vulnerable. We should give people reason to suspect that Jesus is coming.

> **Do people know that "Jesus is coming" by the way you use power, material goods, and in your treatment of others?**

SECOND READING » ROMANS 15:4-9

That's exactly what Jesus did. He didn't make it easy for himself by avoiding people's troubles, but waded right in and helped out. "I took on the troubles of the troubled," is the way Scripture puts it. Even if it was written in Scripture long ago, you can be sure it's written for us. God wants the combination of his steady, constant calling and warm, personal counsel in Scripture to come to characterize us, keeping us alert for whatever he will do next. May our dependably steady and warmly personal God develop maturity in you so that you get along with each other as well as Jesus gets along with us all. Then we'll be a choir—not our voices only, but our very lives singing in harmony in a stunning anthem to the God and Father of our Master Jesus!

So reach out and welcome one another to God's glory. Jesus did it; now you do it! Jesus, staying true to God's purposes, reached out in a special way to the Jewish insiders so that the old ancestral promises would come true for them. As a result, the non-Jewish outsiders have been able to experience mercy and to show appreciation to God. Just think of all the Scriptures that will come true in what we do! For instance:

Then I'll join outsiders in a hymn-sing;
I'll sing to your name!
And this one:
Outsiders and insiders, rejoice together!
And again:
People of all nations, celebrate God!
All colors and races, give hearty praise!
And Isaiah's word:
There's the root of our ancestor Jesse,

breaking through the earth and growing tree tall,
Tall enough for everyone everywhere to see and take hope!

Oh! May the God of green hope fill you up with joy, fill you up with peace, so that your believing lives, filled with the life-giving energy of the Holy Spirit, will brim over with hope!

The late Cardinal Bernardin of Chicago worried about the lack of harmony in the modern church. Progressive Catholics who embraced the reforms of the Second Vatican Council seemed determined to take apart, brick by brick, the church that conservative Catholics had always revered. Not only did Bernardin sense the tension between the two groups, but he also observed the lack of respect for the values and perspectives of the other side. The unity that Christ seeks for the church seemed threatened by the widening gulf.

The tension between liberal and conservative Catholics is real, but it's not the first time the church has faced division, even outright hostility, within its ranks. The original factions were Jewish and Gentile Christians who had different ideas about what it meant to embrace the Gospel. Did the Jewish believer in Jesus remain within the covenant of Moses or go beyond it? Did the Gentile believer need to be circumcised and embrace the Law? Paul urged harmony, not uniformity, among the conflicted communities. The glory of God can be served in more ways than one.

> **How do you communicate with those whose spirituality**
> **or theology differs from your own?**

GOSPEL » MATTHEW 3:1-12

While Jesus was living in the Galilean hills, John, called "the Baptizer," was preaching in the desert country of Judea. His message was simple and austere, like his desert surroundings:
"Change your life. God's kingdom is here."
John and his message were authorized by Isaiah's prophecy:
Thunder in the desert!
Prepare for God's arrival!
Make the road smooth and straight!
John dressed in a camel-hair habit tied at the waist by a leather strap. He lived on a diet of locusts and wild field honey. People poured out of Jerusalem, Judea, and the Jordanian countryside to hear and see him in action. There at the Jordan River those who came to confess their sins were baptized into a changed life.
When John realized that a lot of Pharisees and Sadducees were showing up for a baptismal experience because it was becoming the popular thing to do, he exploded: "Brood of snakes! What do you think you're doing slithering down here to the river? Do you think a little water on your snakeskins is going to make any difference? It's your life that must change, not your skin! And don't think you

can pull rank by claiming Abraham as father. Being a descendant of Abraham is neither here nor there. Descendants of Abraham are a dime a dozen. What counts is your life. Is it green and blossoming? Because if it's deadwood, it goes on the fire.

"I'm baptizing you here in the river, turning your old life in for a kingdom life. The real action comes next: The main character in this drama—compared to him I'm a mere stagehand—will ignite the kingdom life within you, a fire within you, the Holy Spirit within you, changing you from the inside out. He's going to clean house—make a clean sweep of your lives. He'll place everything true in its proper place before God; everything false he'll put out with the trash to be burned."

If Jesus is the Lamb of God, John the Baptist is the wolf. He stands alone as an inter-testamental figure, more like the prophets of the Hebrew scriptures than the evangelists of Christianity. There is no evidence that he ever became a disciple of Jesus. In fact, the evidence points to his retaining his own following up to the time of his execution. He is the finger of God, pointing to the new revelation, but he stands apart from it, howling out warnings about the scourge to come.

John was no prophet of gentle messages, of love and forgiveness. He came to drown the devil in the flesh, and raise up a nation of spirit prepared to meet its Maker. He lived in the wild, dressed and ate like a wild man. He hurled untamed words at the powerful people of his day, and they trembled. He was raw authority, and many people walked into the Jordan, convinced by his charisma or afraid of his warnings. In the end, the wolf of God would decrease, as the Lamb would increase. For only a brief hour, they browsed together, sharing the message, "The reign of God is at hand."

> Name figures in Christianity today like John the Baptist.
> Do you find them appealing?

WE RESPOND

Be a wolf in faith: live your convictions unflinchingly and publicly. Be a lamb: bring peace, patience, and the willingness to dialogue with those who see the vision of church differently than you do.

THIRD SUNDAY OF ADVENT

....Must We Wait for Another?

FIRST READING » ISAIAH 35:1-6, 10

Wilderness and desert will sing joyously,
*   the badlands will celebrate and flower—*
Like the crocus in spring, bursting into blossom,
*   a symphony of song and color.*
Mountain glories of Lebanon—a gift.
*   Awesome Carmel, stunning Sharon—gifts.*
God's resplendent glory, fully on display.
*   God awesome, God majestic.*
Energize the limp hands,
*   strengthen the rubbery knees*
Tell fearful souls,
*   "Courage! Take heart!*
God is here, right here,
*   on his way to put things right*
And redress all wrongs.
*   He's on his way! He'll save you!"*
Blind eyes will be opened,
*   deaf ears unstopped,*
Lame men and women will leap like deer,
*   the voiceless break into song.*
Springs of water will burst out in the wilderness,
*   streams flow in the desert.*
Hot sands will become a cool oasis,
*   thirsty ground a splashing fountain.*
Even lowly jackals will have water to drink,
*   and barren grasslands flourish richly.*
There will be a highway
*   called the Holy Road.*
No one rude or rebellious
*   is permitted on this road.*
It's for God's people exclusively—
*   impossible to get lost on this road.*
*   Not even fools can get lost on it.*
No lions on this road,
*   no dangerous wild animals—*
Nothing and no one dangerous or threatening.
*   Only the redeemed will walk on it.*

The people God has ransomed
  will come back on this road.
They'll sing as they make their way home to Zion,
  unfading halos of joy encircling their heads,
Welcomed home with gifts of joy and gladness
  as all sorrows and sighs scurry into the night.

How patient are you? Patient enough to wait for the desert to burst into flowers? For shaking hands to be stilled, for weak knees to be strong again? Patient enough to wait for the blind to see, the deaf to hear, the lame to run, the mute to sing? That kind of patience is a divine quality. For most of us, these things are too wonderful to imagine, much less to expect.

The prophecy to the people of God in exile is that they will return home to their land, a thing as impossible to dream of as a blooming desert. Still the message delivered to the door of God's people is always the same: God will save you. From Egypt, from Babylon, from your sins and yourselves, God will save you. To those who believe, the desert is a garden waiting to awaken. No situation in life is barren, no defeat final. No matter the depth to which we have fallen, God is prepared to raise us up. When our hearts are most frightened, we can lean on this word.

> **What desert-like experiences in your life**
> **turned out to be hidden fields of flowers?**

SECOND READING » JAMES 5:7-10

Meanwhile, friends, wait patiently for the Master's Arrival. You see farmers do this all the time, waiting for their valuable crops to mature, patiently letting the rain do its slow but sure work. Be patient like that. Stay steady and strong. The Master could arrive at any time.

Friends, don't complain about each other. A far greater complaint could be lodged against you, you know. The Judge is standing just around the corner.

Take the old prophets as your mentors. They put up with anything, went through everything, and never once quit, all the time honoring God. What a gift life is to those who stay the course! You've heard, of course, of Job's staying power, and you know how God brought it all together for him at the end. That's because God cares, cares right down to the last detail.

I've never been a farmer, though I've passed through the heartland enough to admire the endless toil of those who plow the land. I am a gardener, though, and with my humble patch of soil I've learned a lot about patience. I've learned about waiting on the seed, carrying the water, praying for the sun, and coddling the tiny life that emerges in its own time. I've learned about mystery and I've learned about trust. I've learned not to give up when a plant looks dead and plays dead. Life clings fiercely to life, and if there is the smallest bit of encouragement, most things will go on living despite the odds.

Parents learn these same lessons from their children, and we all learn these lessons from living the life of faith. The kingdom is the seed that Jesus planted, and through prayer and fidelity we nurture a patch of the kingdom in our own lives. Though we may feel we're losing, that the odds are stacked against the spiritual life, we can turn the corner into outright holiness in a heartbeat. We support one another in patience, prayer, and fidelity to values through the long winters of silence and barrenness. And then, just when we think the ground of our hearts will produce no yield, love emerges into the light.

Who supports you in faithfulness to prayer and Christian values?

GOSPEL » MATTHEW 11:2-11

John, meanwhile, had been locked up in prison. When he got wind of what Jesus was doing, he sent his own disciples to ask, "Are you the One we've been expecting, or are we still waiting?"

Jesus told them, "Go back and tell John what's going on:

The blind see,
The lame walk,
Lepers are cleansed,
The deaf hear,
The dead are raised,
The wretched of the earth learn that God is on their side.

"Is this what you were expecting? Then count yourselves most blessed!"

When John's disciples left to report, Jesus started talking to the crowd about John. "What did you expect when you went out to see him in the wild? A weekend camper? Hardly. What then? A sheik in silk pajamas? Not in the wilderness, not by a long shot. What then? A prophet? That's right, a prophet! Probably the best prophet you'll ever hear. He is the prophet that Malachi announced when he wrote, 'I'm sending my prophet ahead of you, to make the road smooth for you.'

"Let me tell you what's going on here: No one in history surpasses John the Baptizer; but in the kingdom he prepared you for, the lowliest person is ahead of him. For a long time now people have tried to force themselves into God's kingdom. But if you read the books of the Prophets and God's Law closely, you will see them culminate in John, teaming up with him in preparing the way for the Messiah of the kingdom. Looked at in this way, John is the 'Elijah' you've all been expecting to arrive and introduce the Messiah."

No one ever born was greater than John the Baptist, by Jesus' own admission. And yet even John found it hard to keep patience while Jesus wandered through the first season of his ministry. From prison, John heard the reports of Jesus teaching, healing, gathering crowds to hear the word of God. He didn't hear what he had expected: Jesus proclaiming his kingship, claiming Jerusalem as his capitol, denouncing the

Romans or the Temple leaders, and "laying the ax to the root of the tree," once and for all. John had preached the coming destruction, and Jesus seemed, well, more *lamb* than *God*. It was hard for John not to be disappointed, and to wonder for a moment if he had misread Jesus altogether.

Jesus doesn't chide John for lacking faith. Instead, he quotes prophecy to reassure John that God's time of favor has arrived. Then Jesus reminds the crowds that John's greatness in history is surpassed by anyone who arrives at an understanding of the kingdom through faith. If we wait for no other, if we cast our lot with Jesus, we find that we do not have to get to the kingdom at all. The kingdom arrives in us. What circumstances make you impatient? How far might you be willing to follow Jesus and wait for his kingdom?

WE RESPOND

Name the deserts, the blindnesses and crippled areas of your life where new life is needed. Pray for the seed of that life to be planted in you, and resolve to encourage that life in every way.

*"John is the 'Elijah' you've all been expecting
to arrive and introduce the Messiah."*

FOURTH SUNDAY OF ADVENT

FIRST READING » ISAIAH 7:10-14

God spoke again to Ahaz. This time he said, "Ask for a sign from your God. Ask anything. Be extravagant. Ask for the moon!"

But Ahaz said, "I'd never do that. I'd never make demands like that on God!"

So Isaiah told him, "Then listen to this, government of David! It's bad enough that you make people tired with your pious, timid hypocrisies, but now you're making God tired. So the Master is going to give you a sign anyway. Watch for this: A girl who is presently a virgin will get pregnant. She'll bear a son and name him Immanuel (God-With-Us). By the time the child is twelve years old, able to make moral decisions, the threat of war will be over. Relax, those two kings that have you so worried will be out of the picture. But also be warned: God will bring on you and your people and your government a judgment worse than anything since the time the kingdom split, when Ephraim left Judah. The king of Assyria is coming!"

Ahaz was a messy sort of king—though in the history of kings, that makes him pretty normal. When neighboring kingdoms urged alliances on Israel, Isaiah cautioned Ahaz to remain politically neutral. But the king refused, inviting the Assyrians into his country, and Israel became a vassal state to Assyria and its gods.

Ahaz had his chance to do it right, complete with signs from God as to how to proceed. But he chose to ignore all divine indicators, including God's prophet speaking directly into his life, in favor of his own judgment. This makes him very familiar to us, since we also lead rather messy lives in which our own judgment drags us in directions from which all of God's angels would warn us away. Signs, messengers, even the prophetic witness of friends and family are useless to us if we insist on figuring things out in reasonable, logical fashion. Logic dictated that Ahaz make nice with Assyria, which was by far the more powerful nation. But that logical decision led a nation into idolatry and sin. Making the reasonable compromise might seem to us to be the only sensible thing to do; but there are demons lurking in the swamp of mere reason. As anti-intellectual as it sounds, as foolish as it may appear in the eyes of the world, sometimes we have to discern the signs and attend to the prophets that are given to us.

Who are the prophets who speak to your life?
What signs have been given to you to discern your way?

SECOND READING » ROMANS 1:1-7

I, Paul, am a devoted slave of Jesus Christ on assignment, authorized as an apostle to proclaim God's words and acts. I write this letter to all the believers in Rome, God's friends.

*The sacred writings contain preliminary reports by the prophets on God's
Son. His descent from David roots him in history; his unique identity as Son of
God was shown by the Spirit when Jesus was raised from the dead, setting him
apart as the Messiah, our Master. Through him we received both the generous
gift of his life and the urgent task of passing it on to others who receive it by
entering into obedient trust in Jesus. You are who you are through this gift and
call of Jesus Christ! And I greet you now with all the generosity of God our
Father and our Master Jesus, the Messiah.*

**Recently I issued invitations for a party, inviting friends to "a gathering of holy
people."** When people called to RSVP, they each admitted, "I'll come. But I don't really think I belong in such a gathering." Why are we so sure we aren't holy people? Is
it because we're so aware of ourselves as sinners? The two states, of course, are not
mutually exclusive. If we understand the nature of humanity, and sin, we know that
you can't have one without the other. And yet we are "called to holiness"—is this a
call to utter frustration? I can't believe this is a game God is playing with us: doomed
to sin, helpless to be holy. I have to believe, rather, that holiness is possible, or we
wouldn't be called to it.

Holiness isn't about displays of piety, or that halo effect the portrait saints reveal
to us. Holiness is the capacity to reflect God's light in the world. My friends have
each done that for me, shown me a bit more of the divine face in their responsive-
ness to Gospel justice, charity, and fidelity. The quiet heroism of their lives—loving
their spouses, raising their children, not grasping for material success over spiritual
gain—is a constant source of inspiration for me. Even when they falter, in their confusion they raise holy questions: what is God asking me to do? What is right, and
not only beneficial to me? The road to holiness is closer to the path we're walking on
than we think. Let us be light.

**How do you reflect God's light into the world?
What prevents you from revealing more of that light?**

GOSPEL » MATTHEW 1:18-24

*The birth of Jesus took place like this. His mother, Mary, was engaged to be
married to Joseph. Before they came to the marriage bed, Joseph discovered
she was pregnant. (It was by the Holy Spirit, but he didn't know that.) Joseph,
chagrined but noble, determined to take care of things quietly so Mary would not
be disgraced.*

*While he was trying to figure a way out, he had a dream. God's angel
spoke in the dream: "Joseph, son of David, don't hesitate to get married. Mary's
pregnancy is Spirit-conceived. God's Holy Spirit has made her pregnant. She will
bring a son to birth, and when she does, you, Joseph, will name him Jesus—'God
saves'—because he will save his people from their sins." This would bring the
prophet's embryonic sermon to full term:*
Watch for this—a virgin will get pregnant and bear a son;

They will name him Immanuel (Hebrew for "God is with us").

Then Joseph woke up. He did exactly what God's angel commanded in the dream: He married Mary. But he did not consummate the marriage until she had the baby. He named the baby Jesus.

Joseph is a fascinating character in the story of salvation. He only appears in two of the gospels, and even in Matthew, his largest appearance, he has no speaking part. A silent man given a humble role who accepts his task and then disappears from the story on cue—what a fellow, this Joseph! We have no idea what happens to him after Jesus' twelfth year. His role is to bring the savior into his majority, as father-protector. The man himself vanishes behind his vocation.

All we do know of Joseph is that he says yes to his mission. He says yes to a dream he had about an angel. The angel in the dream tells him a thing no self-respecting man would believe, and yet it is enough for Joseph. He's a man of remarkable faith, obedient to dreams, faithful under adversity. How absurd it might have seemed to the people of Nazareth, that a man who worked with his hands could be swayed by something so insubstantial! Yet a man who can look at a piece of wood and envision the serviceable thing it might become under skilled hands understood how God might shape his life for a purpose to which he might be blind. Joseph displayed the same mute trust that wood has in the carpenter's hands. And out of that trust, God built a bridge to heaven.

Merry Christmas.

> **How does the figure of Joseph challenge you
> in your attention to God's call in your own life?**

WE RESPOND

Be like wood in the carpenter's hands. Pray this Christmas that God might shape your life for a holy purpose. Even if you can't see the direction God is leading you, surrender more fully to signs, dreams, prophets and angels that may emerge on your path. If you can't see them, pray to be given eyes to see and ears to hear.

*You are who you are
through this gift and call of Jesus Christ!*

CHRISTMAS SEASON

CHRISTMAS DAY

.... In the Beginning

FIRST READING » ISAIAH 52:7-10

How beautiful on the mountains
  are the feet of the messenger bringing good news,
Breaking the news that all's well,
  proclaiming good times, announcing salvation,
  telling Zion, "Your God reigns!"
Voices! Listen! Your scouts are shouting, thunderclap shouts,
  shouting in joyful unison.
They see with their own eyes
  God coming back to Zion.
Break into song! Boom it out, ruins of Jerusalem:
  "God has comforted his people!
  He's redeemed Jerusalem!"
God has rolled up his sleeves.
  All the nations can see his holy, muscled arm.
Everyone, from one end of the earth to the other,
  sees him at work, doing his salvation work.

In the beginning, there was nothing but beauty, peace, and good news. And there was no need for salvation, because there was nothing to be saved from. Death didn't exist, evil and suffering hadn't been invented. But then came human greed, selfishness, egotism, and the lust for power, all in the package called original sin. We often use *pride* as the shorthand for this sin, which encompasses a hornet's nest of failures to love as we were intended to love. Healthy pride comes in small servings; but if it grows out of bounds like a cancer, pride hardens the heart, isolates us from others, convinces us we're the center of the universe, and makes us unwilling to bow before any authority, including our Maker. This puts us in need of salvation, big-time. Now we need to be saved from ourselves.

In the beginning things were really good. Then we altered the design and the world started to suffer. This is why we long to hear the sound of those beautiful feet approaching, bringing good news to this broken planet that long ago lost its peace.

To what sources do you turn for good news?

SECOND READING » HEBREWS 1:1-6

Going through a long line of prophets, God has been addressing our ancestors in different ways for centuries. Recently he spoke to us directly through his Son. By

his Son, God created the world in the beginning, and it will all belong to the Son at the end. This Son perfectly mirrors God, and is stamped with God's nature. He holds everything together by what he says—powerful words!

After he finished the sacrifice for sins, the Son took his honored place high in the heavens right alongside God, far higher than any angel in rank and rule. Did God ever say to an angel, "You're my Son; today I celebrate you" or "I'm his Father, he's my Son"? When he presents his honored Son to the world, he says, "All angels must worship him."

Today we celebrate new life, because today we hear the sound of beautiful feet running, leaping joyfully in a great dance of good news. God's saving power has been felt in the world before—through events in the lives of Abraham and Moses and David, to name a few. And God's life-giving word has been spoken into the world before by folks like Isaiah and Jeremiah and the rest of the prophets. But the divine power and the word of life have never been felt and heard like this before. What comes into the world in the person of Jesus is utterly new.

The Incarnation of Jesus Christ makes the angels in heaven bow down. We can't fully understand the mystery of incarnation, and we've never seen angels or heaven for that matter. But we grasp from this image the awareness that something profound and wonderful happens as a result of this birth, something that makes a difference on earth as it does in heaven. We talk in the language of children as we describe this event: gates of heaven swinging open, while the barrier of sin and death is finally shattered. Limits are overcome, endings become new beginnings, all because a child is born for us.

> **When have you experienced a known barrier suddenly lifted for you?**

GOSPEL » JOHN 1:1-18

The Word was first,
the Word present to God,
*   God present to the Word.*
The Word was God,
*   in readiness for God from day one.*
Everything was created through him;
*   nothing—not one thing!—*
*   came into being without him.*
What came into existence was Life,
*   and the Life was Light to live by.*
The Life-Light blazed out of the darkness;
*   the darkness couldn't put it out.*

There once was a man, his name John, sent by God to point out the way to the Life-Light. He came to show everyone where to look, who to believe in. John was not himself the Light; he was there to show the way to the Light.

The Life-Light was the real thing:
Every person entering Life
he brings into Light.
He was in the world,
the world was there through him,
and yet the world didn't even notice.
He came to his own people,
but they didn't want him.
But whoever did want him,
who believed he was who he claimed
and would do what he said,
He made to be their true selves,
their child-of-God selves.
These are the God-begotten,
not blood-begotten,
not flesh-begotten,
not sex-begotten.
The Word became flesh and blood,
and moved into the neighborhood.
We saw the glory with our own eyes,
the one-of-a-kind glory,
like Father, like Son,
Generous inside and out,
true from start to finish.

John pointed him out and called, "This is the One! The One I told you was coming after me but in fact was ahead of me. He has always been ahead of me, has always had the first word."
We all live off his generous bounty,
gift after gift after gift.
We got the basics from Moses,
and then this exuberant giving and receiving,
This endless knowing and understanding—
all this came through Jesus, the Messiah.
No one has ever seen God,
not so much as a glimpse.
This one-of-a-kind God-Expression,
who exists at the very heart of the Father,
has made him plain as day.

The Bible famously opens with the phrase, "In the beginning..." This is why John the gospel writer chooses to start his story of Jesus with the same phrase. John reminds us of the creation story, but he goes back even further to the time-before-time when there was yet to be a world at all. In the beginning, before light, before day and night, before land and water and fish and birds and animals and human beings, there was only God, Being Itself. And dwelling within God and indistinguishable from God was the divine Word. When this Word was released, everything came into being. The Word is God, and the Word is also life.

John wants us to understand that the Word came into the world twice: once to create everything, and the second time to recreate it, to usher in a new heavens and a new earth, where justice and peace could at last reside. We might say there are two "beginnings," two releases of divine life for our sake. The second one we call Merry Christmas.

What does our present world want for Christmas, most of all?

WE RESPOND

Commit yourself once more to the cause of justice and peace. Cultivate these blessed conditions within your own heart, then practice sharing them with your family, neighbors, co-workers, and strangers.

We got the basics from Moses,
*   and then this exuberant giving and receiving,*
This endless knowing and understanding—
*   all this came through Jesus, the Messiah.*

THE HOLY FAMILY

FIRST READING » SIRACH 3: 2-6, 12-14

Yes, you children, listen to the advice of your parents. Follow it and you'll be saved. Parents should be honored and respected by their children. Honor your mother and father and God will wipe out your past sins; he'll help you deal with the occasions of present sins; he'll hear your daily prayer. Honor your mother and it's like putting money in the bank. Honor your father and your own children will honor you. Your prayers will be answered. You'll live a longer life. Obey your father and your mother will rest well.

Child, support your father in his old age; don't do something that will make him sad. If he shows signs of senility, give him a pass. Don't turn from him in his last days. Caring for a father won't go unnoticed. If your mother lashes out, give her some space. Your reputation will increase. In the day of trial you'll be remembered and your sins will melt like ice in the sun.

Today we celebrate the Holy Family. Not the perfect family, but the holy family. This is good, because most of us don't come from perfect families, nor are we very good about building perfect families ourselves. Holy families are characterized by the virtues Sirach speaks of: honoring its members, respecting authority, comforting one another, caring for and protecting the weak, and kindness above all. If kindness is not available in our families, we will search for it in vain in our society.

Most families are ragged around the edges. They have their histories of pain, broken pieces, problematic personalities. They recount their losses in the deep wounds of the heart. They also have their shared triumphs and happy memories, built on the efforts of those who understand the value of fidelity and forgiveness. Holy families don't just happen; it's not a simple matter of chemistry. Holy families are built on faith, hope, and love, like everything else that lasts. And as Jean Vanier, the founder of the L'Arche communities has written, at the center of every successful relationship is the mystery of forgiveness. Without respect for this mystery, even a family can be reduced to just a group of people.

> **How do you contribute to the holiness of your family or community by your commitment to faith, hope, love, and forgiveness?**

SECOND READING » COLOSSIANS 3:12-21

So, chosen by God for this new life of love, dress in the wardrobe God picked out for you: compassion, kindness, humility, quiet strength, discipline. Be even-tempered, content with second place, quick to forgive an offense. Forgive as quickly and completely as the Master forgave you. And regardless of what else you put on, wear love. It's your basic, all-purpose garment. Never be without it.

Let the peace of Christ keep you in tune with each other, in step with each other. None of this going off and doing your own thing. And cultivate thankfulness. Let the Word of Christ—the Message—have the run of the house. Give it plenty of room in your lives. Instruct and direct one another using good common sense. And sing, sing your hearts out to God! Let every detail in your lives—words, actions, whatever—be done in the name of the Master, Jesus, thanking God the Father every step of the way.

Wives, understand and support your husbands by submitting to them in ways that honor the Master.

Husbands, go all out in love for your wives. Don't take advantage of them.

Children, do what your parents tell you. This delights the Master no end.

Parents, don't come down too hard on your children or you'll crush their spirits.

Paul gives us another list of virtues to consider as we reflect our call to be the "holy and beloved" of God. Patience and forbearance make an appearance here, as well as peace and thankfulness. It's interesting to note that psychologists call thankfulness, or the ability to be grateful, one of the signs of mental wellness. Those who cannot be grateful are on the road to mental illness. Paul advises that we allow our gratefulness to burst forth into song, like people in musicals do who cannot keep their passions to themselves. A woman once told me of a dream she had of waltzing with Jesus by the side of the ocean. Our fervor should be this spontaneous and lyrical, since it is great good news that we carry in our hearts.

It may be hard to square this image of proclaiming our passion with the dull regulations of submission and obedience that follow. As with the injunctions in Sirach, we have to expand our notions of love and respect to include all the members of a family or community—and not get locked into a hierarchy of submission that reflects earlier presuppositions about the way things are supposed to be. Let's give the Holy Spirit room to breathe, shall we? Love and respect, an absence of bitterness and nagging, are good ideas across the spectrum of husband and wife, parents and children. Losing heart comes naturally to any oppressed member of a family. The word of Christ, rich as it is, calls us to lift up the lowly member and to make the last ever first.

Who in your family or community may be losing heart?
Brainstorm ways to lift that person or people up.

GOSPEL » MATTHEW 2:13-15, 19-23

After the scholars were gone, God's angel showed up again in Joseph's dream and commanded, "Get up. Take the child and his mother and flee to Egypt. Stay until further notice. Herod is on the hunt for this child, and wants to kill him."

Joseph obeyed. He got up, took the child and his mother under cover of darkness. They were out of town and well on their way by daylight. They lived in Egypt until Herod's death. This Egyptian exile fulfilled what Hosea had preached: "I called my son out of Egypt."

Later, when Herod died, God's angel appeared in a dream to Joseph in Egypt: "Up, take the child and his mother and return to Israel. All those out to murder the child are dead."

Joseph obeyed. He got up, took the child and his mother, and reentered Israel. When he heard, though, that Archelaus had succeeded his father, Herod, as king in Judea, he was afraid to go there. But then Joseph was directed in a dream to go to the hills of Galilee. On arrival, he settled in the village of Nazareth. This move was a fulfillment of the prophetic words, "He shall be called a Nazarene."

Holy families, we've said, are not perfect families. Matthew's story of Joseph and his family is modeled on an earlier story of another Joseph and his far-from-perfect family in the book of Genesis. In Genesis 37-50, we hear about the dreamer who listened to his dreams and paid a high price for that, going down into Egypt as a slave at the hands of his brothers. Still God raised him up through the power of dreams to become one of the most exalted figures in the land. Just as Israel was drawn into Egypt with Joseph, so too would the nation be restored to their land by the hand of God.

The story of Joseph and Mary echoes that earlier journey, as Joseph's dreams guide his family to flee like refugees into that old, unfriendly territory, and then to return to their land by the will of God. Once again, a dreamer becomes the salvation of his people, by attending to what others might call stuff and nonsense. Joseph's willingness to accept the circumstances of Mary's pregnancy, and Mary's willingness to flee with her husband at the summons of a dream, demonstrates the perfect submission of husband and wife, not to one another, but to the will of God for their lives. That may be the ultimate definition of the holy family.

What can you do to encourage your family or community to be more like the holy family?

WE RESPOND

Use religious imagination to allow thankfulness to bloom in your heart. Sing, dance, draw, cook, build, plant, create something new to express a grateful heart.

Let every detail in your lives—words, actions, whatever—be done in the name of the Master, Jesus.

JANUARY I: MARY, MOTHER OF GOD

FIRST READING » NUMBERS 6:22-27

God spoke to Moses: "Tell Aaron and his sons, This is how you are to bless the
People of Israel. Say to them,
  God bless you and keep you,
  God smile on you and gift you,
  God look you full in the face
    and make you prosper.
  In so doing, they will place my name on the People of Israel—
  I will confirm it by blessing them."

How do you start off fresh in the New Year? A lot of people make resolutions to lose weight and exercise, put their finances in order, or pray more. Some will decide this is the year to clean up their language, get sober, get married, or get serious about their career path. January 1 is simply the day after December 31, but it feels significantly different, as if time has turned a page. When the year is new, anything seems possible.

We might hope that our world leaders wake up today with the same resolve to start fresh. Of course, not all cultures operate according to our calendar, but for everyone who's celebrating the dawn of a new year and trying to make a fresh start, let's offer a blessing. May we be faithful to our resolutions, and supported in our desire to change. And may we find the peace that passes all understanding, which God alone can give.

How will you embrace new possibilities for yourself this year?

SECOND READING » GALATIANS 4:4-7

But when the time arrived that was set by God the Father, God sent his Son,
born among us of a woman, born under the conditions of the law so that he
might redeem those of us who have been kidnapped by the law. Thus we have
been set free to experience our rightful heritage. You can tell for sure that you
are now fully adopted as his own children because God sent the Spirit of his
Son into our lives crying out, "Papa! Father!" Doesn't that privilege of intimate
conversation with God make it plain that you are not a slave, but a child? And if
you are a child, you're also an heir, with complete access to the inheritance.

On polar ends of Paul's society were two kinds of people: slaves and heirs. A slave did not even possess his or her own life, but a male child possessed the promise of all the wealth in the household. Paul uses the two terms "slave" and "heir" to demonstrate the spiritual distinctions between the person enslaved by sin and the inheritance of eternal life gained by the person living in Christ. If you had to choose between fear and favor, who wouldn't want to be favored?

Of all the ways we might be enslaved in the modern world, the chains that bind us to the past are perhaps the most difficult to loosen. Due to our experiences through the years, we may have developed habitual and problematic tendencies toward fear, greed, coldness, melancholy, bitterness, unforgiveness. A slave will say: I cannot change. I am not free. This is how things are with me. An heir says: I can do all things because of the name I bear.

In what ways do you live as an heir,
and how are you still a slave to the past?

GOSPEL » LUKE 2:16-21

As the angel choir withdrew into heaven, the sheepherders talked it over. "Let's get over to Bethlehem as fast as we can and see for ourselves what God has revealed to us." They left, running, and found Mary and Joseph, and the baby lying in the manger. Seeing was believing. They told everyone they met what the angels had said about this child. All who heard the sheepherders were impressed.

Mary kept all these things to herself, holding them dear, deep within herself. The sheepherders returned and let loose, glorifying and praising God for everything they had heard and seen. It turned out exactly the way they'd been told!

When the eighth day arrived, the day of circumcision, the child was named Jesus, the name given by the angel before he was conceived.

The church considers the stories of the past as part of its holy legacy. We continue to read these stories aloud every time we gather because we believe they're not simply ancient tales about our spiritual ancestors—they're also guideposts for our own journey in faith. But Scripture is not the only sacred story given to us. We have at our disposal our own personal story, given to us by God and inspired with wisdom and symbols and teaching that it is our task to ponder and unravel.

People who don't stop and contemplate their personal journeys, as we know, are doomed to walk in circles through the same bleak scenarios until they do. All the wisdom of the ages is available to us—including the near and present revelation of our experiences as confirmation of the whole. No blessing is complete until we ponder its meaning and take it to heart.

How is my story a holy story?

WE RESPOND

Take five minutes for silence every day and breathe deeply. You may want to focus on a religious object or the view from your window, or close your eyes. Tell your story to God, and ask for a blessing on your journey.

EPIPHANY

FIRST READING » ISAIAH 60:1-6

Nations shall walk by your light. "Get out of bed, Jerusalem!
    Wake up. Put your face in the sunlight.
    God's bright glory has risen for you.
The whole earth is wrapped in darkness,
    all people sunk in deep darkness,
But God rises on you,
    his sunrise glory breaks over you.
Nations will come to your light,
    kings to your sunburst brightness.
Look up! Look around!
    Watch as they gather, watch as they approach you:
Your sons coming from great distances,
    your daughters carried by their nannies.
When you see them coming you'll smile—big smiles!
    Your heart will swell and, yes, burst!
All those people returning by sea for the reunion,
    a rich harvest of exiles gathered in from the nations!
And then streams of camel caravans as far as the eye can see,
    young camels of nomads in Midian and Ephah,
Pouring in from the south from Sheba,
    loaded with gold and frankincense,
    preaching the praises of God.
And yes, a great roundup
    of flocks from the nomads in Kedar and Nebaioth,
Welcome gifts for worship at my altar
    as I bathe my glorious Temple in splendor.

Put your face in the sunlight! That's quite an invitation for a new year. If it weren't for the reality of taxes, some of us would hardly distinguish one year from another. What makes January different from December, except that some of us are deeper in debt? What makes this year different from the last one, except that we are older?

Prophecy speaks to the sluggishness in the human heart that tends to see more of the same wherever it looks. "Been there, done that," is the national yawn. "There is nothing new under the sun" was the Hebrew version of our modern saying. And yet God is always saying, "Behold, I make all things new." How can this be?

What we see has a lot to do with the quality of the light. If we sit in a darkened room, we're not attentive to the details. When we open our eyes to God's light, we become radiant at what we see, and it's *never been there, never done that before* as far as the eye can see.

> **What new thing have you seen today?**
> **What new thing are you open to seeing?**

SECOND READING » EPHESIANS 3:2-3, 5-6

This is why I, Paul, am in jail for Christ, having taken up the cause of you outsiders, so-called. I take it that you're familiar with the part I was given in God's plan for including everybody. I got the inside story on this from God himself, as I just wrote you in brief.

As you read over what I have written to you, you'll be able to see for yourselves into the mystery of Christ. None of our ancestors understood this. Only in our time has it been made clear by God's Spirit through his holy apostles and prophets of this new order. The mystery is that people who have never heard of God and those who have heard of him all their lives (what I've been calling outsiders and insiders) stand on the same ground before God. They get the same offer, same help, same promises in Christ Jesus. The Message is accessible and welcoming to everyone, across the board.

What new thing did Paul see, that God's secret plan was revealed to him? He was a fervent man who originally pursued his beliefs to bloody ends. And then something changed for him. He put down his sword, and picked up the cross. Single-handedly, Paul advanced the cause of Christianity more than anyone in history, expanding its message to all the earth.

Paul was not a particularly flexible thinker. In fact, his behavior before and after his conversion demonstrates a fundamentalist leaning. It was his way or the highway, orthodoxy or bust—though at times he spun a new orthodoxy out of his being like a spider as he went along. Paul was a man of contradictions, but not of frail convictions. If he seemed yielding, even radical by his contemporaries' standards, it was because the Spirit was bending him like a tree in high wind. This means there's hope for those who feel too old to change, too set in old ways to think in new ways. Even if we stand perfectly still, God's Spirit can move us into position quite nicely.

> **How do you respond to the call to change?**

GOSPEL » MATTHEW 2:1-12

After Jesus was born in Bethlehem village, Judah territory— this was during Herod's kingship—a band of scholars arrived in Jerusalem from the East. They asked around, "Where can we find and pay homage to the newborn King of the Jews? We observed a star in the eastern sky that signaled his birth. We're on pilgrimage to worship him."

When word of their inquiry got to Herod, he was terrified—and not Herod alone, but most of Jerusalem as well. Herod lost no time. He gathered all the high priests and religion scholars in the city together and asked, "Where is the Messiah supposed to be born?"

They told him, "Bethlehem, Judah territory. The prophet Micah wrote it plainly:

It's you, Bethlehem, in Judah's land,
     no longer bringing up the rear.
From you will come the leader
     who will shepherd-rule my people, my Israel."

Herod then arranged a secret meeting with the scholars from the East. Pretending to be as devout as they were, he got them to tell him exactly when the birth-announcement star appeared. Then he told them the prophecy about Bethlehem, and said, "Go find this child. Leave no stone unturned. As soon as you find him, send word and I'll join you at once in your worship."

Instructed by the king, they set off. Then the star appeared again, the same star they had seen in the eastern skies. It led them on until it hovered over the place of the child. They could hardly contain themselves: They were in the right place! They had arrived at the right time!

They entered the house and saw the child in the arms of Mary, his mother. Overcome, they kneeled and worshiped him. Then they opened their luggage and presented gifts: gold, frankincense, myrrh.

In a dream, they were warned not to report back to Herod. So they worked out another route, left the territory without being seen, and returned to their own country.

These seekers define epiphany in their willingness to walk by the light. Through weeks and lands they traveled to honor an unknown king, with only a star for their guide. As the late William Stafford wrote in his poem *Star Guides*: "Any star is enough, if you know which one it is." These scholars knew their star. And because they persevered, the manifestation of God was revealed to them.

We call these men wise for wandering in search of the unknown, when their own people might have called them foolish. Yet we who know our king are less likely to risk that journey of faith, and we have much more than starlight to guide us. What holds us back? Fear, ignorance, or simple laziness? The main motivation in our well-fed society is selfishness: why risk anything when we can stay right where we are and be comfortable? Why give our wealth to a king when we can keep it for ourselves? The three we call wise are distinguished by their generosity. Generosity in itself is a kind of wisdom.

> **To whose generosity have you been beholden?**
> **How do you practice generosity?**

WE RESPOND

Christmas giving is over. Time for a new kind of giving—not an exchange of gifts, but a free giving to those who cannot return your kindness. Give your attention, talent, or material wealth to someone who needs it, and do not let one hand know what the other is doing.

*The Message is accessible
and welcoming to everyone, across the board.*

LENT

ASH WEDNESDAY

FIRST READING » JOEL 2:12–18

But there's also this, it's not too late—
    God's personal Message!—
"Come back to me and really mean it!
    Come fasting and weeping, sorry for your sins!"
Change your life, not just your clothes.
    Come back to God, your God.
And here's why: God is kind and merciful.
    He takes a deep breath, puts up with a lot,
This most patient God, extravagant in love,
    always ready to cancel catastrophe.
Who knows? Maybe he'll do it now,
    maybe he'll turn around and show pity.
Maybe, when all's said and done,
    there'll be blessings full and robust for your God!
Blow the ram's horn trumpet in Zion!
    Declare a day of repentance, a holy fast day.
Call a public meeting.
    Get everyone there. Consecrate the congregation.
Make sure the elders come,
    but bring in the children, too, even the nursing babies,
Even men and women on their honeymoon—
    interrupt them and get them there.
Between Sanctuary entrance and altar,
    let the priests, God's servants, weep tears of repentance.
Let them intercede: "Have mercy, God, on your people!
    Don't abandon your heritage to contempt.
Don't let the pagans take over and rule them
    and sneer, 'And so where is this God of theirs?'"
At that, God went into action to get his land back.
    He took pity on his people.
God answered and spoke to his people,
    "Look, listen—I'm sending a gift:
Grain and wine and olive oil.
    The fast is over—eat your fill!
I won't expose you any longer

to contempt among the pagans.
I'll head off the final enemy coming out of the north
    and dump them in a wasteland.
Half of them will end up in the Dead Sea,
    the other half in the Mediterranean.
There they'll rot, a stench to high heaven.
    The bigger the enemy, the stronger the stench!"

Lent isn't a season for loners. While we often think of it as private penitential time, these weeks are inaugurated with the summons to gather. Blow the horn and get everyone there! What we do in these forty days, we do together. Our fasting, prayer, and almsgiving are a communal effort. Just as the world will know practicing Catholics today by that smudge on our foreheads, we recognize and appreciate each other every Friday as we circumvent the burger in favor of the fish. Or see fellow parishioners among the swelled numbers for daily Mass, Stations of the Cross, Adoration, the Lenten parish mission, and Reconciliation services. We notice the Rice Bowl on the office desk, the extra effort given to service projects, the decreased time spent watching TV, the foregoing of dessert. When you're tempted to cheat on your resolutions this Lent, remember: you support the whole Catholic gang with your fidelity.

> **How do I intend to change my life,**
> **and not just a few temporary habits,**
> **by observing Lenten disciplines?**

SECOND READING » 2 CORINTHIANS 5:20—6:2

Because of this decision we don't evaluate people by what they have or how they look. We looked at the Messiah that way once and got it all wrong, as you know. We certainly don't look at him that way anymore. Now we look inside, and what we see is that anyone united with the Messiah gets a fresh start, is created new. The old life is gone; a new life burgeons! Look at it! All this comes from the God who settled the relationship between us and him, and then called us to settle our relationships with each other. God put the world square with himself through the Messiah, giving the world a fresh start by offering forgiveness of sins. God has given us the task of telling everyone what he is doing. We're Christ's representatives. God uses us to persuade men and women to drop their differences and enter into God's work of making things right between them. We're speaking for Christ himself now: Become friends with God; he's already a friend with you.

How? you ask. In Christ. God put the wrong on him who never did anything wrong, so we could be put right with God.

Companions as we are in this work with you, we beg you, please don't squander one bit of this marvelous life God has given us. God reminds us,

I heard your call in the nick of time;
  The day you needed me, I was there to help.

Well, now is the right time to listen, the day to be helped. Don't put it off; don't frustrate God's work by showing up late, throwing a question mark over everything we're doing. Our work as God's servants gets validated—or not—in the details. People are watching us as we stay at our post, alertly, unswervingly... in hard times, tough times, bad times; when we're beaten up, jailed, and mobbed; working hard, working late, working without eating; with pure heart, clear head, steady hand; in gentleness, holiness, and honest love; when we're telling the truth, and when God's showing his power; when we're doing our best setting things right; when we're praised, and when we're blamed; slandered, and honored; true to our word, though distrusted; ignored by the world, but recognized by God; terrifically alive, though rumored to be dead; beaten within an inch of our lives, but refusing to die; immersed in tears, yet always filled with deep joy; living on handouts, yet enriching many; having nothing, having it all.

The first meaning of church is "gathering." *Ecclesia* or assembly is how Christians originally defined themselves—which is where we get our word "ecclesial" today. Jesus made it clear we couldn't be church alone when he said "when two or three of you are together because of me, you can be sure that I'll be there" (Matt 18:20).

Saint Paul further reminds us that church isn't something we can do without God. That may sound obvious: but aren't we sometimes tempted to think our religion is all about what we do *for* God, and not the other way around? Going to Mass isn't our little weekly gift to God. Eucharist, which means thanksgiving, is our thank-you to God for the many gifts God's already given to us. Church isn't just about getting together with our fellow parishioners. It's about all of us getting on the same page with the God who befriends us first.

Who is at the center of my religious life: God, or me?
How do I befriend the God who befriends me?

GOSPEL » MATTHEW 6:1–6, 16–18

"Be especially careful when you are trying to be good so that you don't make a performance out of it. It might be good theater, but the God who made you won't be applauding.

"When you do something for someone else, don't call attention to yourself. You've seen them in action, I'm sure—'play-actors' I call them—treating prayer meeting and street corner alike as a stage, acting compassionate as long as someone is watching, playing to the crowds. They get applause, true, but that's all they get. When you help someone out, don't think about how it looks. Just do it— quietly and unobtrusively. That is the way your God, who conceived you in love, working behind the scenes, helps you out.

THIS TRANSFORMING WORD

"And when you come before God, don't turn that into a theatrical production either. All these people making a regular show out of their prayers, hoping for stardom! Do you think God sits in a box seat?

"Here's what I want you to do: Find a quiet, secluded place so you won't be tempted to role-play before God. Just be there as simply and honestly as you can manage. The focus will shift from you to God, and you will begin to sense his grace.

"When you practice some appetite-denying discipline to better concentrate on God, don't make a production out of it. It might turn you into a small-time celebrity but it won't make you a saint. If you 'go into training' inwardly, act normal outwardly. Shampoo and comb your hair, brush your teeth, wash your face. God doesn't require attention-getting devices. He won't overlook what you are doing; he'll reward you well.

Religious ritual isn't meant to be a theater performance. High formal liturgies can seem stagey at times—just think of Vatican ceremonies, viewed by millions on television—but the main purpose is never to impress or to be observed. Ritual is a participatory event. Liturgy actually means public work or duty. We do ritual as a public service, for the sake of the world. Even if no one is watching. We give our thanks and praise to God and receive the graces available in each sacramental hour. So we can think of the stages of ritual as follows: We act. God acts. We return to the greater community to share what we've received.

While ritual is a public act, humility obliges us not to take credit for this "good deed." It *is* good for us to gather, to give thanks, but it's always in response to what God has done for us. In the same way, taking credit for our fasting, prayer, and almsgiving in this season is like wanting to be thanked for sending a thank-you card. When it comes to religious activity, we are always on the receiving end of the bargain.

What have I received from God today? How have I shown my gratitude?

WE RESPOND

Choose a way to observe each of the traditional categories during these forty days: fasting, prayer, giving alms. Let's do it together!

Find a quiet, secluded place so you won't be tempted to role-play before God.

FIRST SUNDAY OF LENT

FIRST READING » GENESIS 2:7-9; 3:1-7

At the time God made Earth and Heaven, before any grasses or shrubs had sprouted from the ground—God hadn't yet sent rain on Earth, nor was there anyone around to work the ground (the whole Earth was watered by underground springs)—God formed Man out of dirt from the ground and blew into his nostrils the breath of life. The Man came alive—a living soul!

Then God planted a garden in Eden, in the east. He put the Man he had just made in it. God made all kinds of trees grow from the ground, trees beautiful to look at and good to eat. The Tree-of-Life was in the middle of the garden, also the Tree-of-Knowledge-of-Good-and-Evil.

The serpent was clever, more clever than any wild animal God had made. He spoke to the Woman: "Do I understand that God told you not to eat from any tree in the garden?"

The Woman said to the serpent, "Not at all. We can eat from the trees in the garden. It's only about the tree in the middle of the garden that God said, 'Don't eat from it; don't even touch it or you'll die.'"

The serpent told the Woman, "You won't die. God knows that the moment you eat from that tree, you'll see what's really going on. You'll be just like God, knowing everything, ranging all the way from good to evil."

When the Woman saw that the tree looked like good eating and realized what she would get out of it—she'd know everything!—she took and ate the fruit and then gave some to her husband, and he ate.

Immediately the two of them did "see what's really going on"—saw themselves naked! They sewed fig leaves together as makeshift clothes for themselves.

Sin is indeed an eye-opening experience. While we are in a state of relative innocence, we see the world in straightforward ways. We deal with people honestly, and expect forthrightness from them. We extend kindness and good will, and anticipate its return. Much of the time, benevolence is met with open-heartedness (if astonishment) on the other side. But not always immediately. Which is why, in Christian terms, we're taught to turn the other cheek. Sometimes, as we know too well, good is answered with evil in the short run. The cross is the central witness to that reality. But the resurrection, of course, is God's last word on the subject, the final turn of the wheel toward goodness.

Sin changes the dynamic of give-and-take altogether. If we act in the world with malice in our hearts, there's a stellar change in what's returned to us. Some religions call that karma. If you are stingy, expect little to be returned to you, like the man who buries his talents in the ground and grows no profit. Jesus promises that the one who loves much, is forgiven much, and so he taught us to pray, "Forgive us our trespasses, as we forgive those who trespass against us." If we choose the ways of sin—mistrust, ill will, greed, bitterness—our eyes will be opened to the full reality of evil present in the world around us, and we will become disillusioned, reinforced in our belief in sin and doubts about grace. Seek and ye shall find, Jesus also said. If we travel along the path of sin, we shouldn't wonder if sin is under every rock and behind every tree.

What avenues of sin hold the most attraction for you: greed, lust, indifference, or some other commonly traveled road?

SECOND READING » ROMANS 5:12-19

You know the story of how Adam landed us in the dilemma we're in—first sin, then death, and no one exempt from either sin or death. That sin disturbed relations with God in everything and everyone, but the extent of the disturbance was not clear until God spelled it out in detail to Moses. So death, this huge abyss separating us from God, dominated the landscape from Adam to Moses. Even those who didn't sin precisely as Adam did by disobeying a specific command of God still had to experience this termination of life, this separation from God. But Adam, who got us into this, also points ahead to the One who will get us out of it.

Yet the rescuing gift is not exactly parallel to the death-dealing sin. If one man's sin put crowds of people at the dead-end abyss of separation from God, just think what God's gift poured through one man, Jesus Christ, will do! There's no comparison between that death-dealing sin and this generous, life-giving gift. The verdict on that one sin was the death sentence; the verdict on the many sins that followed was this wonderful life sentence. If death got the upper hand through one man's wrongdoing, can you imagine the breathtaking recovery life makes, sovereign life, in those who grasp with both hands this wildly extravagant life-gift, this grand setting-everything-right, that the one man Jesus Christ provides?

Here it is in a nutshell: Just as one person did it wrong and got us in all this trouble with sin and death, another person did it right and got us out of it. But more than just getting us out of trouble, he got us into life! One man said no to God and put many people in the wrong; one man said yes to God and put many in the right.

History teaches us that leaders do count. Crowds tend to go this way or that according to societal norms and values. The majority of us are drifters much of the time. We don't think; we just behave on auto-pilot, like sleep-walkers. It takes a crisis, personal or national, to wake us up to what we're doing and what's really going on. Though we have free will, we exercise it rarely. Much of the time, we're bound by the world around us and our personal histories, which dictate who we are and "should" be.

By contrast, leaders make a difference. Leaders are people who wake up to the world as it is and become free choosers in the stream of history. Leaders aren't afraid to change things, to dictate new terms into the way things are. Leaders are terrifying, because they threaten the status quo. Leaders cause problems for those established in power, and that's why real leaders are often imprisoned or eliminated.

Jesus led us out of the darkness of sin and into grace with the same transforming authority, and powerful people continue to be threatened by the message of the gospel.

> **Real leaders are not to be confused with the people in power.**
> **Who are the real leaders in your family, parish, community?**

GOSPEL » MATTHEW 4:1-11

Next Jesus was taken into the wild by the Spirit for the Test. The Devil was ready to give it. Jesus prepared for the Test by fasting forty days and forty nights. That left him, of course, in a state of extreme hunger, which the Devil took advantage of in the first test: "Since you are God's Son, speak the word that will turn these stones into loaves of bread."

Jesus answered by quoting Deuteronomy: "It takes more than bread to stay alive. It takes a steady stream of words from God's mouth."

For the second test the Devil took him to the Holy City. He sat him on top of the Temple and said, "Since you are God's Son, jump." The Devil goaded him by quoting Psalm 91: "He has placed you in the care of angels. They will catch you so that you won't so much as stub your toe on a stone."

Jesus countered with another citation from Deuteronomy: "Don't you dare test the Lord your God."

For the third test, the Devil took him to the peak of a huge mountain. He gestured expansively, pointing out all the earth's kingdoms, how glorious they all were. Then he said, "They're yours—lock, stock, and barrel. Just go down on your knees and worship me, and they're yours."

Jesus' refusal was curt: "Beat it, Satan!" He backed his rebuke with a third quotation from Deuteronomy: "Worship the Lord your God, and only him. Serve him with absolute single-heartedness."

The Test was over. The Devil left. And in his place, angels! Angels came and took care of Jesus' needs.

Israel wandered for decades in the desert, not yet having learned how to be a faithful, holy people. They demanded that God "turn stones into bread," or at least to send bread from heaven and water from a rock. Israel demanded continual signs of God's intervention and interest. They even worshipped the golden calf, hoping that it would safeguard them better than Moses and *his* God.

When Jesus enters the desert, he faces the same Exodus temptations. But where Israel falters, Jesus remains steadfast. What does this single victory over the devil mean, against the sad tabulation of centuries of failure on the part of the rest of us? What can Jesus' victory mean, when I fall to the lure of sin again and again?

The example of Jesus' faithfulness may keep the saints on course during great trials; but a common sinner like me can keep an eye on Jesus' example while still fainting under the spell of self-interest. The real power of Jesus' victory over temptation is that it destroyed the necessary relationship between sin and death. I may fall to sin along the way, but the ultimate victory belongs to God.

What form does the golden calf take in my life:
security? paycheck? spouse? children?

WE RESPOND

Tackle your demons! Address the "golden calf" in your life by resisting its false exercise of power over you. Don't let your false god make decisions for you, and bend you to its counterfeit purposes. Follow the real leader, Jesus!

"Worship the Lord your God, and only him.
Serve him with absolute single-heartedness."

SECOND SUNDAY OF LENT

FIRST READING » GENESIS 12:1-4

*God told Abram: "Leave your country, your family, and your father's home for a
land that I will show you.*
I'll make you a great nation
        and bless you.
    I'll make you famous;
        you'll be a blessing.
    I'll bless those who bless you;
        those who curse you I'll curse.
    All the families of the Earth
        will be blessed through you."
*So Abram left just as God said, and Lot left with him. Abram was seventy-five
years old when he left Haran. Abram took his wife Sarai and his nephew Lot
with him, along with all the possessions and people they had gotten in Haran,
and set out for the land of Canaan and arrived safe and sound.*

*Abram passed through the country as far as Shechem and the Oak of Moreh.
At that time the Canaanites occupied the land.*

God makes seven promises to Abram in this close encounter of the divine kind. A
nation will derive from Abram. God will personally bless him. The name of Abram
will become famous, and he himself will become a blessing for others. Those who
are good to this servant of God will know divine favor. Those who harm Abram will
know God's wrath. And one more thing: the blessing that comes from Abram will not
be just for his own people, but for all of the world.

Look how God's promises have been fulfilled! The generations descend from
Abraham like a waterfall, and his journey of faith was greatly rewarded in his own
time. Twenty centuries later, several great religions claim his story as part of their
own: Judaism, Christianity, and Islam. Abraham's faithfulness to God became the
blessing from which countless blessings have emerged from those who follow his
way of faith. The story of Abraham's journey to the promise has become a worldwide inspiration for all who journey in the direction of God's purposes, wild and
unlikely though they may be.

> **What kind of promises might God be making with you,
> as wonderful as those made to Abram?**

SECOND READING » 2 TIMOTHY 1:8-10

*So don't be embarrassed to speak up for our Master or for me, his prisoner.
Take your share of suffering for the Message along with the rest of us. We can
only keep on going, after all, by the power of God, who first saved us and then*

called us to this holy work. We had nothing to do with it. It was all his idea, a gift prepared for us in Jesus long before we knew anything about it. But we know it now. Since the appearance of our Savior, nothing could be plainer: death defeated, life vindicated in a steady blaze of light, all through the work of Jesus.

Does God have a plan for you? It's tempting to answer with sarcasm: "Not very likely!" Maybe you're not the perfect child your parents were hoping for, or the perfect man or woman you had hopes of being yourself. You may not be as rich, as strong, as lovely, or as smart as those people in the ads. You may not be as kind, sympathetic, or helpful as the boy or girl scout you trained to be. Yet God has a plan, which includes you. Trust in that.

So what does it mean for us to contemplate God's plan? In parochial school, vocation seemed a kind of shell game that I tried to win: does God want me to be a priest, a sister, or a brother? (Being a girl, the answer was supposed to be obvious.) In my teens and twenties, the shell game became even more intense: does God want me to be a wife, a mother? And *which* fellow was the right fellow, the partner ordained for me? These days, I have come to understand that the divine design is no shell game at all. God does not have the one-and-only right choice for my life hidden someplace where I have to find it or lose big. God wants only that I choose God. God's plan for me is that I choose grace. And grace flows in many directions as God invites me to be a free chooser, a free creature called to glorify God through holy choices.

> Describe the roads you have walked in your life so far:
> your original family, education, independence,
> work, present family or community.
> How many of these roads were freely chosen?
> Which of these feel God-inspired or grace-filled?

GOSPEL » MATTHEW 17:1-9

Six days later, three of them saw that glory. Jesus took Peter and the brothers, James and John, and led them up a high mountain. His appearance changed from the inside out, right before their eyes. Sunlight poured from his face. His clothes were filled with light. Then they realized that Moses and Elijah were also there in deep conversation with him.

Peter broke in, "Master, this is a great moment! What would you think if I built three memorials here on the mountain—one for you, one for Moses, one for Elijah?"

While he was going on like this, babbling, a light-radiant cloud enveloped them, and sounding from deep in the cloud a voice: "This is my Son, marked by my love, focus of my delight. Listen to him."

When the disciples heard it, they fell flat on their faces, scared to death. But Jesus came over and touched them. "Don't be afraid." When they opened their eyes and looked around all they saw was Jesus, only Jesus.

Coming down the mountain, Jesus swore them to secrecy. "Don't breathe a word of what you've seen. After the Son of Man is raised from the dead, you are free to talk."

Jesus was changed before their eyes. Have you ever seen a transfiguration? Have you ever seen a simple thing become a holy thing, like bread become sacred flesh? Have you ever seen a plain face become a radiant beauty when seen through the eyes of love? Have you ever seen a timid person become a lion when circumstances required strength beyond fear? Transfiguration is not an isolated incident, a one-time deal in salvation history. Transfigurations happen around us in surprising places, for those who have eyes to see.

Sitting with my dying friend for many weeks, I watched how a weakening body can become a temple of great holiness. The spiritual strength of a failing mortal life was so much stronger than the physical vigor he once displayed. Before his illness, he scaled mountains for pleasure. In his last illness, he ascended to spiritual heights that astonished me with their breathtaking vistas. Once, he saw the view from the peaks of the Sierras, and hoped to climb Mount Kilimanjaro. Now, his vision is on higher places, and the things he sees are lovelier than all of earth's delights. This is transfiguration, as surely as what Peter, James and John saw on that fateful day.

When and how have you see transfigurations in yourself, in others, or in situations around you?

WE RESPOND

Get ready to participate in some powerful transfigurations! Ask God to change the rough, ugly, or impossible roads in your life into freeways for grace. Invite the Holy Spirit to make the valleys smooth, and the mountains low.

"Don't breathe a word of what you've seen. After the Son of Man is raised from the dead, you are free to talk."

THIRD SUNDAY OF LENT

FIRST READING » EXODUS 17:3-7

But the people were thirsty for water there. They complained to Moses, "Why did you take us from Egypt and drag us out here with our children and animals to die of thirst?"

Moses cried out in prayer to God, "What can I do with these people? Any minute now they'll kill me!"

God said to Moses, "Go on out ahead of the people, taking with you some of the elders of Israel. Take the staff you used to strike the Nile. And go. I'm going to be present before you there on the rock at Horeb. You are to strike the rock. Water will gush out of it and the people will drink."

Moses did what he said, with the elders of Israel right there watching. He named the place Massah (Testing-Place) and Meribah (Quarreling) because of the quarreling of the Israelites and because of their testing of God when they said, "Is God here with us, or not?"

Before Moses ever began his historic mission as the moral guide of Israel, the God of Sinai transformed his shepherd's staff into a sign of authority. The staff was not simply a symbol of power: it had divine power invested in it. When thrown in front of Pharaoh, the staff became a fearful serpent. When dipped into the Nile, it turned the river to blood. When lifted over the Red Sea, the sea parted before all Israel. No wonder, then, that when Moses struck the rock at Horeb, water flowed in the desert for people to drink.

Moses guided the people of Israel for forty years through the desert, but as moral guardian he would lead the Jews for centuries to come. The staff that would continue to shepherd the people would be the law that Moses brought down from heaven. The authority of Moses runs so deep, even Jesus does not dispute it: "I have come not to abolish the law, but to fulfill it." Rather than serving as a contradiction to Moses, Jesus in many ways imitates this shepherd's role by parting the power of death itself and leading God's people to freedom and salvation. What unites us to the story of the Jews is so much more than what divides us.

> **How much do you know about Jewish-Christian relations?**
> **Does your local community or parish provide opportunities**
> **to participate in interfaith dialogue or service?**

SECOND READING » ROMANS 5:1-2, 5-8

By entering through faith into what God has always wanted to do for us—set us right with him, make us fit for him—we have it all together with God because of our Master Jesus. And that's not all: We throw open our doors to God and discover at the same moment that he has already thrown open his door to us. We find ourselves standing where we always hoped we might stand—out in the wide-open spaces of God's grace and glory, standing tall and shouting our praise.

There's more to come: We continue to shout our praise even when we're hemmed in with troubles, because we know how troubles can develop passionate patience in us, and how that patience in turn forges the tempered steel of virtue, keeping us alert for whatever God will do next. In alert expectancy such as this, we're never left feeling shortchanged. Quite the contrary—we can't round up enough containers to hold everything God generously pours into our lives through the Holy Spirit!

Christ arrives right on time to make this happen. He didn't, and doesn't, wait for us to get ready. He presented himself for this sacrificial death when we were far too weak and rebellious to do anything to get ourselves ready. And even if we hadn't been so weak, we wouldn't have known what to do anyway. We can understand someone dying for a person worth dying for, and we can understand how someone good and noble could inspire us to selfless sacrifice. But God put his love on the line for us by offering his Son in sacrificial death while we were of no use whatever to him.

Some time ago, a friend of mine underwent a medical crisis. In love and friendship, I naturally dropped everything to be at his bedside to care for him. Who wouldn't? When you love someone, you will do just about anything to assist that person in time of need. Maybe if you loved him or her enough, you might go so far as to donate a kidney. And in the most critical case, you might even risk your life.

But it's quite a different thing to behave this way in the case of someone you know only slightly, or a stranger, or an enemy. This is what Paul marvels at when he considers the extraordinary behavior of Jesus. Jesus died for sinners, who are by definition estranged from God—we could even say the enemies of the divine will. Jesus gave his life and love for sinners—for us—even as we turn our backs on love and are indifferent to God's way. As I ministered to my sick friend through those long weeks of his illness, I kept wondering if I could do this for someone I did not love as much, who did not hold as much love in his heart for me. His love made helping him so easy and natural. But if he had been hostile to me, who can say? I am not as good as God.

> **Whom do you love best?**
> **What would you be willing to sacrifice for his or her sake?**
> **How much would you sacrifice for a stranger? An enemy?**

GOSPEL » JOHN 4:5-42

To get there, he had to pass through Samaria. He came into Sychar, a Samaritan village that bordered the field Jacob had given his son Joseph. Jacob's well was still there. Jesus, worn out by the trip, sat down at the well. It was noon.

A woman, a Samaritan, came to draw water. Jesus said, "Would you give me a drink of water?" (His disciples had gone to the village to buy food for lunch.)

The Samaritan woman, taken aback, asked, "How come you, a Jew, are asking me, a Samaritan woman, for a drink?" (Jews in those days wouldn't be caught dead talking to Samaritans.)

Jesus answered, "If you knew the generosity of God and who I am, you would be asking me for a drink, and I would give you fresh, living water."

The woman said, "Sir, you don't even have a bucket to draw with, and this well is deep. So how are you going to get this 'living water'? Are you a better man than our ancestor Jacob, who dug this well and drank from it, he and his sons and livestock, and passed it down to us?"

Jesus said, "Everyone who drinks this water will get thirsty again and again. Anyone who drinks the water I give will never thirst—not ever. The water I give will be an artesian spring within, gushing fountains of endless life."

The woman said, "Sir, give me this water so I won't ever get thirsty, won't ever have to come back to this well again!"

He said, "Go call your husband and then come back."

"I have no husband," she said.

"That's nicely put: 'I have no husband.' You've had five husbands, and the man you're living with now isn't even your husband. You spoke the truth there, sure enough."

"Oh, so you're a prophet! Well, tell me this: Our ancestors worshiped God at this mountain, but you Jews insist that Jerusalem is the only place for worship, right?"

"Believe me, woman, the time is coming when you Samaritans will worship the Father neither here at this mountain nor there in Jerusalem. You worship guessing in the dark; we Jews worship in the clear light of day. God's way of salvation is made available through the Jews. But the time is coming—it has, in fact, come—when what you're called will not matter and where you go to worship will not matter.

"It's who you are and the way you live that count before God. Your worship must engage your spirit in the pursuit of truth. That's the kind of people the Father is out looking for: those who are simply and honestly themselves before him in their worship. God is sheer being itself—Spirit. Those who worship him must do it out of their very being, their spirits, their true selves, in adoration."

The woman said, "I don't know about that. I do know that the Messiah is coming. When he arrives, we'll get the whole story."

"I am he," said Jesus. "You don't have to wait any longer or look any further."

Just then his disciples came back. They were shocked. They couldn't believe he was talking with that kind of a woman. No one said what they were all thinking, but their faces showed it.

The woman took the hint and left. In her confusion she left her water pot. Back in the village she told the people, "Come see a man who knew all about the things I did, who knows me inside and out. Do you think this could be the

Messiah?" And they went out to see for themselves.

In the meantime, the disciples pressed him, "Rabbi, eat. Aren't you going to eat?"

He told them, "I have food to eat you know nothing about."

The disciples were puzzled. "Who could have brought him food?"

Jesus said, "The food that keeps me going is that I do the will of the One who sent me, finishing the work he started. As you look around right now, wouldn't you say that in about four months it will be time to harvest? Well, I'm telling you to open your eyes and take a good look at what's right in front of you. These Samaritan fields are ripe. It's harvest time!

"The Harvester isn't waiting. He's taking his pay, gathering in this grain that's ripe for eternal life. Now the Sower is arm in arm with the Harvester, triumphant. That's the truth of the saying, 'This one sows, that one harvests.' I sent you to harvest a field you never worked. Without lifting a finger, you have walked in on a field worked long and hard by others."

Many of the Samaritans from that village committed themselves to him because of the woman's witness: "He knew all about the things I did. He knows me inside and out!" They asked him to stay on, so Jesus stayed two days. A lot more people entrusted their lives to him when they heard what he had to say. They said to the woman, "We're no longer taking this on your say-so. We've heard it for ourselves and know it for sure. He's the Savior of the world!"

Still waters run deep! The well in Samaria may have been dug down to a level of 200 feet below the grade of the town, but it was not as deep as the water of which Jesus speaks to the woman that day. Jesus is a wellspring of living water, leaping up to eternal life. Now *that's* deep.

Water talk in the Bible is always significant, because the Middle East is one large desert with a few important rivers running through it. Water determined everything biblical: where cities were built, if the people prospered or languished, who would win a battle, whether life could go on. The best way for an enemy to defeat you was to destroy your well or cut off your access to it. Then victory was only days away.

Jesus and the woman both know, better than we do in a land where water is on tap, that water means life. We know that the woman drinks deeply of the message Jesus gives her when she leaves her water jar behind at the well. She experienced exactly what he told her: that if she listened to him, she would never be thirsty again.

> **What does water mean to you?**
> **What does your experience of water teach you**
> **about the life that Jesus offers?**

WE RESPOND

Get involved in the interfaith movement! The Church is talking with the synagogue, and so should we. Join or organize a local effort. Invite a local rabbi to speak at your parish about the faith of God's first people.

FOURTH SUNDAY OF LENT

...."I'm the One, All Right."

FIRST READING » 1 SAMUEL 16:6-7, 10-13

When they arrived, Samuel took one look at Eliab and thought, "Here he is! God's anointed!"

But God told Samuel, "Looks aren't everything. Don't be impressed with his looks and stature. I've already eliminated him. God judges persons differently than humans do. Men and women look at the face; God looks into the heart."

Jesse presented his seven sons to Samuel. Samuel was blunt with Jesse, "God hasn't chosen any of these."

Then he asked Jesse, "Is this it? Are there no more sons?"

"Well, yes, there's the runt. But he's out tending the sheep."

Samuel ordered Jesse, "Go get him. We're not moving from this spot until he's here."

Jesse sent for him. He was brought in, the very picture of health—bright-eyed, good-looking.

God said, "Up on your feet! Anoint him! This is the one."

Samuel took his flask of oil and anointed him, with his brothers standing around watching. The Spirit of God entered David like a rush of wind, God vitally empowering him for the rest of his life.

Samuel left and went home to Ramah.

Even the prophet Samuel was swayed by worldly appearances, so we shouldn't be surprised that we are. Samuel took one look at Jesse's first son Eliab and said to himself, "This is the next king of Israel!" But he was mistaken. It was David, called from the fields, intentionally uninvited to the sacrifice, whom God had chosen. God chose the baby of the family over the eldest, the shepherd boy over the apparent heir. Isn't this always God's way, to choose the unlikely one for the mission?

Still we keep on choosing the apparent leaders among us. We put giants in charge, forgetful that God chooses little ones. We prefer Philistines, while God likes kids with slingshots. We seek powerful people to fill powerful roles, while God chooses a barren couple to produce a nation (Abraham and Sarah), a stammerer for a mouthpiece (Moses), and a virgin to bring forth salvation (Mary). If you are small, weak, and passed up by the world, God expects great things from you. If you are big, strong, and important, God expects you to follow the meek ones.

Who are the weak and small ones God has chosen to lead you along your way?

SECOND READING » EPHESIANS 5:8-14

You groped your way through that murk once, but no longer. You're out in the open now. The bright light of Christ makes your way plain. So no more stumbling around. Get on with it! The good, the right, the true—these are the actions appropriate for daylight hours. Figure out what will please Christ, and then do it.

Don't waste your time on useless work, mere busywork, the barren pursuits of darkness. Expose these things for the sham they are. It's a scandal when people waste their lives on things they must do in the darkness where no one will see. Rip the cover off those frauds and see how attractive they look in the light of Christ.

Wake up from your sleep,
Climb out of your coffins;
Christ will show you the light!

So watch your step. Use your head. Make the most of every chance you get. These are desperate times!

Once we were all in darkness, we can agree. I remember my darkness well. I grew up a timid sort of female, prone to self-doubt and depression. I was the kind of person destined to be pushed around by self-asserting personalities as early as the playground. I was a mouse in the land of lions that roared. I was the wallflower at dances, the quiet girl with glasses, the one few knew and no one dated.

But like you, I was called to live in the light. Light produces the good, the right, and the true, Paul tells us. In my case, it produced self-knowledge, a sense of my own worth, learning to see myself in God's eyes. Once I did that, I became the mouse that roared. Now I'm happy to be a flower in God's garden, a useful tool in divine hands. My story is also yours. Nothing changes except the names and details.

> **Through what darkness have you been led so far?**
> **How is God using your weakness to powerful advantage?**

GOSPEL » JOHN 9:1-41

Walking down the street, Jesus saw a man blind from birth. His disciples asked, "Rabbi, who sinned: this man or his parents, causing him to be born blind?" Jesus said, "You're asking the wrong question. You're looking for someone to blame. There is no such cause-effect here. Look instead for what God can do. We need to be energetically at work for the One who sent me here, working while the sun shines. When night falls, the workday is over. For as long as I am in the world, there is plenty of light. I am the world's Light."

He said this and then spit in the dust, made a clay paste with the saliva, rubbed the paste on the blind man's eyes, and said, "Go, wash at the Pool of Siloam" (Siloam means "Sent"). The man went and washed—and saw.

Soon the town was buzzing. His relatives and those who year after year had seen him as a blind man begging were saying, "Why, isn't this the man we knew, who sat here and begged?"

Others said, "It's him all right!"

But others objected, "It's not the same man at all. It just looks like him."

He said, "It's me, the very one."

They said, "How did your eyes get opened?"

"A man named Jesus made a paste and rubbed it on my eyes and told me, 'Go to Siloam and wash.' I did what he said. When I washed, I saw."

"So where is he?"

"I don't know."

They marched the man to the Pharisees. This day when Jesus made the paste and healed his blindness was the Sabbath. The Pharisees grilled him again on how he had come to see. He said, "He put a clay paste on my eyes, and I washed, and now I see."

Some of the Pharisees said, "Obviously, this man can't be from God. He doesn't keep the Sabbath."

Others countered, "How can a bad man do miraculous, God-revealing things like this?" There was a split in their ranks.

They came back at the blind man, "You're the expert. He opened your eyes. What do you say about him?"

He said, "He is a prophet."

The Jews didn't believe it, didn't believe the man was blind to begin with. So they called the parents of the man now bright-eyed with sight. They asked them, "Is this your son, the one you say was born blind? So how is it that he now sees?"

His parents said, "We know he is our son, and we know he was born blind. But we don't know how he came to see—haven't a clue about who opened his eyes. Why don't you ask him? He's a grown man and can speak for himself." (His parents were talking like this because they were intimidated by the Jewish leaders, who had already decided that anyone who took a stand that this was the Messiah would be kicked out of the meeting place. That's why his parents said, "Ask him. He's a grown man.")

They called the man back a second time—the man who had been blind—and told him, "Give credit to God. We know this man is an impostor."

He replied, "I know nothing about that one way or the other. But I know one thing for sure: I was blind…I now see."

They said, "What did he do to you? How did he open your eyes?"

"I've told you over and over and you haven't listened. Why do you want to hear it again? Are you so eager to become his disciples?"

With that they jumped all over him. "You might be a disciple of that man, but we're disciples of Moses. We know for sure that God spoke to Moses, but we have no idea where this man even comes from."

The man replied, "This is amazing! You claim to know nothing about him, but the fact is, he opened my eyes! It's well known that God isn't at the beck and call of sinners, but listens carefully to anyone who lives in reverence and does his will. That someone opened the eyes of a man born blind has never been heard of—ever. If this man didn't come from God, he wouldn't be able to do anything."

They said, "You're nothing but dirt! How dare you take that tone with us!"
Then they threw him out in the street.

Jesus heard that they had thrown him out, and went and found him. He asked him, "Do you believe in the Son of Man?"

The man said, "Point him out to me, sir, so that I can believe in him."

Jesus said, "You're looking right at him. Don't you recognize my voice?"

"Master, I believe," the man said, and worshiped him.

Jesus then said, "I came into the world to bring everything into the clear light of day, making all the distinctions clear, so that those who have never seen will see, and those who have made a great pretense of seeing will be exposed as blind."

Some Pharisees overheard him and said, "Does that mean you're calling us blind?"

Jesus said, "If you were really blind, you would be blameless, but since you claim to see everything so well, you're accountable for every fault and failure."

The fellow who used to sit and beg becomes the one who stands and gives witness. The one they knew as the man born blind becomes the only one with clear sight. Are we surprised? This is the way with God's people. The last are first. The meek inherit the earth. The loser takes all, and the crucified one is raised from the dead. It all makes Christian sense.

The Pharisees who question the man call themselves disciples of Moses, but in fact they follow their own sense of how the world works. Blind men stay blind; sinners break Sabbath law. For Jesus to come and cure a blind man on the Sabbath upsets the apple cart of reason and piety. This is unacceptable to those who consider themselves religious. Even God, after all, has to keep to the divine place! It can be particularly true of religious people that we want the Sacred to remain inert in the Tabernacle to be worshipped. If Holy Power escapes into the world, who can be safe from its freedom to act?

> **Have you ever seen a holy thing**
> **that doesn't fit into the usual pious categories,**
> **like the love between an unwed mother and her child?**

WE RESPOND

God likes to color outside the lines. Invite God to expand your sense of what is right, acceptable and good. Ask that your blindness be healed, and that you be given clear sight.

FIFTH SUNDAY OF LENT

FIRST READING » EZEKIEL 37:12-14

"Therefore, prophesy. Tell them, 'God, the Master, says: I'll dig up your graves and bring you out alive—O my people! Then I'll take you straight to the land of Israel. When I dig up graves and bring you out as my people, you'll realize that I am God. I'll breathe my life into you and you'll live. Then I'll lead you straight back to your land and you'll realize that I am God. I've said it and I'll do it. God's Decree.'"

Somewhere in your life, a part of you lies buried. It could be some part of your love that was wounded or never sought out, and in pain and silence you buried it stillborn. Perhaps there's an artist in you that was censored early on, or an adventurer that was held down on the farm. Part of you was said "no" to, and you believed the word that was spoken. Maybe in fear, or maybe with resignation, you let that part of you die away.

But a prophet comes to speak to that part of us and to call it forth: "I'll dig up your graves and bring you out alive!" Our God is the God of life, and not of death. The God who created us does not labor in vain, and there's no part of who we are that was "a mistake" or unnecessary. So let your love flow, let the poet out, let the traveler roam free. God calls us from a common grave into a new land where all that we are is blessed for service.

What part of you needs to be awakened to life?
What can you do to encourage this awakening?

SECOND READING » ROMANS 8:8-11

Those who think they can do it on their own end up obsessed with measuring their own moral muscle but never get around to exercising it in real life. Those who trust God's action in them find that God's Spirit is in them—living and breathing God! Obsession with self in these matters is a dead end; attention to God leads us out into the open, into a spacious, free life. Focusing on the self is the opposite of focusing on God. Anyone completely absorbed in self ignores God, ends up thinking more about self than God. That person ignores who God is and what he is doing. And God isn't pleased at being ignored.

But if God himself has taken up residence in your life, you can hardly be thinking more of yourself than of him. Anyone, of course, who has not welcomed this invisible but clearly present God, the Spirit of Christ, won't know what we're talking about. But for you who welcome him, in whom he dwells—even though you still experience all the limitations of sin—you yourself experience life on God's terms. It stands to reason, doesn't it, that if the alive-and-present God who raised Jesus from the dead moves into your life, he'll do the same thing in you that he did in Jesus, bringing you alive to himself? When God lives and breathes in you (and he does, as surely as he did in Jesus), you are delivered from that dead life. With his Spirit living in you, your body will be as alive as Christ's!

Paul seems harsh about "the self" in this passage—often translated as "the flesh." A misinterpretation here could easily wind up contradicting Ezekiel's prophecy in the previous reading. Maybe we *should* bury some impulses, sacrifice parts of our "self" for the sake of purity, we might think. This kind of thinking comes to us for a reason, especially if you've spent any time in the pre-1960s church. For a good many generations, the religious-minded were awfully suspicious of the body. And "the flesh" was an old Catholic euphemism for sex, which was considered the very threshold of evil.

Libertine lifestyles are definitely "out" for Christians, but there's a whole lot of space between libertines and Puritans. It's simply insupportable by biblical standards to say that the experience of our senses is "always" bad, anymore than it's biblical to claim everything in the world of spirit as "good." The reality of the flesh can be the best thing in the world, as was the conception of Jesus in the womb of Mary. And spirit can be quite evil, as anyone who has wrestled with a private demon can tell you.

> How healthy is your life "in the flesh"?
> How healthy is your life "in the spirit"? What needs to change?

GOSPEL » JOHN 11:1-45

A man was sick, Lazarus of Bethany, the town of Mary and her sister Martha. This was the same Mary who massaged the Lord's feet with aromatic oils and then wiped them with her hair. It was her brother Lazarus who was sick. So the sisters sent word to Jesus, "Master, the one you love so very much is sick."

When Jesus got the message, he said, "This sickness is not fatal. It will become an occasion to show God's glory by glorifying God's Son."

Jesus loved Martha and her sister and Lazarus, but oddly, when he heard that Lazarus was sick, he stayed on where he was for two more days. After the two days, he said to his disciples, "Let's go back to Judea."

They said, "Rabbi, you can't do that. The Jews are out to kill you, and you're going back?"

Jesus replied, "Are there not twelve hours of daylight? Anyone who walks in daylight doesn't stumble because there's plenty of light from the sun. Walking at night, he might very well stumble because he can't see where he's going."

He said these things, and then announced, "Our friend Lazarus has fallen asleep. I'm going to wake him up."

The disciples said, "Master, if he's gone to sleep, he'll get a good rest and wake up feeling fine." Jesus was talking about death, while his disciples thought he was talking about taking a nap.

Then Jesus became explicit: "Lazarus died. And I am glad for your sakes that I wasn't there. You're about to be given new grounds for believing. Now let's go to him."

That's when Thomas, the one called the Twin, said to his companions, "Come along. We might as well die with him."

When Jesus finally got there, he found Lazarus already four days dead. Bethany was near Jerusalem, only a couple of miles away, and many of the Jews were visiting Martha and Mary, sympathizing with them over their brother. Martha heard Jesus was coming and went out to meet him. Mary remained in the house.

Martha said, "Master, if you'd been here, my brother wouldn't have died. Even now, I know that whatever you ask God he will give you."

Jesus said, "Your brother will be raised up."

Martha replied, "I know that he will be raised up in the resurrection at the end of time."

"You don't have to wait for the End. I am, right now, Resurrection and Life. The one who believes in me, even though he or she dies, will live. And everyone who lives believing in me does not ultimately die at all. Do you believe this?"

"Yes, Master. All along I have believed that you are the Messiah, the Son of God who comes into the world."

After saying this, she went to her sister Mary and whispered in her ear, "The Teacher is here and is asking for you."

The moment she heard that, she jumped up and ran out to him. Jesus had not yet entered the town but was still at the place where Martha had met him. When her sympathizing Jewish friends saw Mary run off, they followed her, thinking she was on her way to the tomb to weep there. Mary came to where Jesus was waiting and fell at his feet, saying, "Master, if only you had been here, my brother would not have died."

When Jesus saw her sobbing and the Jews with her sobbing, a deep anger welled up within him. He said, "Where did you put him?"

"Master, come and see," they said. Now Jesus wept.

The Jews said, "Look how deeply he loved him."

Others among them said, "Well, if he loved him so much, why didn't he do something to keep him from dying? After all, he opened the eyes of a blind man."

Then Jesus, the anger again welling up within him, arrived at the tomb. It was a simple cave in the hillside with a slab of stone laid against it. Jesus said, "Remove the stone."

The sister of the dead man, Martha, said, "Master, by this time there's a stench. He's been dead four days!"

Jesus looked her in the eye. "Didn't I tell you that if you believed, you would see the glory of God?"

Then, to the others, "Go ahead, take away the stone."

They removed the stone. Jesus raised his eyes to heaven and prayed, "Father, I'm grateful that you have listened to me. I know you always do listen, but on account of this crowd standing here I've spoken so that they might believe that you sent me."

Then he shouted, "Lazarus, come out!" And he came out, a cadaver, wrapped from head to toe, and with a kerchief over his face.

Jesus told them, "Unwrap him and let him loose."

That was a turnaround for many of the Jews who were with Mary. They saw what Jesus did, and believed in him. But some went back to the Pharisees and told on Jesus. The high priests and Pharisees called a meeting of the Jewish ruling body. "What do we do now?" they asked. "This man keeps on doing things, creating God-signs. If we let him go on, pretty soon everyone will be believing in him and the Romans will come and remove what little power and privilege we still have."

How we long to hear these words of Jesus when those we love become ill: "This sickness is not fatal." How we want to believe our loved ones will not leave us, and how betrayed we may feel when our loving arms are not enough to hold them in life. Human life is a passing shadow. We're not called mortal for nothing.

So what are we to make of this story of Lazarus? He's not saved from death in the long run; Lazarus will surely die again. But Jesus demonstrates graphically what it means to be the Lord of life. The Son of Man has power over death. No one passes beyond the limits of his kingdom. None of us is lost to life by moving beyond its tangible boundaries. Even the dead respond to the sound of Christ's voice. The shepherd knows his sheep, and they know him. The gift of Christianity is this assurance in the continuance of life, its fulfillment and transfiguration beyond mortality. Our loved ones are not lost. They are called into more and greater life.

> **When have you encountered the nearness of death,**
> **in your own experience or with those you love?**
> **Do you respond to the reality of death in faith or fear or both?**

WE RESPOND

Pray for the courage to be called out of death, fear, and sin. Pray for the wisdom to walk into the new light of God's life urgent to be born in you.

THIS TRANSFORMING WORD

HOLY WEEK AND THE TRIDUUM

PASSION SUNDAY

FIRST READING » ISAIAH 50:4-7

The Master, God, has given me
a well-taught tongue,
So I know how to encourage tired people.
He wakes me up in the morning,
Wakes me up, opens my ears
to listen as one ready to take orders.
The Master, God, opened my ears,
and I didn't go back to sleep,
didn't pull the covers back over my head.
I followed orders,
stood there and took it while they beat me,
held steady while they pulled out my beard,
Didn't dodge their insults,
faced them as they spit in my face.
And the Master, God, stays right there and helps me,
so I'm not disgraced.
Therefore I set my face like flint,
confident that I'll never regret this.
My champion is right here.
Let's take our stand together!
Who dares bring suit against me?
Let him try!
Look! the Master, God, is right here.
Who would dare call me guilty?
Look! My accusers are a clothes bin of threadbare
socks and shirts, fodder for moths!

The human body is a miracle of creativity. Even if we can scientifically name all of its chemicals and trace its functions, we cannot hope to duplicate its mystery. Sensation and emotion can be physiologically located, but there are wonders beyond what we know. Human beings are simply amazing.

And yet, how fragile and vulnerable is life! We can be conquered by the smallest microbe, a lifetime cut short by a moment of inattention. We may be hale and strong, and yet a small bullet can stop our hearts. Though we're smart or powerful or young, there are no guarantees that we'll survive beyond the present hour.

Such is the human body, both astonishing and transitory. Isaiah's suffering servant bears testimony to the best and most vulnerable aspects of human life. Eloquent speech and fierce resolve encounter beatings and abuse. The will of righteousness cannot be destroyed, even as the body wears away.

What are the strengths and virtues of your body?
What are its weaknesses?

SECOND READING » PHILIPPIANS 2:6-11

Think of yourselves the way Christ Jesus thought of himself. He had equal status with God but didn't think so much of himself that he had to cling to the advantages of that status no matter what. Not at all. When the time came, he set aside the privileges of deity and took on the status of a slave, became human! Having become human, he stayed human. It was an incredibly humbling process. He didn't claim special privileges. Instead, he lived a selfless, obedient life and then died a selfless, obedient death—and the worst kind of death at that—a crucifixion.

Because of that obedience, God lifted him high and honored him far beyond anyone or anything, ever, so that all created beings in heaven and on earth— even those long ago dead and buried—will bow in worship before this Jesus Christ, and call out in praise that he is the Master of all, to the glorious honor of God the Father.

The body of Christ, the minister of Eucharist says to us. Amen, we respond, and receive the bread of life. These are simple words, easily exchanged, and sometimes rotely recited. But inherent in them is a world of meaning.

The body of Christ is in itself a marvel. God has a body! God *chose* to have a body, the One who had no need of one as we do. God chose to accept the limitation and inconvenience and outright peril of bodily existence in order to be like us "in all ways but sin." God chose, in Christ, to accept even death, the natural fate of every body. And yet there is nothing natural about crucifixion. The particular death suffered by the body of Christ is unnatural, dreamt up by the cruelty of human imagination.

We are the body of Christ. We reverence his body in the Eucharist, and take on the identity of his body by our baptism. Within the identity of that body, our death is transformed, and our life has wonderful new meaning.

How does the Eucharist you receive live on beyond the Mass?

GOSPEL » MATTHEW 26:14—27:66

That is when one of the Twelve, the one named Judas Iscariot, went to the cabal of high priests and said, "What will you give me if I hand him over to you?" They settled on thirty silver pieces. He began looking for just the right moment to hand him over.

On the first of the Days of Unleavened Bread, the disciples came to Jesus and

THIS TRANSFORMING WORD

said, "Where do you want us to prepare your Passover meal?"

He said, "Enter the city. Go up to a certain man and say, 'The Teacher says, My time is near. I and my disciples plan to celebrate the Passover meal at your house.'" The disciples followed Jesus' instructions to the letter, and prepared the Passover meal.

After sunset, he and the Twelve were sitting around the table. During the meal, he said, "I have something hard but important to say to you: One of you is going to hand me over to the conspirators."

They were stunned, and then began to ask, one after another, "It isn't me, is it, Master?"

Jesus answered, "The one who hands me over is someone I eat with daily, one who passes me food at the table. In one sense the Son of Man is entering into a way of treachery well-marked by the Scriptures—no surprises here. In another sense that man who turns him in, turns traitor to the Son of Man—better never to have been born than do this!"

Then Judas, already turned traitor, said, "It isn't me, is it, Rabbi?"

Jesus said, "Don't play games with me, Judas."

During the meal, Jesus took and blessed the bread, broke it, and gave it to his disciples:

Take, eat.
This is my body.

Taking the cup and thanking God, he gave it to them:

Drink this, all of you.
This is my blood,
God's new covenant poured out for many people
  for the forgiveness of sins.

"I'll not be drinking wine from this cup again until that new day when I'll drink with you in the kingdom of my Father."

They sang a hymn and went directly to Mount Olives.

Then Jesus told them, "Before the night's over, you're going to fall to pieces because of what happens to me. There is a Scripture that says,

I'll strike the shepherd;
helter-skelter the sheep will be scattered.

But after I am raised up, I, your Shepherd, will go ahead of you, leading the way to Galilee."

Peter broke in, "Even if everyone else falls to pieces on account of you, I won't."

"Don't be so sure," Jesus said. "This very night, before the rooster crows up the dawn, you will deny me three times."

Peter protested, "Even if I had to die with you, I would never deny you." All the others said the same thing.

Then Jesus went with them to a garden called Gethsemane and told his disciples, "Stay here while I go over there and pray." Taking along Peter and the two sons of Zebedee, he plunged into an agonizing sorrow. Then he said, "This sorrow is crushing my life out. Stay here and keep vigil with me."

Going a little ahead, he fell on his face, praying, "My Father, if there is any way, get me out of this. But please, not what I want. You, what do you want?"

When he came back to his disciples, he found them sound asleep. He said to Peter, "Can't you stick it out with me a single hour? Stay alert; be in prayer so you don't wander into temptation without even knowing you're in danger. There is a part of you that is eager, ready for anything in God. But there's another part that's as lazy as an old dog sleeping by the fire."

He then left them a second time. Again he prayed, "My Father, if there is no other way than this, drinking this cup to the dregs, I'm ready. Do it your way."

When he came back, he again found them sound asleep. They simply couldn't keep their eyes open. This time he let them sleep on, and went back a third time to pray, going over the same ground one last time.

When he came back the next time, he said, "Are you going to sleep on and make a night of it? My time is up, the Son of Man is about to be handed over to the hands of sinners. Get up! Let's get going! My betrayer is here."

The words were barely out of his mouth when Judas (the one from the Twelve) showed up, and with him a gang from the high priests and religious leaders brandishing swords and clubs. The betrayer had worked out a sign with them: "The one I kiss, that's the one—seize him." He went straight to Jesus, greeted him, "How are you, Rabbi?" and kissed him.

Jesus said, "Friend, why this charade?"

Then they came on him—grabbed him and roughed him up. One of those with Jesus pulled his sword and, taking a swing at the Chief Priest's servant, cut off his ear.

Jesus said, "Put your sword back where it belongs. All who use swords are destroyed by swords. Don't you realize that I am able right now to call to my Father, and twelve companies—more, if I want them—of fighting angels would be here, battle-ready? But if I did that, how would the Scriptures come true that say this is the way it has to be?"

Then Jesus addressed the mob: "What is this—coming out after me with swords and clubs as if I were a dangerous criminal? Day after day I have been sitting in the Temple teaching, and you never so much as lifted a hand against me. You've done it this way to confirm and fulfill the prophetic writings."

Then all the disciples cut and ran.

The gang that had seized Jesus led him before Caiaphas the Chief Priest, where the religion scholars and leaders had assembled. Peter followed at a safe distance until they got to the Chief Priest's courtyard. Then he slipped in and mingled with the servants, watching to see how things would turn out.

The high priests, conspiring with the Jewish Council, tried to cook up charges against Jesus in order to sentence him to death. But even though many stepped up, making up one false accusation after another, nothing was believable.

Finally two men came forward with this: "He said, 'I can tear down this Temple of God and after three days rebuild it.'"

The Chief Priest stood up and said, "What do you have to say to the accusation?"

Jesus kept silent.

Then the Chief Priest said, "I command you by the authority of the living God to say if you are the Messiah, the Son of God."

Jesus was curt: "You yourself said it. And that's not all. Soon you'll see it for yourself:

The Son of Man seated at the right hand of the Mighty One,
Arriving on the clouds of heaven."

At that, the Chief Priest lost his temper, ripping his robes, yelling, "He blasphemed! Why do we need witnesses to accuse him? You all heard him blaspheme! Are you going to stand for such blasphemy?"

They all said, "Death! That seals his death sentence."

Then they were spitting in his face and banging him around. They jeered as they slapped him: "Prophesy, Messiah: Who hit you that time?"

All this time, Peter was sitting out in the courtyard. One servant girl came up to him and said, "You were with Jesus the Galilean."

In front of everybody there, he denied it. "I don't know what you're talking about."

As he moved over toward the gate, someone else said to the people there, "This man was with Jesus the Nazarene."

Again he denied it, salting his denial with an oath: "I swear, I never laid eyes on the man."

Shortly after that, some bystanders approached Peter. "You've got to be one of them. Your accent gives you away."

Then he got really nervous and swore. "I don't know the man!"

Just then a rooster crowed. Peter remembered what Jesus had said: "Before the rooster crows, you will deny me three times." He went out and cried and cried and cried.

In the first light of dawn, all the high priests and religious leaders met and put the finishing touches on their plot to kill Jesus. Then they tied him up and paraded him to Pilate, the governor.

Judas, the one who betrayed him, realized that Jesus was doomed. Overcome with remorse, he gave back the thirty silver coins to the high priests, saying, "I've sinned. I've betrayed an innocent man."

They said, "What do we care? That's your problem!"

Judas threw the silver coins into the Temple and left. Then he went out and hung himself.

The high priests picked up the silver pieces, but then didn't know what to do with them. "It wouldn't be right to give this—a payment for murder!—as an offering in the Temple." They decided to get rid of it by buying the "Potter's Field" and use it as a burial place for the homeless. That's how the field got called "Murder Meadow," a name that has stuck to this day. Then Jeremiah's words became history:

> They took the thirty silver pieces,
> The price of the one priced by some sons of Israel,
> And they purchased the potter's field.

And so they unwittingly followed the divine instructions to the letter.

Jesus was placed before the governor, who questioned him: "Are you the 'King of the Jews'?"

Jesus said, "If you say so."

But when the accusations rained down hot and heavy from the high priests and religious leaders, he said nothing. Pilate asked him, "Do you hear that long list of accusations? Aren't you going to say something?" Jesus kept silence—not a word from his mouth. The governor was impressed, really impressed.

It was old custom during the Feast for the governor to pardon a single prisoner named by the crowd. At the time, they had the infamous Jesus Barabbas in prison. With the crowd before him, Pilate said, "Which prisoner do you want me to pardon: Jesus Barabbas, or Jesus the so-called Christ?" He knew it was through sheer spite that they had turned Jesus over to him.

While court was still in session, Pilate's wife sent him a message: "Don't get mixed up in judging this noble man. I've just been through a long and troubled night because of a dream about him."

Meanwhile, the high priests and religious leaders had talked the crowd into asking for the pardon of Barabbas and the execution of Jesus.

The governor asked, "Which of the two do you want me to pardon?"

They said, "Barabbas!"

"Then what do I do with Jesus, the so-called Christ?"

They all shouted, "Nail him to a cross!"

He objected, "But for what crime?"

But they yelled all the louder, "Nail him to a cross!"

When Pilate saw that he was getting nowhere and that a riot was imminent, he took a basin of water and washed his hands in full sight of the crowd, saying, "I'm washing my hands of responsibility for this man's death. From now on, it's in your hands. You're judge and jury."

The crowd answered, "We'll take the blame, we and our children after us."

Then he pardoned Barabbas. But he had Jesus whipped, and then handed over for crucifixion.

The soldiers assigned to the governor took Jesus into the governor's palace and got the entire brigade together for some fun. They stripped him and dressed him in a red toga. They plaited a crown from branches of a thorn bush and set it on his head. They put a stick in his right hand for a scepter. Then they knelt before him in mocking reverence: "Bravo, King of the Jews!" they said. "Bravo!" Then they spit on him and hit him on the head with the stick. When they had had their fun, they took off the toga and put his own clothes back on him. Then they proceeded out to the crucifixion.

Along the way they came on a man from Cyrene named Simon and made him carry Jesus' cross. Arriving at Golgotha, the place they call "Skull Hill," they offered him a mild painkiller (a mixture of wine and myrrh), but when he tasted it he wouldn't drink it.

After they had finished nailing him to the cross and were waiting for him to die, they whiled away the time by throwing dice for his clothes. Above his head they had posted the criminal charge against him: THIS IS JESUS, THE KING OF THE JEWS. Along with him, they also crucified two criminals, one to his right, the other to his left. People passing along the road jeered, shaking their heads in mock lament: "You bragged that you could tear down the Temple and then rebuild it in three days—so show us your stuff! Save yourself! If you're really God's Son, come down from that cross!"

The high priests, along with the religion scholars and leaders, were right there mixing it up with the rest of them, having a great time poking fun at him: "He saved others—he can't save himself! King of Israel, is he? Then let him get down from that cross. We'll all become believers then! He was so sure of God—well, let him rescue his 'Son' now—if he wants him! He did claim to be God's Son, didn't he?" Even the two criminals crucified next to him joined in the mockery.

From noon to three, the whole earth was dark. Around midafternoon Jesus groaned out of the depths, crying loudly, "Eli, Eli, lama sabachthani?" which means, "My God, my God, why have you abandoned me?"

Some bystanders who heard him said, "He's calling for Elijah." One of them ran and got a sponge soaked in sour wine and lifted it on a stick so he could drink. The others joked, "Don't be in such a hurry. Let's see if Elijah comes and saves him."

But Jesus, again crying out loudly, breathed his last.

At that moment, the Temple curtain was ripped in two, top to bottom. There was an earthquake, and rocks were split in pieces. What's more, tombs were opened up, and many bodies of believers asleep in their graves were raised. (After Jesus' resurrection, they left the tombs, entered the holy city, and appeared to many.)

The captain of the guard and those with him, when they saw the earthquake and everything else that was happening, were scared to death. They said, "This has to be the Son of God!"

There were also quite a few women watching from a distance, women who had followed Jesus from Galilee in order to serve him. Among them were Mary Magdalene, Mary the mother of James and Joseph, and the mother of the Zebedee brothers.

Late in the afternoon a wealthy man from Arimathea, a disciple of Jesus, arrived. His name was Joseph. He went to Pilate and asked for Jesus' body. Pilate granted his request. Joseph took the body and wrapped it in clean linens, put it in his own tomb, a new tomb only recently cut into the rock, and rolled a large stone across the entrance. Then he went off. But Mary Magdalene and the other Mary stayed, sitting in plain view of the tomb.

After sundown, the high priests and Pharisees arranged a meeting with Pilate. They said, "Sir, we just remembered that that liar announced while he was still alive, 'After three days I will be raised.' We've got to get that tomb sealed until the third day. There's a good chance his disciples will come and steal the corpse and then go around saying, 'He's risen from the dead.' Then we'll be worse off than before, the final deceit surpassing the first."

Pilate told them, "You will have a guard. Go ahead and secure it the best you can." So they went out and secured the tomb, sealing the stone and posting guards.

Jesus offers his disciples bread and wine, which is what they expected him to do as table host. But he offers them also his body and blood, which they did not expect and receive in confusion and distress.

And then Jesus goes into the night, to face his betrayer and accusers. His body is handed over, spat upon in the presence of the high priest, sold for a bag of silver. The crowds cry out to see his body crucified. His flesh is whipped and his brow is crushed by a crown of thorns. His thirst is mocked by vinegar on a sponge, and his limbs are torn by nails. And finally, the body of Jesus is murdered on the cross, and taken down and carried away for burial. One would have thought that would have been the end of it, and mercifully so.

But the body of Christ rises from the dead, and lives on in our community of faith. Jesus offers his body again and again to those who would be his disciples. And now we claim this body as our own, and offer it to a world which longs to see the face of love.

> **What is your primary reaction to the passion of Christ:**
> **horror, fear, discomfort, love?**
> **What is your *response* to the passion of Christ in your daily life?**

WE RESPOND

Spend some time reflecting on the Eucharist. If you are able, attend the Exposition of the Sacrament on Holy Thursday night at your parish. Sit before the tabernacle in a quiet hour, and contemplate how the body of Christ lives in you.

The captain of the guard and those with him,
when they saw the earthquake
and everything else that was happening,
were scared to death.
They said, "This has to be the Son of God!"

HOLY THURSDAY
EVENING MASS OF THE LORD'S SUPPER

.... God's Life Is Ours

FIRST READING » EXODUS 12:1-8, 11-14

God said to Moses and Aaron while still in Egypt, "This month is to be the first month of the year for you. Address the whole community of Israel; tell them that on the tenth of this month each man is to take a lamb for his family, one lamb to a house. If the family is too small for a lamb, then share it with a close neighbor, depending on the number of persons involved. Be mindful of how much each person will eat. Your lamb must be a healthy male, one year old; you can select it from either the sheep or the goats. Keep it penned until the fourteenth day of this month and then slaughter it—the entire community of Israel will do this—at dusk. Then take some of the blood and smear it on the two doorposts and the lintel of the houses in which you will eat it. You are to eat the meat, roasted in the fire, that night, along with bread, made without yeast, and bitter herbs. Don't eat any of it raw or boiled in water; make sure it's roasted—the whole animal, head, legs, and innards. Don't leave any of it until morning; if there are leftovers, burn them in the fire.

"And here is how you are to eat it: Be fully dressed with your sandals on and your stick in your hand. Eat in a hurry; it's the Passover to God.

"I will go through the land of Egypt on this night and strike down every firstborn in the land of Egypt, whether human or animal, and bring judgment on all the gods of Egypt. I am God. The blood will serve as a sign on the houses where you live. When I see the blood I will pass over you—no disaster will touch you when I strike the land of Egypt.

"This will be a memorial day for you; you will celebrate it as a festival to God down through the generations, a fixed festival celebration to be observed always. You will eat unraised bread (matzoth) for seven days: On the first day get rid of all yeast from your houses—anyone who eats anything with yeast from the first day to the seventh day will be cut off from Israel. The first and the seventh days are set aside as holy; do no work on those days. Only what you have to do for meals; each person can do that.

"The life of every animal is its blood—the blood is its life" (Lev. 17:14). This saying is older than the law of Moses. Blood is equated with life for the observable reason that sufficient loss of blood results in loss of life. Cradling the divine gift of vitality, blood was therefore sacred. Animals had to be drained of blood before eaten, which is still a kosher law. The blood was poured into the ground, the origin and destination of all life in Genesis.

Blood was deemed a kind of divinely determined off-limits marker. Women were not to be touched in the time of their blood flow. Newborns had to undergo a period

THIS TRANSFORMING WORD

of purification after birth. Those who came into contact with a corpse underwent a period of untouchability. Blood rituals marking the ears, hands, and feet were used to ordain the priests of Aaron. A nearly identical procedure pronounced a leper cured. Blood was splashed liberally against altars of sacrifice, and sacrificial animals themselves were vehicles for offering life back to God. The marking of houses with blood was enough to turn the angel of death aside.

> How do I honor the gift of life in myself, in others,
> and even in the creatures of earth?

SECOND READING » 1 CORINTHIANS 11:23−26

Let me go over with you again exactly what goes on in the Lord's Supper and why it is so centrally important. I received my instructions from the Master himself and passed them on to you. The Master, Jesus, on the night of his betrayal, took bread. Having given thanks, he broke it and said,
This is my body, broken for you.
Do this to remember me.
After supper, he did the same thing with the cup:
This cup is my blood, my new covenant with you.
Each time you drink this cup, remember me.
What you must solemnly realize is that every time you eat this bread and every time you drink this cup, you reenact in your words and actions the death of the Master. You will be drawn back to this meal again and again until the Master returns. You must never let familiarity breed contempt.

Compare the attitude toward blood in the old covenant with the self-offering Jesus makes of it in the new! As it was forbidden to consume blood or to touch it casually because of its sacred and life-containing property, old-covenant blood had to be poured on the ground or rendered to God at the altar. Jesus does not deny that there's "life in the blood," or that his blood is anything less than a sacred substance. Yet in a marvelous reversal, he urges his followers to drink the cup of his blood in order to share this divine vitality. Rather than becoming "unclean" or "impure" as a result of an unworthy contact, the cup of blood Jesus shares with us makes us whole and consecrates us for holy purposes.

It's no wonder that early Jewish Christians would have appreciated the sign of Eucharist for its remarkable new revelation in meaning. It's also no surprise that many Jews of the time would have found in it a horror and a stumbling block to acceptance. How you understand the sacrificial blood of Christ is the linchpin of faith.

> When we eat this bread and drink this cup, divine life is in us.
> What implications does this have for all of life?

GOSPEL » JOHN 13:1–15

Just before the Passover Feast, Jesus knew that the time had come to leave this world to go to the Father. Having loved his dear companions, he continued to love them right to the end. It was suppertime. The Devil by now had Judas, son of Simon the Iscariot, firmly in his grip, all set for the betrayal.

Jesus knew that the Father had put him in complete charge of everything, that he came from God and was on his way back to God. So he got up from the supper table, set aside his robe, and put on an apron. Then he poured water into a basin and began to wash the feet of the disciples, drying them with his apron. When he got to Simon Peter, Peter said, "Master, you wash my feet?"

Jesus answered, "You don't understand now what I'm doing, but it will be clear enough to you later."

Peter persisted, "You're not going to wash my feet—ever!"

Jesus said, "If I don't wash you, you can't be part of what I'm doing."

"Master!" said Peter. "Not only my feet, then. Wash my hands! Wash my head!"

Jesus said, "If you've had a bath in the morning, you only need your feet washed now and you're clean from head to toe. My concern, you understand, is holiness, not hygiene. So now you're clean. But not every one of you." (He knew who was betraying him. That's why he said, "Not every one of you.") After he had finished washing their feet, he took his robe, put it back on, and went back to his place at the table.

Then he said, "Do you understand what I have done to you? You address me as 'Teacher' and 'Master,' and rightly so. That is what I am. So if I, the Master and Teacher, washed your feet, you must now wash each other's feet. I've laid down a pattern for you. What I've done, you do. I'm only pointing out the obvious. A servant is not ranked above his master; an employee doesn't give orders to the employer. If you understand what I'm telling you, act like it—and live a blessed life.

The pattern Jesus lays down for us is one of humble, loving service. It may seem odd that two very different signs are offered to us on the night before Jesus died. On the one hand, Eucharist tells us that God-life is in us, and that it makes us bearers of divine vitality into the world. On the other hand, the foot washing of the disciples makes it plain that we are exalted to share in God-life for the purpose of humbling ourselves to the role of servanthood. Glory and humility, up and down. Grace is always a balancing act between the two. Christian self-knowledge means we know full well the grandness of our calling—and we also embrace its ego-diminishing obligations cheerfully.

Saint Francis of Assisi appreciated the "perfect joy" found in the most humiliating circumstances. While rough treatment is certainly unpleasant, knowing how Jesus was treated made the likeness delightful to Francis. Having our egos polished down on humbling occasions is a spiritual lesson better than a mountain of praise.

THIS TRANSFORMING WORD

When has my ego been sorely "polished" by circumstances?
What did I learn about myself on that occasion?

WE RESPOND

"I'm washed and prepared for service. What, Lord, would you have me do?" Pray for discernment to offer the service that will be required of you in every situation.

"I've laid down a pattern for you.
What I've done, you do.
I'm only pointing out the obvious."

GOOD FRIDAY OF THE LORD'S PASSION

FIRST READING » ISAIAH 52:13—53:12

"Just watch my servant blossom!
  Exalted, tall, head and shoulders above the crowd!
But he didn't begin that way.
  At first everyone was appalled.
He didn't even look human—
  a ruined face, disfigured past recognition.
Nations all over the world will be in awe, taken aback,
  kings shocked into silence when they see him.
For what was unheard of they'll see with their own eyes,
  what was unthinkable they'll have right before them."
Who believes what we've heard and seen?
  Who would have thought God's saving power would look like this?
The servant grew up before God—a scrawny seedling,
  a scrubby plant in a parched field.
There was nothing attractive about him,
  nothing to cause us to take a second look.
He was looked down on and passed over,
  a man who suffered, who knew pain firsthand.
One look at him and people turned away.
  We looked down on him, thought he was scum.
But the fact is, it was our pains he carried—
  our disfigurements, all the things wrong with us.
We thought he brought it on himself,
  that God was punishing him for his own failures.
But it was our sins that did that to him,
  that ripped and tore and crushed him—our sins!
He took the punishment, and that made us whole.
  Through his bruises we get healed.
We're all like sheep who've wandered off and gotten lost.
  We've all done our own thing, gone our own way.
And God has piled all our sins, everything we've done wrong,
  on him, on him.
He was beaten, he was tortured,
  but he didn't say a word.
Like a lamb taken to be slaughtered
  and like a sheep being sheared,
  he took it all in silence.

Justice miscarried, and he was led off—
*   and did anyone really know what was happening?*
He died without a thought for his own welfare,
*   beaten bloody for the sins of my people.*
They buried him with the wicked,
*   threw him in a grave with a rich man,*
Even though he'd never hurt a soul
*   or said one word that wasn't true.*
Still, it's what God had in mind all along,
*   to crush him with pain.*
The plan was that he give himself as an offering for sin
*   so that he'd see life come from it—life, life, and more life.*
*   And God's plan will deeply prosper through him.*
Out of that terrible travail of soul,
*   he'll see that it's worth it and be glad he did it.*
Through what he experienced, my righteous one, my servant,
*   will make many "righteous ones,"*
*   as he himself carries the burden of their sins.*
Therefore I'll reward him extravagantly—
*   the best of everything, the highest honors—*
Because he looked death in the face and didn't flinch,
*   because he embraced the company of the lowest.*
He took on his own shoulders the sin of the many,
*   he took up the cause of all the black sheep.*

Life, life, and more life. The Lord of life has nothing less planned for the beloved world and all its inhabitants. As free choosers, of course, we may have other plans. God will not obstruct our liberty even when we've got death and destruction on our minds. So we may abuse our health, commit our infidelities, wage our wars, and neglect the poor with no apparent consequences—at first. Heaven awaits the change of heart and converted mind that might still lead to renewed life. But time forecloses, and we do arrive at a tipping point when the consequences of our death-dealing choices cannot be overturned in the short run. Our health may be ruined, our relationships irretrievably broken, communities destroyed, and the silent poor lost, one by one. Only in the eternal realm may we still have hope for more life. And that's something! God's generosity in offering us life was hard-won by the suffering servant who forced open the door of death for us. But you and I must still deliberately choose to walk through it.

> **How many of my daily choices celebrate life?**
> **Which ones reap harm, intentionally or not?**

SECOND READING » HEBREWS 4:14–16; 5:7–9

Now that we know what we have—Jesus, this great High Priest with ready access to God—let's not let it slip through our fingers. We don't have a priest who is out of touch with our reality. He's been through weakness and testing, experienced it all—all but the sin. So let's walk right up to him and get what he is so ready to give. Take the mercy, accept the help.

While he lived on earth, anticipating death, Jesus cried out in pain and wept in sorrow as he offered up priestly prayers to God. Because he honored God, God answered him. Though he was God's Son, he learned trusting-obedience by what he suffered, just as we do. Then, having arrived at the full stature of his maturity and having been announced by God as high priest in the order of Melchizedek, he became the source of eternal salvation to all who believingly obey him.

"Take the mercy and accept the help." When I go into the tee shirt and bumper sticker business some day, this phrase will find a wider audience. In our self-reliant, lone-ranger culture, we view mercy and help as a sign of weakness. Well, let me be the first to assign myself to the Am-Weak-Need-Mercy column in the ledgers of heaven! If eternal life could be earned only by our own merits, I wouldn't stand a chance. I cling to the Christian story because it's the only one that can save me. As Saint Paul says in Romans, "I realize that I don't have what it takes. I can will it, but I can't do it. I decide to do good, but I don't *really* do it; I decide not to do bad, but then I do it anyway" (7:18-19).

In many ways we "good-enough" Christians are the most vulnerable species of all. We have an airbrushed look about us that, compared with the great scoundrels of history, makes us seem positively virtuous. Skirting wickedness puts us only at the trailhead of virtue. How little we realize that the failure to do good is an evil all its own!

> **How do I seek the help available to me through the church?**
> **When I pray, "Lord have mercy," am I aware how much I need it?**

GOSPEL » JOHN 18:1—19:42

Jesus, having prayed this prayer, left with his disciples and crossed over the brook Kidron at a place where there was a garden. He and his disciples entered it.

Judas, his betrayer, knew the place because Jesus and his disciples went there often. So Judas led the way to the garden, and the Roman soldiers and police sent by the high priests and Pharisees followed. They arrived there with lanterns and torches and swords. Jesus, knowing by now everything that was coming down on him, went out and met them. He said, "Who are you after?"

They answered, "Jesus the Nazarene."

He said, "That's me." The soldiers recoiled, totally taken aback. Judas, his betrayer, stood out like a sore thumb.

Jesus asked again, "Who are you after?"

They answered, "Jesus the Nazarene."

"I told you," said Jesus, "that's me. I'm the one. So if it's me you're after, let these others go." (This validated the words in his prayer, "I didn't lose one of those you gave.")

Just then Simon Peter, who was carrying a sword, pulled it from its sheath and struck the Chief Priest's servant, cutting off his right ear. Malchus was the servant's name.

Jesus ordered Peter, "Put back your sword. Do you think for a minute I'm not going to drink this cup the Father gave me?"

Then the Roman soldiers under their commander, joined by the Jewish police, seized Jesus and tied him up. They took him first to Annas, father-in-law of Caiaphas. Caiaphas was the Chief Priest that year. It was Caiaphas who had advised the Jews that it was to their advantage that one man die for the people.

Simon Peter and another disciple followed Jesus. That other disciple was known to the Chief Priest, and so he went in with Jesus to the Chief Priest's courtyard. Peter had to stay outside. Then the other disciple went out, spoke to the doorkeeper, and got Peter in.

The young woman who was the doorkeeper said to Peter, "Aren't you one of this man's disciples?"

He said, "No, I'm not."

The servants and police had made a fire because of the cold and were huddled there warming themselves. Peter stood with them, trying to get warm.

Annas interrogated Jesus regarding his disciples and his teaching. Jesus answered, "I've spoken openly in public. I've taught regularly in meeting places and the Temple, where the Jews all come together. Everything has been out in the open. I've said nothing in secret. So why are you treating me like a conspirator? Question those who have been listening to me. They know well what I have said. My teachings have all been aboveboard."

When he said this, one of the policemen standing there slapped Jesus across the face, saying, "How dare you speak to the Chief Priest like that!"

Jesus replied, "If I've said something wrong, prove it. But if I've spoken the plain truth, why this slapping around?"

Then Annas sent him, still tied up, to the Chief Priest Caiaphas.

Meanwhile, Simon Peter was back at the fire, still trying to get warm. The others there said to him, "Aren't you one of his disciples?"

He denied it, "Not me."

One of the Chief Priest's servants, a relative of the man whose ear Peter had cut off, said, "Didn't I see you in the garden with him?"

Again, Peter denied it. Just then a rooster crowed.

They led Jesus then from Caiaphas to the Roman governor's palace. It was early morning. They themselves didn't enter the palace because they didn't want to be disqualified from eating the Passover. So Pilate came out to them and spoke. "What charge do you bring against this man?"

They said, "If he hadn't been doing something evil, do you think we'd be here bothering you?"

Pilate said, "You take him. Judge him by your law."

The Jews said, "We're not allowed to kill anyone." (This would confirm Jesus' word indicating the way he would die.)

Pilate went back into the palace and called for Jesus. He said, "Are you the 'King of the Jews'?"

Jesus answered, "Are you saying this on your own, or did others tell you this about me?"

Pilate said, "Do I look like a Jew? Your people and your high priests turned you over to me. What did you do?"

"My kingdom," said Jesus, "doesn't consist of what you see around you. If it did, my followers would fight so that I wouldn't be handed over to the Jews. But I'm not that kind of king, not the world's kind of king."

Then Pilate said, "So, are you a king or not?"

Jesus answered, "You tell me. Because I am King, I was born and entered the world so that I could witness to the truth. Everyone who cares for truth, who has any feeling for the truth, recognizes my voice."

Pilate said, "What is truth?"

Then he went back out to the Jews and told them, "I find nothing wrong in this man. It's your custom that I pardon one prisoner at Passover. Do you want me to pardon the 'King of the Jews'?"

They shouted back, "Not this one, but Barabbas!" Barabbas was a Jewish freedom fighter.

So Pilate took Jesus and had him whipped. The soldiers, having braided a crown from thorns, set it on his head, threw a purple robe over him, and approached him with, "Hail, King of the Jews!" Then they greeted him with slaps in the face.

Pilate went back out again and said to them, "I present him to you, but I want you to know that I do not find him guilty of any crime." Just then Jesus came out wearing the thorn crown and purple robe.

Pilate announced, "Here he is: the Man."

When the high priests and police saw him, they shouted in a frenzy, "Crucify! Crucify!"

Pilate told them, "You take him. You crucify him. I find nothing wrong with him."

The Jews answered, "We have a law, and by that law he must die because he claimed to be the Son of God."

When Pilate heard this, he became even more scared. He went back into the palace and said to Jesus, "Where did you come from?"

Jesus gave no answer.

Pilate said, "You won't talk? Don't you know that I have the authority to pardon you, and the authority to—crucify you?"

Jesus said, "You haven't a shred of authority over me except what has been given you from heaven. That's why the one who betrayed me to you has committed a far greater fault."

At this, Pilate tried his best to pardon him, but the Jews shouted him down: "If you pardon this man, you're no friend of Caesar's. Anyone setting himself up as 'king' defies Caesar."

When Pilate heard those words, he led Jesus outside. He sat down at the judgment seat in the area designated Stone Court (in Hebrew, Gabbatha). It was the preparation day for Passover. The hour was noon. Pilate said to the Jews, "Here is your king."

They shouted back, "Kill him! Kill him! Crucify him!"

Pilate said, "I am to crucify your king?"

The high priests answered, "We have no king except Caesar."

Pilate caved in to their demand. He turned him over to be crucified.

They took Jesus away. Carrying his cross, Jesus went out to the place called Skull Hill (the name in Hebrew is Golgotha), where they crucified him, and with him two others, one on each side, Jesus in the middle. Pilate wrote a sign and had it placed on the cross. It read:

JESUS THE NAZARENE
THE KING OF THE JEWS.

Many of the Jews read the sign because the place where Jesus was crucified was right next to the city. It was written in Hebrew, Latin, and Greek. The Jewish high priests objected. "Don't write," they said to Pilate, "'The King of the Jews.' Make it, 'This man said, "I am the King of the Jews."'"

Pilate said, "What I've written, I've written."

When they crucified him, the Roman soldiers took his clothes and divided them up four ways, to each soldier a fourth. But his robe was seamless, a single piece of weaving, so they said to each other, "Let's not tear it up. Let's throw dice to see who gets it." This confirmed the Scripture that said, "They divided up my clothes among them and threw dice for my coat." (The soldiers validated the Scriptures!)

While the soldiers were looking after themselves, Jesus' mother, his aunt, Mary the wife of Clopas, and Mary Magdalene stood at the foot of the cross. Jesus saw his mother and the disciple he loved standing near her. He said to his mother, "Woman, here is your son." Then to the disciple, "Here is your mother." From that moment the disciple accepted her as his own mother.

Jesus, seeing that everything had been completed so that the Scripture record might also be complete, then said, "I'm thirsty."

A jug of sour wine was standing by. Someone put a sponge soaked with the wine on a javelin and lifted it to his mouth. After he took the wine, Jesus said, "It's done...complete." Bowing his head, he offered up his spirit.

Then the Jews, since it was the day of Sabbath preparation, and so the bodies wouldn't stay on the crosses over the Sabbath (it was a high holy day that year), petitioned Pilate that their legs be broken to speed death, and the bodies taken down. So the soldiers came and broke the legs of the first man crucified with Jesus, and then the other. When they got to Jesus, they saw that he was already dead, so they didn't break his legs. One of the soldiers stabbed him in the side with his spear. Blood and water gushed out.

The eyewitness to these things has presented an accurate report. He saw it himself and is telling the truth so that you, also, will believe.

These things that happened confirmed the Scripture, "Not a bone in his body was broken," and the other Scripture that reads, "They will stare at the one they pierced."

After all this, Joseph of Arimathea (he was a disciple of Jesus, but secretly, because he was intimidated by the Jews) petitioned Pilate to take the body of Jesus. Pilate gave permission. So Joseph came and took the body.

Nicodemus, who had first come to Jesus at night, came now in broad daylight carrying a mixture of myrrh and aloes, about seventy-five pounds. They took Jesus' body and, following the Jewish burial custom, wrapped it in linen with the spices. There was a garden near the place he was crucified, and in the garden a new tomb in which no one had yet been placed. So, because it was Sabbath preparation for the Jews and the tomb was convenient, they placed Jesus in it.

Pilate pops the question: "What is truth?" Maybe he's being glib. Or maybe he really wants to know. The Passion narrative suggests that he'd sincerely like to know what to do with Jesus. The judgment rests on Pilate's shoulders and he'd rather shift the weight elsewhere. Being the Roman governor of a troublesome province means he's constantly beset with decisions big and small. Pilate seems unsure in the gospel accounts whether this Jesus business counts as a big decision or a small one. So he takes his cue from the crowds below. Do they seem stirred up about this Jesus? Does his fate matter enough to cause more unrest if he's released or put to death?

When Pilate wonders about truth, he's not reflecting on the innocence or guilt of Jesus. He already admits Jesus is innocent of any crime. No, truth to Pilate is an expedient judgment: one which removes this item from his agenda for a season, or at least for today. He settles on his truth shortly. Our creed affixes it to him for all time in the phrase: "crucified under Pontius Pilate."

> What kind of truth am I seeking?
> What might my epitaph be if this truth were attached to me for keeps?

WE RESPOND

Jesus says, "I am the way, the truth, and the life." If we seek Jesus, we will find truth.

EASTER VIGIL

FIRST READING » GENESIS 1:1—2:2

First this: God created the Heavens and Earth—all you see, all you don't see.
Earth was a soup of nothingness, a bottomless emptiness, an inky blackness.
God's Spirit brooded like a bird above the watery abyss.
God spoke: "Light!"
    And light appeared.
  God saw that light was good
    and separated light from dark.
  God named the light Day,
    he named the dark Night.
  It was evening, it was morning—
  Day One.
God spoke: "Sky! In the middle of the waters;
    separate water from water!"
  God made sky.
  He separated the water under sky
    from the water above sky.
  And there it was:
    he named sky the Heavens;
  It was evening, it was morning—
  Day Two.
God spoke: "Separate!
    Water-beneath-Heaven, gather into one place;
Land, appear!"
    And there it was.
  God named the land Earth.
    He named the pooled water Ocean.
  God saw that it was good.
God spoke: "Earth, green up! Grow all varieties
    of seed-bearing plants,
Every sort of fruit-bearing tree."
    And there it was.
  Earth produced green seed-bearing plants,
    all varieties,
And fruit-bearing trees of all sorts.
    God saw that it was good.
  It was evening, it was morning—
  Day Three.

God spoke: "Lights! Come out!
Shine in Heaven's sky!
Separate Day from Night.
Mark seasons and days and years,
Lights in Heaven's sky to give light to Earth."
And there it was.
God made two big lights, the larger
to take charge of Day,
The smaller to be in charge of Night;
and he made the stars.
God placed them in the heavenly sky
to light up Earth
And oversee Day and Night,
to separate light and dark.
God saw that it was good.
It was evening, it was morning—
Day Four.
God spoke: "Swarm, Ocean, with fish and all sea life!
Birds, fly through the sky over Earth!"
God created the huge whales,
all the swarm of life in the waters,
And every kind and species of flying birds.
God saw that it was good.
God blessed them: "Prosper! Reproduce! Fill Ocean!
Birds, reproduce on Earth!"
It was evening, it was morning—
Day Five.
God spoke: "Earth, generate life! Every sort and kind:
cattle and reptiles and wild animals—all kinds."
And there it was:
wild animals of every kind,
Cattle of all kinds, every sort of reptile and bug.
God saw that it was good.
God spoke: "Let us make human beings in our image, make them
reflecting our nature
So they can be responsible for the fish in the sea,
the birds in the air, the cattle,
And, yes, Earth itself,
and every animal that moves on the face of Earth."
God created human beings;
he created them godlike,
Reflecting God's nature.

He created them male and female.
God blessed them:
   "Prosper! Reproduce! Fill Earth! Take charge!
Be responsible for fish in the sea and birds in the air,
   for every living thing that moves on the face of Earth."
Then God said, "I've given you
   every sort of seed-bearing plant on Earth
And every kind of fruit-bearing tree,
   given them to you for food.
To all animals and all birds,
   everything that moves and breathes,
I give whatever grows out of the ground for food."
   And there it was.
God looked over everything he had made;
   it was so good, so very good!
It was evening, it was morning—
Day Six.
Heaven and Earth were finished,
   down to the last detail.
By the seventh day
   God had finished his work.
On the seventh day
   he rested from all his work.
God blessed the seventh day.
   He made it a Holy Day
Because on that day he rested from his work,
   all the creating God had done.
This is the story of how it all started,
   of Heaven and Earth when they were created.

God speaks, and things happen to fill the world with goodness. Human speech is not always so productive. And when it is, it doesn't always result in goodness. Can we choose our words with more care? Can we mean what we say, and bring only truth, kindness, encouragement, and compassion into the world?

SECOND READING » GENESIS 22:1-18

After all this, God tested Abraham. God said, "Abraham!"
   "Yes?" answered Abraham. "I'm listening."
   He said, "Take your dear son Isaac whom you love and go to the land of Moriah. Sacrifice him there as a burnt offering on one of the mountains that I'll point out to you."
   Abraham got up early in the morning and saddled his donkey. He took two

of his young servants and his son Isaac. He had split wood for the burnt offering. He set out for the place God had directed him. On the third day he looked up and saw the place in the distance. Abraham told his two young servants, "Stay here with the donkey. The boy and I are going over there to worship; then we'll come back to you."

Abraham took the wood for the burnt offering and gave it to Isaac his son to carry. He carried the flint and the knife. The two of them went off together.

Isaac said to Abraham his father, "Father?"

"Yes, my son."

"We have flint and wood, but where's the sheep for the burnt offering?"

Abraham said, "Son, God will see to it that there's a sheep for the burnt offering." And they kept on walking together.

They arrived at the place to which God had directed him. Abraham built an altar. He laid out the wood. Then he tied up Isaac and laid him on the wood. Abraham reached out and took the knife to kill his son.

Just then an angel of God called to him out of Heaven, "Abraham! Abraham!"

"Yes, I'm listening."

"Don't lay a hand on that boy! Don't touch him! Now I know how fearlessly you fear God; you didn't hesitate to place your son, your dear son, on the altar for me."

Abraham looked up. He saw a ram caught by its horns in the thicket. Abraham took the ram and sacrificed it as a burnt offering instead of his son.

Abraham named that place God-Yireh (God-Sees-to-It). That's where we get the saying, "On the mountain of God, he sees to it."

The angel of God spoke from Heaven a second time to Abraham: "I swear—God's sure word!—because you have gone through with this, and have not refused to give me your son, your dear, dear son, I'll bless you—oh, how I'll bless you! And I'll make sure that your children flourish—like stars in the sky! like sand on the beaches! And your descendants will defeat their enemies. All nations on Earth will find themselves blessed through your descendants because you obeyed me."

God speaks, and Abraham obeys. This episode is called a test, and it's one of the eeriest and most discomforting passages in the Old Testament. Job will later say, "God gives and God takes"—but we still have trouble understanding what we are to make of this. Would God deliberately take what we most love, precisely because we do love it? If we lose what we love best, will we be as faithful as Abraham?

THIRD READING » EXODUS 14:15—15:1

God said to Moses: "Why cry out to me? Speak to the Israelites. Order them to get moving. Hold your staff high and stretch your hand out over the sea: Split the sea! The Israelites will walk through the sea on dry ground.

"Meanwhile I'll make sure the Egyptians keep up their stubborn chase—I'll use Pharaoh and his entire army, his chariots and horsemen, to put my Glory on display so that the Egyptians will realize that I am God."

The angel of God that had been leading the camp of Israel now shifted and got behind them. And the Pillar of Cloud that had been in front also shifted to the rear. The Cloud was now between the camp of Egypt and the camp of Israel. The Cloud enshrouded one camp in darkness and flooded the other with light. The two camps didn't come near each other all night.

Then Moses stretched out his hand over the sea and God, with a terrific east wind all night long, made the sea go back. He made the sea dry ground. The seawaters split.

The Israelites walked through the sea on dry ground with the waters a wall to the right and to the left. The Egyptians came after them in full pursuit, every horse and chariot and driver of Pharaoh racing into the middle of the sea. It was now the morning watch. God looked down from the Pillar of Fire and Cloud on the Egyptian army and threw them into a panic. He clogged the wheels of their chariots; they were stuck in the mud.

The Egyptians said, "Run from Israel! God is fighting on their side and against Egypt!"

God said to Moses, "Stretch out your hand over the sea and the waters will come back over the Egyptians, over their chariots, over their horsemen."

Moses stretched his hand out over the sea: As the day broke and the Egyptians were running, the sea returned to its place as before. God dumped the Egyptians in the middle of the sea. The waters returned, drowning the chariots and riders of Pharaoh's army that had chased after Israel into the sea. Not one of them survived.

But the Israelites walked right through the middle of the sea on dry ground, the waters forming a wall to the right and to the left. God delivered Israel that day from the oppression of the Egyptians. And Israel looked at the Egyptian dead, washed up on the shore of the sea, and realized the tremendous power that God brought against the Egyptians. The people were in reverent awe before God and trusted in God and his servant Moses.

Then Moses and the Israelites sang this song to God, giving voice together,
I'm singing my heart out to God—what a victory!
    He pitched horse and rider into the sea.
God is my strength, God is my song,
    and, yes! God is my salvation.
This is the kind of God I have
    and I'm telling the world!
This is the God of my father—

> I'm spreading the news far and wide!
> God is a fighter,
>   pure God, through and through.
> Pharaoh's chariots and army
>   he dumped in the sea,
> The elite of his officers
>   he drowned in the Red Sea.
> Wild ocean waters poured over them;
>   they sank like a rock in the deep blue sea.
> Your strong right hand, God, shimmers with power;
>   your strong right hand shatters the enemy.
> In your mighty majesty
>   you smash your upstart enemies,
> You let loose your hot anger
>   and burn them to a crisp.
> At a blast from your nostrils
>   the waters piled up;
> Tumbling streams dammed up,
>   wild oceans curdled into a swamp.

"Stuck in the mud" is how Pharaoh's chariots and drivers are described. The opposite is true of the Israelites, who move swiftly through the walls of water from the territory of Egypt to the safe shore of the Sinai peninsula. At this time in our lives, are we stuck in the mud, or on the move? Do we go swiftly to the shore where God leads us, even if we don't know what awaits us there?

FOURTH READING » ISAIAH 54:5–14

> "Sing, barren woman, who has never had a baby.
>   Fill the air with song, you who've never experienced childbirth!
> You're ending up with far more children
>   than all those childbearing women." God says so!
> "Clear lots of ground for your tents!
>   Make your tents large. Spread out! Think big!
> Use plenty of rope,
>   drive the tent pegs deep.
> You're going to need lots of elbow room
>   for your growing family.
> You're going to take over whole nations;
>   you're going to resettle abandoned cities.
> Don't be afraid—you're not going to be embarrassed.
>   Don't hold back—you're not going to come up short.
> You'll forget all about the humiliations of your youth,

and the indignities of being a widow will fade from memory.
For your Maker is your bridegroom,
    his name, God-of-the-Angel-Armies!
Your Redeemer is The Holy of Israel,
    known as God of the whole earth.
You were like an abandoned wife, devastated with grief,
    and God welcomed you back,
Like a woman married young
    and then left," says your God.
Your Redeemer God says:
"I left you, but only for a moment.
    Now, with enormous compassion, I'm bringing you back.
In an outburst of anger I turned my back on you—
    but only for a moment.
It's with lasting love
    that I'm tenderly caring for you.
"This exile is just like the days of Noah for me:
    I promised then that the waters of Noah
    would never again flood the earth.
I'm promising now no more anger,
    no more dressing you down.
For even if the mountains walk away
    and the hills fall to pieces,
My love won't walk away from you,
    my covenant commitment of peace won't fall apart."
    The God who has compassion on you says so.
"Afflicted city, storm-battered, unpitied:
    I'm about to rebuild you with stones of turquoise,
Lay your foundations with sapphires,
    construct your towers with rubies,
Your gates with jewels,
    and all your walls with precious stones.
All your children will have God for their teacher—
    what a mentor for your children!
You'll be built solid, grounded in righteousness,
    far from any trouble—nothing to fear!
    far from terror—it won't even come close!
If anyone attacks you,
    don't for a moment suppose that I sent them,
And if any should attack,
    nothing will come of it.
I create the blacksmith

who fires up his forge
and makes a weapon designed to kill.
I also create the destroyer—
but no weapon that can hurt you has ever been forged.
Any accuser who takes you to court
will be dismissed as a liar.
This is what God's servants can expect.
I'll see to it that everything works out for the best."
God's Decree.

One of God's many names is "Lord of Hosts," rendered here as "God-of-the-Angel-Armies." Scripture often warns against trusting too much in the power of governments and their armies. An Angel Army, however, is a different matter. God's protection is absolute, though mountains fall and hills turn to dust. Do we trust more in Angel Armies, or in the power of our own forces?

FIFTH READING » ISAIAH 55:1–11

"Hey there! All who are thirsty,
come to the water!
Are you penniless?
Come anyway—buy and eat!
Come, buy your drinks, buy wine and milk.
Buy without money—everything's free!
Why do you spend your money on junk food,
your hard-earned cash on cotton candy?
Listen to me, listen well: Eat only the best,
fill yourself with only the finest.
Pay attention, come close now,
listen carefully to my life-giving, life-nourishing words.
I'm making a lasting covenant commitment with you,
the same that I made with David: sure, solid, enduring love.
I set him up as a witness to the nations,
made him a prince and leader of the nations,
And now I'm doing it to you:
You'll summon nations you've never heard of,
and nations who've never heard of you
will come running to you
Because of me, your God,
because The Holy of Israel has honored you."
Seek God while he's here to be found,
pray to him while he's close at hand.
Let the wicked abandon their way of life

and the evil their way of thinking.
Let them come back to God, who is merciful,
come back to our God, who is lavish with forgiveness.
"I don't think the way you think.
The way you work isn't the way I work."
God's Decree.
"For as the sky soars high above earth,
so the way I work surpasses the way you work,
and the way I think is beyond the way you think.
Just as rain and snow descend from the skies
and don't go back until they've watered the earth,
Doing their work of making things grow and blossom,
producing seed for farmers and food for the hungry,
So will the words that come out of my mouth
not come back empty-handed.
They'll do the work I sent them to do,
they'll complete the assignment I gave them.

Thank heaven God doesn't think the way we do! We live in a Me-First world with Even-Steven justice being the best we can hope for—and it's all down hill from there. Most of the time we count ourselves lucky to wind up in the black. But when God's word goes out into the world, it brings back a hundredfold in graces. Dare we become the soil in which that fertile word is planted?

SIXTH READING » BARUCH 3:9–15, 32—4:4

Hear, Israel, the commandments of life;
keep your ears open, and you'll pick up some wisdom.
What's your story, Israel?
How come you find yourself in enemy territory?
You've grown gray hairs in a foreign land; you're good as dead;
you're written off as though you were already in the world below.
You've left behind the fountain of wisdom!
If you walked in the way of God, you'd live in peace forever.
Learn how to find prudence, fortitude, intellect;
once found, you'll what life means, what wisdom means, and what peace is.
Has anyone found where wisdom hangs out?
Has anyone dipped a tentative hand into her treasury?
But there's one person who truly knows where she is;
he's the one who made the earth and filled it with four-footed beasts.
He turned the sun on and turned the sun off;
it followed the path laid down for it; it dared not wander.
Stars twinked and blinked and seemed quite happy in his company.

When he calls, they say, "we're already here,"
winking and twinking with joy at the one who made them.
This is our God;
there's not another like him;
he laid out the thruways to wisdom
and gave it to Jacob his faithful servant
and Israel his beloved son.
    Since then she's been spotted regularly on earth,
pausing now and then to chat with her admirers.
Wisdom is a book that contains the commandments of God,
which are also the law of God; both will last forever.
Everyone who keeps the laws will live;
those who don't will die.
Turn your life around, tribe of Jacob; welcome wisdom while you can;
let her be your chandelier.
Don't waste your worship on some other god;
don't spend your good offerings on a bad altar.
We're blessed, people of Israel,
because we know what pleases God.

Wisdom is our chandelier. When things are at their darkest, only wisdom can bring light to the subject and show us our options with clarity. We often struggle to make decisions with the facts in hand—forgetting that we must also discern with wisdom as our guide. We have to ask not simply: "what's best for me?," but "what's best for the common good?"

SEVENTH READING » EZEKIEL 36:16–17A, 18–28

God's Message came to me: "Son of man, when the people of Israel lived in their land, they polluted it by the way they lived. I poured out my anger on them because of the polluted blood they poured out on the ground. And so I got thoroughly angry with them polluting the country with their wanton murders and dirty gods. I kicked them out, exiled them to other countries. I sentenced them according to how they had lived. Wherever they went, they gave me a bad name. People said, 'These are God's people, but they got kicked off his land.' I suffered much pain over my holy reputation, which the people of Israel blackened in every country they entered.
    "Therefore, tell Israel, 'Message of God, the Master: I'm not doing this for you, Israel. I'm doing it for me, to save my character, my holy name, which you've blackened in every country where you've gone. I'm going to put my great and holy name on display, the name that has been ruined in so many countries, the name that you blackened wherever you went. Then the nations will realize who I really am, that I am God, when I show my holiness through you so that they can

see it with their own eyes.

"'For here's what I'm going to do: I'm going to take you out of these countries, gather you from all over, and bring you back to your own land. I'll pour pure water over you and scrub you clean. I'll give you a new heart, put a new spirit in you. I'll remove the stone heart from your body and replace it with a heart that's God-willed, not self-willed. I'll put my Spirit in you and make it possible for you to do what I tell you and live by my commands. You'll once again live in the land I gave your ancestors. You'll be my people! I'll be your God!'"

There's a wide chasm between self-will and God's will. Often we find ourselves doing a tightrope dance between the two. I know what God's will requires in every situation: love, patience, forgiveness, kindness, honesty, fidelity. My will seeks comfort, satisfaction, admiration, personal profit. It's not safe to dash back and forth between the two wills, I know. When will I surrender to God's will, and stick with it?

EPISTLE » ROMANS 6:3–11

So what do we do? Keep on sinning so God can keep on forgiving? I should hope not! If we've left the country where sin is sovereign, how can we still live in our old house there? Or didn't you realize we packed up and left there for good? That is what happened in baptism. When we went under the water, we left the old country of sin behind; when we came up out of the water, we entered into the new country of grace—a new life in a new land!

That's what baptism into the life of Jesus means. When we are lowered into the water, it is like the burial of Jesus; when we are raised up out of the water, it is like the resurrection of Jesus. Each of us is raised into a light-filled world by our Father so that we can see where we're going in our new grace-sovereign country.

Could it be any clearer? Our old way of life was nailed to the cross with Christ, a decisive end to that sin-miserable life—no longer at sin's every beck and call! What we believe is this: If we get included in Christ's sin-conquering death, we also get included in his life-saving resurrection. We know that when Jesus was raised from the dead it was a signal of the end of death-as-the-end. Never again will death have the last word. When Jesus died, he took sin down with him, but alive he brings God down to us. From now on, think of it this way: Sin speaks a dead language that means nothing to you; God speaks your mother tongue, and you hang on every word. You are dead to sin and alive to God. That's what Jesus did.

Sin speaks a dead language. God speaks our mother tongue. If we listen to the gibberish spouted all around us, we'll be convinced that money, celebrity, power, and stuff will make our lives sublime. They don't. They all lead to dead ends. If we listen to the word of life, we will find happiness forever. This isn't rocket science. It's religion!

GOSPEL » MATTHEW 28:1-10

After the Sabbath, as the first light of the new week dawned, Mary Magdalene and the other Mary came to keep vigil at the tomb. Suddenly the earth reeled and rocked under their feet as God's angel came down from heaven, came right up to where they were standing. He rolled back the stone and then sat on it. Shafts of lightning blazed from him. His garments shimmered snow-white. The guards at the tomb were scared to death. They were so frightened, they couldn't move.

The angel spoke to the women: "There is nothing to fear here. I know you're looking for Jesus, the One they nailed to the cross. He is not here. He was raised, just as he said. Come and look at the place where he was placed.

"Now, get on your way quickly and tell his disciples, 'He is risen from the dead. He is going on ahead of you to Galilee. You will see him there.' That's the message."

The women, deep in wonder and full of joy, lost no time in leaving the tomb. They ran to tell the disciples. Then Jesus met them, stopping them in their tracks. "Good morning!" he said. They fell to their knees, embraced his feet, and worshiped him. Jesus said, "You're holding on to me for dear life! Don't be frightened like that. Go tell my brothers that they are to go to Galilee, and that I'll meet them there."

A stone, a tomb, a missing person. A seeker, a messenger, an impossible message. While the gospel accounts of the resurrection differ in the arithmetic of the Easter event—how many women? how many angels?—the fundamentals of the scene remain the same. Someone is seeking, someone is telling. The tomb is open and empty. Where did Jesus go? More importantly, where is he today? Are we the ones seeking, and are we telling?

> **What aspect of your life has been dead or dormant?**
> **What can you do to allow it to be raised up?**

WE RESPOND

Someone near you needs hope. You are the designated messenger of Easter hope and joy.

EASTER SEASON

EASTER SUNDAY

FIRST READING » ACTS OF THE APOSTLES 10:34A, 37-43

Peter fairly exploded with his good news: "It's God's own truth, nothing could be plainer: God plays no favorites! It makes no difference who you are or where you're from—if you want God and are ready to do as he says, the door is open. The Message he sent to the children of Israel—that through Jesus Christ everything is being put together again—well, he's doing it everywhere, among everyone.

"You know the story of what happened in Judea. It began in Galilee after John preached a total life-change. Then Jesus arrived from Nazareth, anointed by God with the Holy Spirit, ready for action. He went through the country helping people and healing everyone who was beaten down by the Devil. He was able to do all this because God was with him.

"And we saw it, saw it all, everything he did in the land of the Jews and in Jerusalem where they killed him, hung him from a cross. But in three days God had him up, alive, and out where he could be seen. Not everyone saw him—he wasn't put on public display. Witnesses had been carefully handpicked by God beforehand—us! We were the ones, there to eat and drink with him after he came back from the dead. He commissioned us to announce this in public, to bear solemn witness that he is in fact the One whom God destined as Judge of the living and dead. But we're not alone in this. Our witness that he is the means to forgiveness of sins is backed up by the witness of all the prophets."

How far are you willing to take your faith? To family, friends, neighbors, coworkers? Peter addresses a group of foreigners in the household of a Roman soldier, the enemy of his people. He is going way out on a limb here, breaking with Jewish piety by entering the man's house. Peter has no particular love for foreigners, especially those responsible for the crucifixion of his Lord. Like the other disciples, he had a hard time getting it when Jesus stopped to help outsiders.

But the resurrection has changed things. Peter, once slow-witted about the Gospel, is now the leader of the Christian movement. Once willing to deny his faith to save his skin, he's now prepared to take great risks to speak about "this man God raised." Peter feels a keen sense of mission about witnessing to what he saw and knows to be true. What keeps us from taking risks like that? Is it that we haven't "seen and known" Jesus, or that we are still afraid of what we might lose?

Within which circles of your society are you willing to be known as a Christian? Where are you less comfortable claiming that identity?

SECOND READING » COLOSSIANS 3:1-4

So if you're serious about living this new resurrection life with Christ, act like it. Pursue the things over which Christ presides. Don't shuffle along, eyes to the ground, absorbed with the things right in front of you. Look up, and be alert to what is going on around Christ—that's where the action is. See things from his perspective.

Your old life is dead. Your new life, which is your real life—even though invisible to spectators—is with Christ in God. He is your life. When Christ (your real life, remember) shows up again on this earth, you'll show up, too—the real you, the glorious you. Meanwhile, be content with obscurity, like Christ.

Some forms of piety abuse this advice from Paul, buying insurance in the next world while ignoring this one. It's easy to "get spiritual" by paying more attention to pious practices while taking a pass on the pragmatism of the Gospel: feeding the hungry, forgiving those who wrong us, speaking out for justice. When Paul says "look up and be alert," his intention is HIGHLY practical. Heavenly values drive us to pay more attention to the way we live in the world, not less.

Our death to the material world doesn't lead us to otherworldliness, like people who float above reality, but to wisdom. Hidden with Christ in the mystery of the cross, Christians should be the most grounded people of all.

How do the "spiritual" things you do affect your "earthly" life?

GOSPEL » JOHN 20:1-9

Early in the morning on the first day of the week, while it was still dark, Mary Magdalene came to the tomb and saw that the stone was moved away from the entrance. She ran at once to Simon Peter and the other disciple, the one Jesus loved, breathlessly panting, "They took the Master from the tomb. We don't know where they've put him."

Peter and the other disciple left immediately for the tomb. They ran, neck and neck. The other disciple got to the tomb first, outrunning Peter. Stooping to look in, he saw the pieces of linen cloth lying there, but he didn't go in. Simon Peter arrived after him, entered the tomb, observed the linen cloths lying there, and the kerchief used to cover his head not lying with the linen cloths but separate, neatly folded by itself. Then the other disciple, the one who had gotten there first, went into the tomb, took one look at the evidence, and believed. No one yet knew from the Scripture that he had to rise from the dead. The disciples then went back home.

What if Mary hadn't gone to the tomb that day?

John tells us she got up in the darkness, the day after the Sabbath, as soon as religion allowed for work to be done. She had waited with great longing for the end of Saturday, so that she could return to the burial place and anoint the body of one she loved. When she arrived in that dark hour, she found the stone rolled away, and her fear propelled her into the presence of the disciples. Jesus' body was stolen!

Her report mobilized the men, and so Easter came into being. But what if Mary had not returned to the site because of discouragement, fear, or sheer exhaustion? Would anyone have discovered the miracle? Often we reach the end of our own personal passion week, and never make it to the empty tomb. Lots of things conspire to keep us away. Love is the only reason to go forward, to find that the night is ended and a new world has dawned.

What difference does the resurrection of Jesus make to you?

WE RESPOND

Raise up a fallen friend. Lift up a lonely heart. Bring the morning to someone who is wrapped in darkness. Take one step beyond discouragement and fear, and find Easter.

*So if you're serious about living
this new resurrection life with Christ,
act like it.*

SECOND SUNDAY OF EASTER

FIRST READING » ACTS OF THE APOSTLES 2:42-47

That day about three thousand took him at his word, were baptized and were signed up. They committed themselves to the teaching of the apostles, the life together, the common meal, and the prayers.

Everyone around was in awe—all those wonders and signs done through the apostles! And all the believers lived in a wonderful harmony, holding everything in common. They sold whatever they owned and pooled their resources so that each person's need was met.

They followed a daily discipline of worship in the Temple followed by meals at home, every meal a celebration, exuberant and joyful, as they praised God. People in general liked what they saw. Every day their number grew as God added those who were saved.

Think about the closest bunch of friends you ever made. Maybe they were the kids on the playground, the gang in the tree house. Maybe it was your high school buddies or college crowd, or even the group you hang around with today. That's the group the early disciples resembled. They did everything together, shared what they had in common, laughed and cried and dreamed of a better world together. They studied, ate, and talked far into the night about what had happened to them through Jesus. They shared a vision, the way every generation has its own way of imagining the future they hope to bring into being.

Unlike most generations, which eventually surrender idealism for profit, the Christian dream continues to present an image of the way things could be—the reign of God—which is also the way things WILL be, world without end. And we can all say amen to that.

> **Who is, or was, your "gang," the closest circle of friends? What were your dreams, and have they been realized?**

SECOND READING » 1 PETER 1:3-9

What a God we have! And how fortunate we are to have him, this Father of our Master Jesus! Because Jesus was raised from the dead, we've been given a brand-new life and have everything to live for, including a future in heaven—and the future starts now! God is keeping careful watch over us and the future. The Day is coming when you'll have it all—life healed and whole.

I know how great this makes you feel, even though you have to put up with every kind of aggravation in the meantime. Pure gold put in the fire comes out of it proved pure; genuine faith put through this suffering comes out proved genuine. When Jesus wraps this all up, it's your faith, not your gold, that God will have on display as evidence of his victory.

THIS TRANSFORMING WORD

You never saw him, yet you love him. You still don't see him, yet you trust him—with laughter and singing. Because you kept on believing, you'll get what you're looking forward to: total salvation.

An inheritance may come in many forms: a house, a piece of land, a bank account, personal effects. But whatever it is we may expect to gain from departing relatives and friends, the same holds true for us: we'll be passing it all along to someone else soon enough.

Most of what we stand to gain in this world, we must lose. Most of what is valued in this world is remarkably transient. Still we hear stories of friends who fought viciously with family members over some anticipated inheritance that did not come through as expected. We spend far less energy fighting for our imperishable inheritance, "total salvation." We forget there are only three things that last—faith, hope, and love. These are the only things we CAN take with us when we go.

> **What is the spiritual legacy you inherit from your family?**
> **What do you hope your spiritual legacy might be?**

GOSPEL » JOHN 20:19-31

Later on that day, the disciples had gathered together, but, fearful of the Jews, had locked all the doors in the house. Jesus entered, stood among them, and said, "Peace to you." Then he showed them his hands and side.

The disciples, seeing the Master with their own eyes, were exuberant. Jesus repeated his greeting: "Peace to you. Just as the Father sent me, I send you."

Then he took a deep breath and breathed into them. "Receive the Holy Spirit," he said. "If you forgive someone's sins, they're gone for good. If you don't forgive sins, what are you going to do with them?"

But Thomas, sometimes called the Twin, one of the Twelve, was not with them when Jesus came. The other disciples told him, "We saw the Master."

But he said, "Unless I see the nail holes in his hands, put my finger in the nail holes, and stick my hand in his side, I won't believe it."

Eight days later, his disciples were again in the room. This time Thomas was with them. Jesus came through the locked doors, stood among them, and said, "Peace to you."

Then he focused his attention on Thomas. "Take your finger and examine my hands. Take your hand and stick it in my side. Don't be unbelieving. Believe."

Thomas said, "My Master! My God!"

Jesus said, "So, you believe because you've seen with your own eyes. Even better blessings are in store for those who believe without seeing."

Jesus provided far more God-revealing signs than are written down in this book. These are written down so you will believe that Jesus is the Messiah, the Son of God, and in the act of believing, have real and eternal life in the way he personally revealed it.

Thomas' challenge to his friends was graphic and harsh. If Jesus had indeed returned, he wanted to see the marks of his crucifixion. And Thomas got his wish, though he certainly hadn't counted on it.

Many bear the marks of crucifixion as they make their way through the world. The abused child, the jaded adult, the dying elder all show signs of the suffering they endure. We can, like Thomas, reach out and finger these wounds in others if we doubt their existence. But more useful is the healing touch Jesus demonstrated on so many occasions in his ministry. We may not have a miraculous gift for healing, but we do have within our grasp the capacity to kiss; hold a hand; spend some time; speak a word of kindness. The sheer amount of suffering in the world can overwhelm us and lead to inaction. But a Christian has a clear calling to the signs of suffering in others. With the cross as our inheritance, we know even wounds can be glorified.

> What are your wounds?
> How might they become "glorified wounds"?

WE RESPOND

Contemplate in prayer the marks of crucifixion in your neighborhood, parish, or city. Consider assisting a group which addresses these concerns in any way your resources allow.

"Even better blessings are in store
for those who believe without seeing."

THIRD SUNDAY OF EASTER

FIRST READING » ACTS OF THE APOSTLES 2:14, 22-33

That's when Peter stood up and, backed by the other eleven, spoke out with bold urgency: "Fellow Jews, all of you who are visiting Jerusalem, listen carefully and get this story straight. These people aren't drunk as some of you suspect. They haven't had time to get drunk—it's only nine o'clock in the morning. This is what the prophet Joel announced would happen:

> *"In the Last Days," God says,*
> *"I will pour out my Spirit*
>> *on every kind of people:*
> *Your sons will prophesy,*
>> *also your daughters;*
> *Your young men will see visions,*
>> *your old men dream dreams.*
> *When the time comes,*
>> *I'll pour out my Spirit*
> *On those who serve me, men and women both,*
>> *and they'll prophesy.*
> *I'll set wonders in the sky above*
>> *and signs on the earth below,*
> *Blood and fire and billowing smoke,*
>> *the sun turning black and the moon blood-red,*
> *Before the Day of the Lord arrives,*
>> *the Day tremendous and marvelous;*
> *And whoever calls out for help*
>> *to me, God, will be saved."*

"Fellow Israelites, listen carefully to these words: Jesus the Nazarene, a man thoroughly accredited by God to you—the miracles and wonders and signs that God did through him are common knowledge—this Jesus, following the deliberate and well-thought-out plan of God, was betrayed by men who took the law into their own hands, and was handed over to you. And you pinned him to a cross and killed him. But God untied the death ropes and raised him up. Death was no match for him. David said it all:

> *I saw God before me for all time.*
>> *Nothing can shake me; he's right by my side.*
> *I'm glad from the inside out, ecstatic;*
>> *I've pitched my tent in the land of hope.*
> *I know you'll never dump me in Hades;*

> I'll never even smell the stench of death.
> You've got my feet on the life-path,
>   with your face shining sun-joy all around.

"Dear friends, let me be completely frank with you. Our ancestor David is dead and buried—his tomb is in plain sight today. But being also a prophet and knowing that God had solemnly sworn that a descendant of his would rule his kingdom, seeing far ahead, he talked of the resurrection of the Messiah—'no trip to Hades, no stench of death.' This Jesus, God raised up. And every one of us here is a witness to it. Then, raised to the heights at the right hand of God and receiving the promise of the Holy Spirit from the Father, he poured out the Spirit he had just received. That is what you see and hear."

What do you hope for? Peace of mind, relief from debt, healing, love, meaningful work for your hands? We all have something we're longing for—that's part of the human condition. There is always a piece missing from the puzzle. Mortality by definition isn't perfect.

When Peter speaks his message in the crowded streets of Jerusalem, he speaks to the human longing for life itself. "God untied the death ropes" so that all of us can be spared the final abandonment that flesh is heir to. In this Easter season, we celebrate the gift of life, both now and forever. We celebrate the restoration of the missing piece of the puzzle. Though our present circumstance may fail us, the promise of life revealed in Jesus will not fail. Our hearts have every reason to hold fast to hope.

> **Within which circles of your society**
> **are you willing to be known as a Christian?**
> **Where are you less comfortable claiming that identity?**

SECOND READING » 1 PETER 1:17-21

You call out to God for help and he helps—he's a good Father that way. But don't forget, he's also a responsible Father, and won't let you get by with sloppy living.

Your life is a journey you must travel with a deep consciousness of God. It cost God plenty to get you out of that dead-end, empty-headed life you grew up in. He paid with Christ's sacred blood, you know. He died like an unblemished, sacrificial lamb. And this was no afterthought. Even though it has only lately—at the end of the ages—become public knowledge, God always knew he was going to do this for you. It's because of this sacrificed Messiah, whom God then raised from the dead and glorified, that you trust God, that you know you have a future in God.

Our salvation isn't rooted in perishable things—but oh, how we love them anyway.
For quite some time I tended to a dying friend, whose body melted like wax despite all that medical science can do. In the course of my care for him, I find myself among his personal effects, opening drawers and closets, uncovering secrets meant for no

eyes but his. He was a holy man; his hidden flaws were minor vanities that in the last hours were touching in their absurdity. I found a box of hair coloring intended to mask his white hair—but alas, radiation had left him with no hair at all. We cried together the day his hair fell away, though that was the least of his suffering.

Hair, skin, mobility, continence will all pass away, and silver and gold will cease to matter. But the precious blood of Christ promises to bring my friend's body to glory. Peter's words, "God always knew he was going to do this for you" mean more to me now. Death is a destination we all approach softly, taking off our shoes.

> What missing pieces of the puzzle in your life do you long for?
> How does your faith speak to your longing?
> What perishable things do you cling to?
> What would it take to let them go?

GOSPEL » LUKE 24:13-35

That same day two of them were walking to the village Emmaus, about seven miles out of Jerusalem. They were deep in conversation, going over all these things that had happened. In the middle of their talk and questions, Jesus came up and walked along with them. But they were not able to recognize who he was.

He asked, "What's this you're discussing so intently as you walk along?"

They just stood there, long-faced, like they had lost their best friend. Then one of them, his name was Cleopas, said, "Are you the only one in Jerusalem who hasn't heard what's happened during the last few days?"

He said, "What has happened?"

They said, "The things that happened to Jesus the Nazarene. He was a man of God, a prophet, dynamic in work and word, blessed by both God and all the people. Then our high priests and leaders betrayed him, got him sentenced to death, and crucified him. And we had our hopes up that he was the One, the One about to deliver Israel. And it is now the third day since it happened. But now some of our women have completely confused us. Early this morning they were at the tomb and couldn't find his body. They came back with the story that they had seen a vision of angels who said he was alive. Some of our friends went off to the tomb to check and found it empty just as the women said, but they didn't see Jesus."

Then he said to them, "So thick-headed! So slow-hearted! Why can't you simply believe all that the prophets said? Don't you see that these things had to happen, that the Messiah had to suffer and only then enter into his glory?" Then he started at the beginning, with the Books of Moses, and went on through all the Prophets, pointing out everything in the Scriptures that referred to him.

They came to the edge of the village where they were headed. He acted as if he were going on but they pressed him: "Stay and have supper with us. It's nearly evening; the day is done." So he went in with them. And here is what happened: He sat down at the table with them. Taking the bread, he blessed and broke and gave it to them. At that moment, open-eyed, wide-eyed, they recognized him. And then he disappeared.

Back and forth they talked. "Didn't we feel on fire as he conversed with us on the road, as he opened up the Scriptures for us?"

They didn't waste a minute. They were up and on their way back to Jerusalem. They found the Eleven and their friends gathered together, talking away: "It's really happened! The Master has been raised up—Simon saw him!"

Then the two went over everything that happened on the road and how they recognized him when he broke the bread.

Church people use a lot of religious language to describe what we believe in: salvation, resurrection, communion. But in our rituals, we use very familiar signs to explain what we mean by all this. Eucharist is one of these. Oh, for the pleasure of a meal with friends!

Friendship is a kind of sacrament all its own. We share histories with our friends. We tell the story of our lives and find common ground. And when we come together, we share food. The warmth and comfort of a meal reflects the nature of our relationship with one another. We celebrate the union of our hearts around the table.

In the unique gathering of our Eucharist, we also acknowledge the great story of God and our relationship with the Holy One through Jesus Christ. Our eyes are opened in this meal to recognize the common ground we hold with divinity: the reign of God itself. Our friendship with God through Christ is true yesterday, today, and forever. This is what our faith means. Everything we need to know about God is in this meal.

> **Think of a meal you recently shared with friends or family.
> What does it teach you about the meaning of Eucharist?**

WE RESPOND

Prepare a special meal for someone you care about. Entertain the Holy One in the breaking of the bread.

FOURTH SUNDAY OF EASTER

FIRST READING » ACTS OF THE APOSTLES 2:14A, 36-41

That's when Peter stood up and, backed by the other eleven, spoke out with bold urgency: "Fellow Jews, all of you who are visiting Jerusalem, listen carefully and get this story straight. These people aren't drunk as some of you suspect. They haven't had time to get drunk—it's only nine o'clock in the morning. This is what the prophet Joel announced would happen:

> *"In the Last Days," God says,*
> *"I will pour out my Spirit*
>   *on every kind of people:*
> *Your sons will prophesy,*
>   *also your daughters;*
> *Your young men will see visions,*
>   *your old men dream dreams.*
> *When the time comes,*
>   *I'll pour out my Spirit*
> *On those who serve me, men and women both,*
>   *and they'll prophesy.*
> *I'll set wonders in the sky above*
>   *and signs on the earth below,*
> *Blood and fire and billowing smoke,*
>   *the sun turning black and the moon blood-red,*
> *Before the Day of the Lord arrives,*
>   *the Day tremendous and marvelous;*
> *And whoever calls out for help*
>   *to me, God, will be saved."*

"Dear friends, let me be completely frank with you. Our ancestor David is dead and buried—his tomb is in plain sight today. But being also a prophet and knowing that God had solemnly sworn that a descendant of his would rule his kingdom, seeing far ahead, he talked of the resurrection of the Messiah—'no trip to Hades, no stench of death.' This Jesus, God raised up. And every one of us here is a witness to it. Then, raised to the heights at the right hand of God and receiving the promise of the Holy Spirit from the Father, he poured out the Spirit he had just received. That is what you see and hear. For David himself did not ascend to heaven, but he did say,

> *God said to my Master, "Sit at my right hand*
> *Until I make your enemies a stool for resting your feet."*

"All Israel, then, know this: There's no longer room for doubt—God made him

Master and Messiah, this Jesus whom you killed on a cross."

Cut to the quick, those who were there listening asked Peter and the other apostles, "Brothers! Brothers! So now what do we do?"

Peter said, "Change your life. Turn to God and be baptized, each of you, in the name of Jesus Christ, so your sins are forgiven. Receive the gift of the Holy Spirit. The promise is targeted to you and your children, but also to all who are far away—whomever, in fact, our Master God invites."

He went on in this vein for a long time, urging them over and over, "Get out while you can; get out of this sick and stupid culture!"

That day about three thousand took him at his word, were baptized and were signed up.

Is our present generation more corrupt than the one before—or any other generation, for that matter? Wars, murders, greed, indifference, prejudice and arrogance abound in the Bible. It is hard to imagine a worse society than the one surrounding Noah, Moses, Isaiah, or John the Baptist. Human nature hasn't evolved much, despite our progress. People haven't gotten better.

So now what do we do, sisters and brothers? Those who hear the call to conversion of the heart in every generation ask the same question addressed to Peter. And the answer is always the same: Repent. Repent means turn around, turn to God, open your heart and be made new. The gift of the Holy Spirit is given to those who do this; consider what your life could be if the Spirit of Holiness lived in you. It's never too late. No matter where the road has led so far, we can always turn around.

When have you experienced a "turning" in your life? What made you change?

SECOND READING » 1 PETER 2:20B-25

You who are servants, be good servants to your masters—not just to good masters, but also to bad ones. What counts is that you put up with it for God's sake when you're treated badly for no good reason. There's no particular virtue in accepting punishment that you well deserve. But if you're treated badly for good behavior and continue in spite of it to be a good servant, that is what counts with God.

This is the kind of life you've been invited into, the kind of life Christ lived. He suffered everything that came his way so you would know that it could be done, and also know how to do it, step-by-step.

He never did one thing wrong,
Not once said anything amiss.

They called him every name in the book and he said nothing back. He suffered in silence, content to let God set things right. He used his servant body to carry our sins to the Cross so we could be rid of sin, free to live the right way. His wounds became your healing. You were lost sheep with no idea who you were or where you were going. Now you're named and kept for good by the Shepherd of your souls.

THIS TRANSFORMING WORD

In a moment of self-examination recently, I noticed how defensive I am to insult and injury. When people push me, I push back. When someone is rude, I want to get ruder. I'm generally prepared to sword-fight verbally with anyone who crosses my will. My fuse is short. I don't suffer fools gladly.

And of course, I also know this kind of behavior just escalates the amount of bad humor in the world. It does nothing to promote the cause of love and goodness. It does not proclaim the gospel to those who haven't heard it. It is a poor witness for a Christian to offer.

I pray for patience like Jesus, to reserve my anger for real injustice and not just to vent my displeasure. May the precious wounds of Jesus heal us all when we stray from his image.

How do you respond to insult?
Compare your response to the example of Jesus as Peter describes it.

GOSPEL » JOHN 10:1-10

"Let me set this before you as plainly as I can. If a person climbs over or through the fence of a sheep pen instead of going through the gate, you know he's up to no good—a sheep rustler! The shepherd walks right up to the gate. The gatekeeper opens the gate to him and the sheep recognize his voice. He calls his own sheep by name and leads them out. When he gets them all out, he leads them and they follow because they are familiar with his voice. They won't follow a stranger's voice but will scatter because they aren't used to the sound of it."

Jesus told this simple story, but they had no idea what he was talking about. So he tried again. "I'll be explicit, then. I am the Gate for the sheep. All those others are up to no good—sheep stealers, every one of them. But the sheep didn't listen to them. I am the Gate. Anyone who goes through me will be cared for— will freely go in and out, and find pasture. A thief is only there to steal and kill and destroy. I came so they can have real and eternal life, more and better life than they ever dreamed of.

Sitting on a plane, I listened to the flight attendant reviewing the usual procedures for emergency exits, something all of us hope we don't have to make. She was pointing out the doors, the floor lights, the flotation devices and all those instructions that frequent fliers have heard countless times. I tried to imagine myself remembering all these details in a crisis, and doubted that I could. Pull WHAT cord? Move in WHICH direction? Even in the best of times, my sense of direction is terrible.

How wonderful that, in the most significant sense of the word, we do not have to make our way to safety on our own. Jesus is the gate, the gatekeeper, and the shepherd. Our only task is to listen for the voice of the Beloved, and to follow where it leads. No harm can come to the one who lives this simple rule. The alternative is, of course, to try to hold all the details in our finite and imperfect hands.

Where are you going? Who or what is leading you?

WE RESPOND

What needs to change in your life? Turn this matter over to God in prayer, and spend some time in a quiet place listening for the Beloved voice to lead you.

You were lost sheep
with no idea who you were
or where you were going.
Now you're named and kept for good
by the Shepherd of your souls.

FIFTH SUNDAY OF EASTER

FIRST READING » ACTS OF THE APOSTLES 6:1-7

During this time, as the disciples were increasing in numbers by leaps and bounds, hard feelings developed among the Greek-speaking believers—"Hellenists"—toward the Hebrew-speaking believers because their widows were being discriminated against in the daily food lines. So the Twelve called a meeting of the disciples. They said, "It wouldn't be right for us to abandon our responsibilities for preaching and teaching the Word of God to help with the care of the poor. So, friends, choose seven men from among you whom everyone trusts, men full of the Holy Spirit and good sense, and we'll assign them this task. Meanwhile, we'll stick to our assigned tasks of prayer and speaking God's Word."

The congregation thought this was a great idea. They went ahead and chose—

Stephen, a man full of faith and the Holy Spirit,

Philip,

Procorus,

Nicanor,

Timon,

Parmenas,

Nicolas, a convert from Antioch.

Then they presented them to the apostles. Praying, the apostles laid on hands and commissioned them for their task.

The Word of God prospered. The number of disciples in Jerusalem increased dramatically. Not least, a great many priests submitted themselves to the faith.

If you had to choose seven trustworthy people to appoint to an important task, who would they be? I was faced with a similar decision when the care of a sick friend grew too much for me. The spirit was willing, but the task was beyond my strength. The sacrifice I was asking my "deacons" to make was considerable, and I needed to be able to delegate serious responsibilities that were literally a matter of life or death.

How quickly a dozen people emerged to offer help! And how abruptly some of them fell away as the burden grew. "The daily distribution" in service to the poor is a great responsibility, impossible to carry alone and tough to bear even within community. Still it's not optional for us to serve the needy in our midst. It's what Jesus commanded us to do.

Whom do you trust? Whom do you serve?

SECOND READING » 1 PETER 2:4-9

Welcome to the living Stone, the source of life. The workmen took one look and threw it out; God set it in the place of honor. Present yourselves as building stones for the construction of a sanctuary vibrant with life, in which you'll serve as holy priests offering Christ-approved lives up to God. The Scriptures provide precedent:

> *Look! I'm setting a stone in Zion,*
> *a cornerstone in the place of honor.*
> *Whoever trusts in this stone as a foundation*
> *will never have cause to regret it.*
> *To you who trust him, he's a Stone to be proud of, but to those who refuse to trust him,*
> *The stone the workmen threw out*
> *is now the chief foundation stone.*
> *For the untrusting it's*
> *...a stone to trip over,*
> *a boulder blocking the way.*
> *They trip and fall because they refuse to obey, just as predicted.*

But you are the ones chosen by God, chosen for the high calling of priestly work, chosen to be a holy people, God's instruments to do his work and speak out for him, to tell others of the night-and-day difference he made for you—from nothing to something, from rejected to accepted.

Where I grew up in the coal region of Pennsylvania, stones were precious. Many of our parents and grandparents made a living mining the earth. Our awareness of geology was heightened by the fact that our destiny was interwoven with the stones under our feet. As kids we all had rock collections, and could spot a bit of quartz in the coal dust as we wandered the hills. We knew sedimentary rock from metamorphic; we knew in which rock beds leaf fossils were most likely to be found.

And we knew what it meant to say we would all one day return to dust, or be built up as stones into a sturdy house. Cornerstones and stumbling blocks were no mere metaphors to us. Contemplate a stone, and you can learn many spiritual lessons.

If you were a stone, where would you be placed within the structure of the Church?

GOSPEL » JOHN 14:1-12

"Don't let this throw you. You trust God, don't you? Trust me. There is plenty of room for you in my Father's home. If that weren't so, would I have told you that I'm on my way to get a room ready for you? And if I'm on my way to get your room ready, I'll come back and get you so you can live where I live. And you already know the road I'm taking."

Thomas said, "Master, we have no idea where you're going. How do you expect us to know the road?"

Jesus said, "I am the Road, also the Truth, also the Life. No one gets to the Father apart from me. If you really knew me, you would know my Father as well.

From now on, you do know him. You've even seen him!"

Philip said, "Master, show us the Father; then we'll be content."

"You've been with me all this time, Philip, and you still don't understand? To see me is to see the Father. So how can you ask, 'Where is the Father?' Don't you believe that I am in the Father and the Father is in me? The words that I speak to you aren't mere words. I don't just make them up on my own. The Father who resides in me crafts each word into a divine act.

"Believe me: I am in my Father and my Father is in me. If you can't believe that, believe what you see—these works. The person who trusts me will not only do what I'm doing but even greater things, because I, on my way to the Father, am giving you the same work to do that I've been doing. You can count on it. From now on, whatever you request along the lines of who I am and what I am doing, I'll do it. That's how the Father will be seen for who he is in the Son. I mean it. Whatever you request in this way, I'll do

Thomas is the practical apostle. He had very little religious imagination. As we know, he couldn't invest himself in the resurrection of Jesus without hands-on experience of it. Here, we find that he isn't going to buy into the reign of God unless he can find it on MapQuest. And Jesus humors him by offering him something better than a roadmap: himself.

Jesus is the way. What does that mean? A generation ago, Christian bumper stickers read, "One Way," with an arrow pointing upwards. But maybe a more theologically accurate sign would point THROUGH—through the heart of the world, into the depths of our humanity until we find that central spot where the Spirit dwells in us. It takes a lot of stillness, a lot of contemplation and quiet, to find that place. We can contemplate the world, in its beauty and suffering, or our own lives, or Scripture or the image of the cross. The mystery of the Kingdom is not "up" from here, but in our midst. We are the Body of Christ. If we're looking for Jesus, and the way, the yellow brick road starts right here.

Where do you go to find stillness?

WE RESPOND

Choose an hour for contemplation this week. (If you can't find an hour, maybe your *We Respond* should focus on why.) Contemplate any image that leads you to the Holy. From where you are in your life right now, let Jesus show you the way.

SIXTH SUNDAY OF EASTER

FIRST READING » ACTS OF THE APOSTLES 8:5-8, 14-17

And Saul just went wild, devastating the church, entering house after house after house, dragging men and women off to jail. Forced to leave home base, the followers of Jesus all became missionaries. Wherever they were scattered, they preached the Message about Jesus. Going down to a Samaritan city, Philip proclaimed the Message of the Messiah. When the people heard what he had to say and saw the miracles, the clear signs of God's action, they hung on his every word. Many who could neither stand nor walk were healed that day. The evil spirits protested loudly as they were sent on their way. And what joy in the city!

When the apostles in Jerusalem received the report that Samaria had accepted God's Message, they sent Peter and John down to pray for them to receive the Holy Spirit. Up to this point they had only been baptized in the name of the Master Jesus; the Holy Spirit hadn't yet fallen on them. Then the apostles laid their hands on them and they did receive the Holy Spirit.

Philip going to Samaria is sort of like Nixon going to China. Despite all the stories Jesus told about Good Samaritans, the pre-Easter disciples never showed much empathy for the enemies of their people. Consider the emotional distance that had to be crossed for Philip to bring the good news to Samaritans! Yet he did, and freedom, healing and joy were the result.

Consider the emotional distance you'd have to cross to bring good things to an enemy. What would enable you to make that journey? And what would happen to them, and to you, if you did?

Who is waiting for you to make the journey toward forgiveness and acceptance?

SECOND READING » 1 PETER 3:15-18

If with heart and soul you're doing good, do you think you can be stopped? Even if you suffer for it, you're still better off. Don't give the opposition a second thought. Through thick and thin, keep your hearts at attention, in adoration before Christ, your Master. Be ready to speak up and tell anyone who asks why you're living the way you are, and always with the utmost courtesy. Keep a clear conscience before God so that when people throw mud at you, none of it will stick. They'll end up realizing that they're the ones who need a bath. It's better to suffer for doing good, if that's what God wants, than to be punished for doing bad. That's what Christ did definitively: suffered because of others' sins, the Righteous One for the unrighteous ones. He went through it all—was put to death and then made alive—to bring us to God.

How would you explain your faith to someone who asks? The philosopher Pascal defined faith as the best wager in the game of life: if you're mistaken, in the end you lose nothing; but if you're correct, you gain eternity. Is faith the "best bet" to you? Or is it something more?

In parochial school, religious faith was often presented simply as The Truth, and it can be a shock in later life to discover that many folks live quite blissfully outside of that certainty. How we understand our faith—as a safe bet, a fond hope, The Truth, or a living experience—shapes too our expression of that faith through our lives. It's worth a moment of consideration.

> **Practice explaining your faith with someone you trust,
> or in front of a mirror. Does it sound convincing?**

GOSPEL » JOHN 14:15-21

"If you love me, show it by doing what I've told you. I will talk to the Father, and he'll provide you another Friend so that you will always have someone with you. This Friend is the Spirit of Truth. The godless world can't take him in because it doesn't have eyes to see him, doesn't know what to look for. But you know him already because he has been staying with you, and will even be in you!

"I will not leave you orphaned. I'm coming back. In just a little while the world will no longer see me, but you're going to see me because I am alive and you're about to come alive. At that moment you will know absolutely that I'm in my Father, and you're in me, and I'm in you.

"The person who knows my commandments and keeps them, that's who loves me. And the person who loves me will be loved by my Father, and I will love him and make myself plain to him."

No lover is fooled by words of love that are not supported by actions. Love is in the evidence. Flowers and poems are good, but holding a feverish child is better. A candlelight dinner or an anniversary present helps, but what's worth more is constancy, fidelity, presence.

Jesus says knowing the commandments is not enough: lovers of God will be known by their observance of a faithful life. We can't fool divinity by ritual acts and pious looks. The One who sees into human hearts knows if our love is lip service or real passion.

> **How do you show your love to those whom you love?**

WE RESPOND

Make your love of God real in three concrete ways this week. Love your neighbor, show unnecessary kindness, bring compassion where there is accusation, remember the poor.

ASCENSION OF THE LORD
.... Don't Just Stand There: DO Something!

FIRST READING » ACTS OF THE APOSTLES 1:1–11

Dear Theophilus, in the first volume of this book I wrote on everything that Jesus began to do and teach until the day he said good-bye to the apostles, the ones he had chosen through the Holy Spirit, and was taken up to heaven. After his death, he presented himself alive to them in many different settings over a period of forty days. In face-to-face meetings, he talked to them about things concerning the kingdom of God. As they met and ate meals together, he told them that they were on no account to leave Jerusalem but "must wait for what the Father promised: the promise you heard from me. John baptized in water; you will be baptized in the Holy Spirit. And soon."

When they were together for the last time they asked, "Master, are you going to restore the kingdom to Israel now? Is this the time?"

He told them, "You don't get to know the time. Timing is the Father's business. What you'll get is the Holy Spirit. And when the Holy Spirit comes on you, you will be able to be my witnesses in Jerusalem, all over Judea and Samaria, even to the ends of the world."

These were his last words. As they watched, he was taken up and disappeared in a cloud. They stood there, staring into the empty sky. Suddenly two men appeared—in white robes! They said, "You Galileans!—why do you just stand here looking up at an empty sky? This very Jesus who was taken up from among you to heaven will come as certainly—and mysteriously—as he left."

I don't know if one can ever grow accustomed to miracles. After years of watching Jesus heal the sick and walk on water and multiply loaves and fishes, it must have gotten familiar, if not exactly routine. Miracles must have seemed the "new normal" under such circumstances. Yet resurrection after crucifixion was still unexpected, despite all the fair warning the friends of Jesus had received. When the time for the ascension rolled around, they were still stunned and awed by what was happening before their eyes.

The angels show up to tell them—and us—to snap out of it. Miracles aren't given for us to say "Wow" and "Whoa" about. God isn't showing off. God is communicating. Jesus is taken from view, so what's the message? We're still here. And we have work to do, between now and when Jesus returns.

> How can you be a witness "to the ends of the earth"
> as Jesus commissioned us to be?
> Whose witness brought you to faith?

SECOND READING » EPHESIANS 1:17–23 OR 4:1–13

That's why, when I heard of the solid trust you have in the Master Jesus and your outpouring of love to all the followers of Jesus, I couldn't stop thanking God for you—every time I prayed, I'd think of you and give thanks. But I do more than thank. I ask—ask the God of our Master, Jesus Christ, the God of glory—to make you intelligent and discerning in knowing him personally, your eyes focused and clear, so that you can see exactly what it is he is calling you to do, grasp the immensity of this glorious way of life he has for his followers, oh, the utter extravagance of his work in us who trust him—endless energy, boundless strength!

All this energy issues from Christ: God raised him from death and set him on a throne in deep heaven, in charge of running the universe, everything from galaxies to governments, no name and no power exempt from his rule. And not just for the time being, but forever. He is in charge of it all, has the final word on everything. At the center of all this, Christ rules the church. The church, you see, is not peripheral to the world; the world is peripheral to the church. The church is Christ's body, in which he speaks and acts, by which he fills everything with his presence.

– OR –

In light of all this, here's what I want you to do. While I'm locked up here, a prisoner for the Master, I want you to get out there and walk—better yet, run!—on the road God called you to travel. I don't want any of you sitting around on your hands. I don't want anyone strolling off, down some path that goes nowhere. And mark that you do this with humility and discipline—not in fits and starts, but steadily, pouring yourselves out for each other in acts of love, alert at noticing differences and quick at mending fences.

You were all called to travel on the same road and in the same direction, so stay together, both outwardly and inwardly. You have one Master, one faith, one baptism, one God and Father of all, who rules over all, works through all, and is present in all. Everything you are and think and do is permeated with Oneness.

But that doesn't mean you should all look and speak and act the same. Out of the generosity of Christ, each of us is given his own gift. The text for this is,

> *He climbed the high mountain,*
> *He captured the enemy and seized the booty,*
> *He handed it all out in gifts to the people.*

Is it not true that the One who climbed up also climbed down, down to the valley of earth? And the One who climbed down is the One who climbed back up, up to highest heaven. He handed out gifts above and below, filled heaven with his gifts, filled earth with his gifts. He handed out gifts of apostle, prophet, evangelist, and pastor-teacher to train Christ's followers in skilled servant work, working within

Christ's body, the church, until we're all moving rhythmically and easily with each other, efficient and graceful in response to God's Son, fully mature adults, fully developed within and without, fully alive like Christ.

God calls each of us into being for a purpose. Some few of us will have a traditionally "religious" vocation, and others will be teachers, community leaders, artists, parents, truth speakers and examples of faithfulness and charity. We may know from an early age precisely what we came into this world to do, or we may wander many paths before we hear and trust the call that is spoken into our lives. Whatever our vocation is, we must seek it. And whatever our path turns out to be, we must have the courage and the confidence in God to pursue it with heart and soul. Because in giving ourselves utterly to that call is hope for us and for the whole world, as grandiose as that may sound. We have our part to play, and our hearts will be restless until we surrender into the gracious truth of who God made us to be.

> How would you describe the vocation that's given to you, or what steps can you take to learn about who God is calling you to be?

GOSPEL » MARK 16:15–20

Still later, as the Eleven were eating supper, he appeared and took them to task most severely for their stubborn unbelief, refusing to believe those who had seen him raised up. Then he said, "Go into the world. Go everywhere and announce the Message of God's good news to one and all. Whoever believes and is baptized is saved; whoever refuses to believe is damned.

"These are some of the signs that will accompany believers: They will throw out demons in my name, they will speak in new tongues, they will take snakes in their hands, they will drink poison and not be hurt, they will lay hands on the sick and make them well."

Then the Master Jesus, after briefing them, was taken up to heaven, and he sat down beside God in the place of honor. And the disciples went everywhere preaching, the Master working right with them, validating the Message with indisputable evidence.

The Ascension of Jesus is an event recorded three times in the New Testament: at the end of Luke, the beginning of Acts, and here, in what's called the longer ending of Mark. (Early manuscripts record several different endings to his gospel.) In each version of the Ascension story, Jesus has different final instructions for the disciples—the ones in "longer Mark" being the most colorful. But in every account we have, Jesus tells the disciples to go and be witnesses of the gospel they have received. On this point, all three speak in one voice. It would seem this mission is non-negotiable.

How we do that is up to us. If you want to knock on doors or preach in the park, suit yourself. If you feel drawn to the foreign missions, the prayer of the church will support you. Maybe the least missionized corner of the world is right where you are. Do you have good news to share?

When you show up, is it "good news" for those around you?
How do you demonstrate the gift of faith that's been given to you?

WE RESPOND

Allow someone's testimony of faith to speak into your life: read a biography of a holy person. Allow your testimony to speak to someone else. Practice the virtues of faith, hope, and charity until they become the "new normal" for you.

"Go into the world.
Go everywhere and announce
the Message of God's good news
to one and all."

SEVENTH SUNDAY OF EASTER

FIRST READING » ACTS OF THE APOSTLES 1:12-14

So they left the mountain called Olives and returned to Jerusalem. It was a little over half a mile. They went to the upper room they had been using as a meeting place:
> *Peter,*
> *John,*
> *James,*
> *Andrew,*
> *Philip,*
> *Thomas,*
> *Bartholomew,*
> *Matthew,*
> *James, son of Alphaeus,*
> *Simon the Zealot,*

Judas, son of James.
They agreed they were in this for good, completely together in prayer, the women included. Also Jesus' mother, Mary, and his brothers.

After the resurrection and ascension of Jesus, the disciples return to Jerusalem to pray... and pray, and pray, and pray. After two astonishing and inconceivable cosmic events, the response of Jesus' followers is prayer. It seems such a quiet reply to salvation history erupting into time. But what else could they do? What would you have done?

A miracle is a hard act to follow. A manifestation of God's pre-eminence over time and nature deserves an acknowledgment on our part, and prayer is the model response. Prayer comes in several colors: breast-beating repentance, intercession for what ails us, thanksgiving for what has been, and praise for the God who is. Chances are the prayer of the disciples was a little bit of each of these in those amazing days.

What circumstances lead you most often to prayer?

SECOND READING » 1 PETER 4:13-16

Friends, when life gets really difficult, don't jump to the conclusion that God isn't on the job. Instead, be glad that you are in the very thick of what Christ experienced. This is a spiritual refining process, with glory just around the corner.

If you're abused because of Christ, count yourself fortunate. It's the Spirit of God and his glory in you that brought you to the notice of others. If they're on you because you broke the law or disturbed the peace, that's a different matter. But if it's because you're a Christian, don't give it a second thought. Be proud of the distinguished status reflected in that name!

We bear the name Christian. There are lots of other names that describe us—our family name, citizenship, and other special affiliations—but taking on the name of Christ is the most penetrating identity of all. Jesus tells his followers many times to be prepared to leave family, town, and all natural ties in order to accompany him. Some protest that they have responsibilities to attend to, plans that are only half-finished. But the call of Jesus remains the same. Come. Follow. Now.

Many cannot accept this kind of summons. It interrupts the flow of expectations, and the cost is considerable. Taking on the name Christian and the identity of a follower was never intended to fit neatly into a Sunday slot in our lives. It is an all or nothing proposition.

> List the names that describe you: family name,
> religious affiliation, or other identities you embrace.
> Rank them in order of significance for you.

GOSPEL » JOHN 17:1-11

Jesus said these things. Then, raising his eyes in prayer, he said:
Father, it's time.
Display the bright splendor of your Son
So the Son in turn may show your bright splendor.
You put him in charge of everything human
So he might give real and eternal life to all in his charge.
And this is the real and eternal life:
That they know you,
The one and only true God,
And Jesus Christ, whom you sent.
I glorified you on earth
By completing down to the last detail
What you assigned me to do.
And now, Father, glorify me with your very own splendor,
The very splendor I had in your presence
Before there was a world.
I spelled out your character in detail
To the men and women you gave me.
They were yours in the first place;
Then you gave them to me,
And they have now done what you said.
They know now, beyond the shadow of a doubt,
That everything you gave me is firsthand from you,
For the message you gave me, I gave them;
And they took it, and were convinced
That I came from you.
They believed that you sent me.

I pray for them.
I'm not praying for the God-rejecting world
But for those you gave me,
For they are yours by right.
Everything mine is yours, and yours mine,
And my life is on display in them.
For I'm no longer going to be visible in the world;
They'll continue in the world
While I return to you.
Holy Father, guard them as they pursue this life
That you conferred as a gift through me,
So they can be one heart and mind
As we are one heart and mind.
As long as I was with them, I guarded them
In the pursuit of the life you gave through me;
I even posted a night watch.
And not one of them got away,
Except for the rebel bent on destruction
(the exception that proved the rule of Scripture).

Books of prayers and books about prayer are very popular. We all know we should pray, and many of us wish we were better pray-ers. Jesus understood that his disciples had a need to learn how to pray, and so he spent a good part of his instruction on the subject. Jesus modeled a life of prayer by retreating often to lonely places. He taught the "Our Father" when his friends asked what they should say when they prayed. He also told stories about people who prayed well, in humility, or badly, with self-satisfaction.

And at the end of his life, when he knew the hour of his passion was near, Jesus raised a prayer to heaven for us. He could have spent his last communion with his Father on the trial to come, but he prayed for our steadfastness instead. And not a word was wasted: we still need a steady spirit for when the trial comes.

Which of Jesus' lessons on prayer teaches you the most about how to pray?

WE RESPOND

Read one of the Gospel stories about prayer: Mt 6:5-8; Mt 6:9-14; Lk 11:5-8; Lk 11:9-13; Lk 18:1-8; Lk 18:9-14. Reflect on how the practice of prayer affects your life.

PENTECOST SUNDAY

FIRST READING » ACTS OF THE APOSTLES 2:1-11

When the Feast of Pentecost came, they were all together in one place. Without warning there was a sound like a strong wind, gale force—no one could tell where it came from. It filled the whole building. Then, like a wildfire, the Holy Spirit spread through their ranks, and they started speaking in a number of different languages as the Spirit prompted them.

There were many Jews staying in Jerusalem just then, devout pilgrims from all over the world. When they heard the sound, they came on the run. Then when they heard, one after another, their own mother tongues being spoken, they were thunderstruck. They couldn't for the life of them figure out what was going on, and kept saying, "Aren't these all Galileans? How come we're hearing them talk in our various mother tongues?

Parthians, Medes, and Elamites;

Visitors from Mesopotamia, Judea, and Cappadocia,

> *Pontus and Asia, Phrygia and Pamphylia,*

> *Egypt and the parts of Libya belonging to Cyrene;*

Immigrants from Rome, both Jews and proselytes;

Even Cretans and Arabs!

"They're speaking our languages, describing God's mighty works!"

Language is a miracle. How you and I can express our distinct experiences to one another meaningfully with sound and gesture, even a roll of the eyes, is one of the most remarkable aspects of being human. Although we take it for granted, human communication is the marvel upon which civilization stands.

That being said, we see in our assemblies today a remarkable diversity of language as our church is gifted with people from all over the world. We are like a modern Tower of Babel in reverse, made one by the miracle of Pentecost, the story of language and nationalism being knit together by a common spirit. If you've ever had a meeting of the minds with someone who didn't speak a word of your language, or bridged a generation gap, you have experienced an aspect of the Pentecost. Beyond the words that can divide us is the language of love which makes us whole.

> **How many ways do you find to communicate**
> **your love to the people you care about?**

SECOND READING » 1 CORINTHIANS 12:3B-7, 12-13

What I want to talk about now is the various ways God's Spirit gets worked into our lives. This is complex and often misunderstood, but I want you to be informed and knowledgeable. Remember how you were when you didn't know God, led from one phony god to another, never knowing what you were doing, just doing it because everybody else did it? It's different in this life. God wants us to use our intelligence, to seek to understand as well as we can. For instance, by using your heads, you know perfectly well that the Spirit of God would never prompt anyone to say "Jesus be damned!" Nor would anyone be inclined to say "Jesus is Master!" without the insight of the Holy Spirit.

God's various gifts are handed out everywhere; but they all originate in God's Spirit. God's various ministries are carried out everywhere; but they all originate in God's Spirit. God's various expressions of power are in action everywhere; but God himself is behind it all. Each person is given something to do that shows who God is: Everyone gets in on it, everyone benefits. All kinds of things are handed out by the Spirit, and to all kinds of people! The variety is wonderful:

> *wise counsel*
> *clear understanding*
> *simple trust*
> *healing the sick*
> *miraculous acts*
> *proclamation*
> *distinguishing between spirits*
> *tongues*
> *interpretation of tongues.*

All these gifts have a common origin, but are handed out one by one by the one Spirit of God. He decides who gets what, and when.

You can easily enough see how this kind of thing works by looking no further than your own body. Your body has many parts—limbs, organs, cells—but no matter how many parts you can name, you're still one body. It's exactly the same with Christ. By means of his one Spirit, we all said good-bye to our partial and piecemeal lives. We each used to independently call our own shots, but then we entered into a large and integrated life in which he has the final say in everything. (This is what we proclaimed in word and action when we were baptized.) Each of us is now a part of his resurrection body, refreshed and sustained at one fountain—his Spirit—where we all come to drink. The old labels we once used to identify ourselves—labels like Jew or Greek, slave or free—are no longer useful. We need something larger, more comprehensive.

Wordless compassion. A kind touch on a sleeve. Flowers sent across a distance. We share so many languages that have nothing to do with words. As Christians, we also share the language of ritual, the extraordinary meaning of bread, wine, oil, and water. No one has to list for us the properties of water for us to know what it means when an infant or an adult receives the three-fold pouring of water. The water we sign ourselves with at the entrance of churches is silently available to us. Water is our life, and calls us beyond ashes to Easter.

The language of water unites Christians across the lines of denomination and citizenship, race, class, and gender. Though we speak more often of our differences,

Paul's call to oneness rings out over the centuries to remind us that our first language in faith is unity.

How is unity (or division) expressed in your family, parish, and community?

GOSPEL » JOHN 20:19-23

Later on that day, the disciples had gathered together, but, fearful of the Jews, had locked all the doors in the house. Jesus entered, stood among them, and said, "Peace to you." Then he showed them his hands and side.

The disciples, seeing the Master with their own eyes, were exuberant. Jesus repeated his greeting: "Peace to you. Just as the Father sent me, I send you."

Then he took a deep breath and breathed into them. "Receive the Holy Spirit," he said. "If you forgive someone's sins, they're gone for good. If you don't forgive sins, what are you going to do with them?"

God created the world with a word, Scripture tells us. God spoke the word BE, and all that is came into being. In the same way, God spoke divinity into human form when Jesus the Word "became flesh and dwelt among us." Finally, the Spirit of Holiness becomes available to us when Jesus breathes the simple words, "Receive the Holy Spirit."

The gifts and fruits of the Holy Spirit are defined by lists of words that school children memorize, but behind those words are powerful realities. Invoking the Spirit of joy, peace, patience, and love will create quite a different world than the one invoked by anger, bitterness, and indifference. Lives are bound together or drawn apart by words spoken or withheld. Stewardship over the power of words is a holy reality.

Look up the fruits of the Holy Spirit in Galatians 5:22-23.
How many of these are expressed in your life?

WE RESPOND

Choose one fruit of the Holy Spirit that is least present in your life, and make conscious decisions to employ it this week.

Each of us is now a part of his resurrection body, refreshed and sustained at one fountain...

TRINITY SUNDAY

FIRST READING » EXODUS 34:4B-6, 8-9

So Moses cut two tablets of stone just like the originals. He got up early in the morning and climbed Mount Sinai as God had commanded him, carrying the two tablets of stone. God descended in the cloud and took up his position there beside him and called out the name, God. God passed in front of him and called out, "God, God, a God of mercy and grace, endlessly patient—so much love, so deeply true—loyal in love for a thousand generations, forgiving iniquity, rebellion, and sin. Still, he doesn't ignore sin. He holds sons and grandsons responsible for a father's sins to the third and even fourth generation."

At once, Moses fell to the ground and worshiped, saying, "Please, O Master, if you see anything good in me, please Master, travel with us, hard-headed as these people are. Forgive our iniquity and sin. Own us, possess us."

In the Hebrew Scriptures, God was pretty easy to identify. A *theophany*, or manifestation of God, was always accompanied by fire, clouds, a mighty voice, and an extraordinary act of power. Often people in the stories were struck dead or blinded by the event. To this day we refer to "acts of God" when describing episodes of remarkable destruction.

In the case of Moses, God appeared with a full-fledged introduction. It was to Moses first that God spoke the divine name. Moses never found himself in the position of "entertaining angels unawares." Nor should we. Knowing that God is love, we can never fail to recognize in the face of love the God who speaks to us.

What events in your life clearly bore the mark of God?

SECOND READING » 2 CORINTHIANS 13:11-13

And that's about it, friends. Be cheerful. Keep things in good repair. Keep your spirits up. Think in harmony. Be agreeable. Do all that, and the God of love and peace will be with you for sure. Greet one another with a holy embrace. All the brothers and sisters here say hello.

Catholics of a certain age will remember the song, "And They'll Know We Are Christians by Our Love." The original Christian presence was known by love, and the sign of peace and holy kiss exchanged between believers became as much a part of their greeting as Paul's invocation of the Trinity. Grace, love, fellowship; Christ, God, and the Holy Spirit. The life that mirrored these attributes reflected the Holy Three in One.

If we know we're dealing with God when love is present, the world can also see the believer in acts of love and service. Faith without works, the evangelist James once declared, is a dead thing. God's life is not revealed in one who will not serve.

Who serves you? Whom do you serve?

GOSPEL » JOHN 3:16-18

"This is how much God loved the world: He gave his Son, his one and only Son. And this is why: so that no one need be destroyed; by believing in him, anyone can have a whole and lasting life. God didn't go to all the trouble of sending his Son merely to point an accusing finger, telling the world how bad it was. He came to help, to put the world right again. Anyone who trusts in him is acquitted; anyone who refuses to trust him has long since been under the death sentence without knowing it. And why? Because of that person's failure to believe in the one-of-a-kind Son of God when introduced to him.

How can we tell it's God in the gospels? There are fewer incidents of fire and cloud there. Look for the sacrifice! Not the animal sacrifice offered in the Temple, but the divine one evident everywhere. Christ emptied himself of divine privileges and took on flesh. Jesus turned from the temptations of wealth and power, and chose service. The King of Kings cast his lot among the poor and ignorant. What might easily have been the golden touch was used to heal lepers. Instead of a career, Jesus had a brief ministry. Sacrifice was spelled out in the silhouette of a cross on a hillside.

The signs of sacrifice are fewer in the world these days, though crosses abound on buildings and dangle from the ends of chains. If we want people to believe we come in the name of God, we'll have to produce the sacrifice.

What sacrifices have you made in the name of Christ?

WE RESPOND

Celebrate the Trinity by creating something in honor of the Source of all creation; sacrificing something in the name of Jesus; and contemplating the Holy Presence in prayer.

God didn't go to all the trouble of sending his Son merely to point an accusing finger.

BODY AND BLOOD OF CHRIST

.... True Food

FIRST READING » DEUTERONOMY 8:2-3, 14B-16A

Keep and live out the entire commandment that I'm commanding you today so that you'll live and prosper and enter and own the land that God promised to your ancestors. Remember every road that God led you on for those forty years in the wilderness, pushing you to your limits, testing you so that he would know what you were made of, whether you would keep his commandments or not. He put you through hard times. He made you go hungry. Then he fed you with manna, something neither you nor your parents knew anything about, so you would learn that men and women don't live by bread only; we live by every word that comes from God's mouth. Your clothes didn't wear out and your feet didn't blister those forty years. You learned deep in your heart that God disciplines you in the same ways a father disciplines his child.

Make sure you don't forget God, your God, by not keeping his commandments, his rules and regulations that I command you today. Make sure that when you eat and are satisfied, build pleasant houses and settle in, see your herds and flocks flourish and more and more money come in, watch your standard of living going up and up—make sure you don't become so full of yourself and your things that you forget God, your God,

the God who delivered you from Egyptian slavery;

the God who led you through that huge and fearsome wilderness,

those desolate, arid badlands crawling with fiery snakes and scorpions;

the God who gave you water gushing from hard rock;

the God who gave you manna to eat in the wilderness, something your ancestors had never heard of, in order to give you a taste of the hard life, to test you so that you would be prepared to live well in the days ahead of you.

Moses is the rock star of Israel's story. He's had his picture on the cover of TIME magazine. He's been portrayed in film by everybody from Charlton Heston to Mel Brooks. He's even got his own Wikipedia page. Not only is he a central figure in three major world religions; but he's totally cool to boot.

What's most remarkable about Moses is not the glitzy role of guiding a nation out of slavery in Egypt. It's his extraordinary relationship with the divine which has not been equaled by a mere mortal since. He carries on a forty-year conversation with God that's full of devotion, tension, trust and conflict. We hear the ins and outs of that relationship in Moses' final speech before the nation crosses over into the promised land. God has done wonderful things, but has also permitted terrible things. Moses isn't a theologian apologizing for God's behavior, or a publicist looking to put a good spin on forty difficult years. He simply reminds the community that God supplied more than food for their hunger. The real gift in the desert was the divine word which reshaped their slave hearts and prepared them for freedom.

As we grope along looking for a relevant savior for our society, Moses stands out as an icon of what freedom means and what it costs. Our slave hearts, bound to material goods and successes, may not be ready to leave Egypt behind.

> **What part of your life binds you
> to spiritual slavery to this world and its values?
> What helps you work toward spiritual freedom?**

SECOND READING » 1 CORINTHIANS 10:16-17

I assume I'm addressing believers now who are mature. Draw your own conclusions: When we drink the cup of blessing, aren't we taking into ourselves the blood, the very life, of Christ? And isn't it the same with the loaf of bread we break and eat? Don't we take into ourselves the body, the very life, of Christ? Because there is one loaf, our many-ness becomes one-ness—Christ doesn't become fragmented in us. Rather, we become unified in him. We don't reduce Christ to what we are; he raises us to what he is. That's basically what happened even in old Israel—those who ate the sacrifices offered on God's altar entered into God's action at the altar.

Look around you at communion time. You are one with all those people in the communion lines. The old woman creeping slowly forward with her walker. The punky young dude in the leather jacket. The painted female in the too-tight skirt, the teenagers dragged here by their parents, the pleasant-looking grandfather, the young mother who could use a week of sleep. Communion means more than accepting the host in our hands or on the tongue. It means accepting our relationship with, even our responsibility toward, all of those people.

Each person in the communion line will hear the words, "The Body of Christ," and each will confirm his or her commitment to being part of that Body with their "Amen." How do we support that Body through our dealings with these people? Do we judge their attire, or sit in judgment over their hearts? Our worshipping community may be small enough to be a real society, or so large that it's only a symbolic one, reminding us of a responsibility to the greater society. In either case, the Sunday assembly is a good place to practice being one with the diverse community around us. If we don't have enough imagination or charity to see our oneness there, it probably won't happen anywhere else.

> **Spend some time reflecting on your Sunday assembly. How is it united?
> What divides it? What role do you play in its unity?**

GOSPEL » JOHN 6:51-58

"I'm telling you the most solemn and sober truth now: Whoever believes in me has real life, eternal life. I am the Bread of Life. Your ancestors ate the manna bread in the desert and died. But now here is Bread that truly comes down out

of heaven. Anyone eating this Bread will not die, ever. I am the Bread—living Bread!—who came down out of heaven. Anyone who eats this Bread will live—and forever! The Bread that I present to the world so that it can eat and live is myself, this flesh-and-blood self."

At this, the Jews started fighting among themselves: "How can this man serve up his flesh for a meal?"

But Jesus didn't give an inch. "Only insofar as you eat and drink flesh and blood, the flesh and blood of the Son of Man, do you have life within you. The one who brings a hearty appetite to this eating and drinking has eternal life and will be fit and ready for the Final Day. My flesh is real food and my blood is real drink. By eating my flesh and drinking my blood you enter into me and I into you. In the same way that the fully alive Father sent me here and I live because of him, so the one who makes a meal of me lives because of me. This is the Bread from heaven. Your ancestors ate bread and later died. Whoever eats this Bread will live always."

We live in an age that invented junk food: food that is not real food because it supplies no nourishment and can be harmful to eat. It's not surprising, then, that we also consume volumes of reporting that is mostly opinion, and inform ourselves from sources we can't even identify. Our culture's popular stories are thin, recycled, and not transformative. A lot of what we take in—to our bodies, our minds, our hearts—is just junk.

Some people awaken to that reality and try to make changes. They train themselves to walk past the processed food aisle in the market. They turn off the TV, forsake prepackaged opinions, seek out stories which lead beyond romance or cynicism. They look for people engaged in vital living, who go beyond the existence loop that many of us have crawled into: work, eat, entertain, sleep. Some folks are looking for true food.

Jesus offers true food to those who believe. Eucharist is how we express that, but the sacrament takes us beyond the sacred elements to the flesh-and-blood avenues of our lives. Jesus gave us the Eucharist to open our eyes to the words he spoke, the stories he told, the transformative action of Spirit that helps us break out of the existence loop and into lives that matter. When we've had enough junk, the true food is on the table.

> **What nourishes your body and your spirit?**
> **How much cultural junk do you consume,**
> **in proportion to the true food of faith?**

WE RESPOND

Consider the ratio of "junk food" in your life to the true food that Jesus offers. Plan a new diet, lessening the amount of time you surrender to useless, lifeless activity. Increase your intake of good food, inspiring stories, real relationships.

ORDINARY TIME

BAPTISM OF THE LORD

FIRST READING » ISAIAH 42:1-4, 6-7

God's Message,
the God who created the cosmos, stretched out the skies,
laid out the earth and all that grows from it,
Who breathes life into earth's people,
makes them alive with his own life:
"I am God. I have called you to live right and well.
I have taken responsibility for you, kept you safe.
I have set you among my people to bind them to me,
and provided you as a lighthouse to the nations,
To make a start at bringing people into the open, into light:
opening blind eyes,
releasing prisoners from dungeons,
emptying the dark prisons.
I am God. That's my name.
I don't franchise my glory,
don't endorse the no-god idols.
Take note: The earlier predictions of judgment have been fulfilled.
I'm announcing the new salvation work.
Before it bursts on the scene,
I'm telling you all about it."

God's faithful servant—from whom Jesus patterned his own mission—was characterized by a spirit of justice. Not by fanfare or a splashy public persona, but by justice. This justice would bring sight to the blind, freedom to prisoners, and light to those in darkness. These are metaphors, of course. The just servant would not be a doctor or defense lawyer or electrician, but a healer of souls. The coming of justice meant that people would change, from the inside out. And once people change, systems change.

There are ways in which you and I are blind, bound, and in the dark. There are truths about ourselves to which we close our eyes. There are fears and old wounds that hold us prisoners to the past. There are lies we've learned to love more than the light of Christ. Baptism signals our acceptance that the servant of justice holds more power over us than all that keeps us from wholeness. The more we accept our baptism, the deeper the healing goes.

Which areas of your life are still in need of the healer of souls?

SECOND READING » ACTS OF THE APOSTLES 10:34-38

Peter fairly exploded with his good news: "It's God's own truth, nothing could be plainer: God plays no favorites! It makes no difference who you are or where you're from—if you want God and are ready to do as he says, the door is open. The Message he sent to the children of Israel—that through Jesus Christ everything is being put together again—well, he's doing it everywhere, among everyone.

"You know the story of what happened in Judea. It began in Galilee after John preached a total life-change. Then Jesus arrived from Nazareth, anointed by God with the Holy Spirit, ready for action. He went through the country helping people and healing everyone who was beaten down by the Devil. He was able to do all this because God was with him.

The way Peter tells the story, it began for Jesus the way it begins for all of us, at baptism. Of course, the baptism of Jesus marks him in a radically different way than ours, since he did not surrender to sin. Instead he's singled out at baptism as the servant who pleases, reminiscent of Isaiah's prophecy. From there Jesus does good works and healing, demonstrating that God is with him. (Emmanuel, remember, means God-with-us.) The devil didn't stand a chance.

In telling this story to the centurion's household, Peter realizes something new: that the power of Jesus heals the rift between Jew and Gentile as well. The fact that Peter is standing in a Gentile's house is something new—the very act should make him unclean. The good news of peace would cross boundaries that Peter could not have imagined. It would mend the breach between heaven and earth itself.

What contemporary breaches might the gospel lead us to mend today?

GOSPEL » MATTHEW 3:13-17

Jesus then appeared, arriving at the Jordan River from Galilee. He wanted John to baptize him. John objected, "I'm the one who needs to be baptized, not you!"

But Jesus insisted. "Do it. God's work, putting things right all these centuries, is coming together right now in this baptism." So John did it.

The moment Jesus came up out of the baptismal waters, the skies opened up and he saw God's Spirit—it looked like a dove—descending and landing on him. And along with the Spirit, a voice: "This is my Son, chosen and marked by my love, delight of my life."

Consider this day Epiphany, Part II. In Eastern rite churches, the feast of Epiphany includes the baptism of Jesus, as this event is the direct manifestation of God in the life of Jesus. Only in the story of the Transfiguration will we get as clear an indication that Jesus is the human face of God.

John is understandably anxious about baptizing "the one who is to come," the one he's already prophesied would bring a baptism of Spirit and fire. But Jesus invites him to surrender that misgiving in favor of doing what God wants. This is excellent advice to anyone on the road of discipleship. We all get anxious about how things ought to be done, what is right and proper and orderly, especially when it comes to religion. But we can't outguess God. Sometimes the least orderly thing we can do is the most in keeping with God's plan. The plan, as we're continually reminded, has little to do with appearances.

> **When has an "improper" or "disorderly" event brought God's will to life in you?**

WE RESPOND

Celebrate your baptism by imitating "the servant who pleases." Be the face of justice for someone this week, righting a wrong, bringing light and freedom to someone in a small but concrete way.

*"This is my Son,
  chosen and marked by my love,
  delight of my life."*

SECOND SUNDAY IN ORDINARY TIME

FIRST READING » ISAIAH 49:3, 5-6

Listen, far-flung islands,
*   pay attention, faraway people:*
God put me to work from the day I was born.
*   The moment I entered the world he named me.*
He gave me speech that would cut and penetrate.
*   He kept his hand on me to protect me.*
He made me his straight arrow
*   and hid me in his quiver.*
He said to me, "You're my dear servant,
*   Israel, through whom I'll shine."*
"And now," God says,
*   this God who took me in hand*
*   from the moment of birth to be his servant,*
To bring Jacob back home to him,
*   to set a reunion for Israel—*
What an honor for me in God's eyes!
*   That God should be my strength!*
He says, "But that's not a big enough job for my servant—
*   just to recover the tribes of Jacob,*
*   merely to round up the strays of Israel.*
I'm setting you up as a light for the nations
*   so that my salvation becomes global!"*

An old exercise is used to reveal one's deepest levels of commitment. It's the story of the lifeboat: if you can only save one other person, who is it going to be? Your spouse or your mother? Your broker or your friend? It's a false dilemma, of course, because no one is being asked to make these spare choices. But what if salvation were up to us, in the broadest possible sense? Whom would we save?

If the matter is left up to God, the choice is clear. Salvation reaches to the ends of the earth. It's not just the property of one people, or a particular nation; all peoples are being invited into the boat. Think of it more like an ark, a floating lifeline to the nations. It is too little, God declares, for this gift to be given only to the few. God's desire is for all people to experience the fullness of life. This might make us rethink the categories of persons we might exclude from our lifeboat.

> **Are there people in your community**
> **who are being "left off the boat" in terms of their needs?**
> **How does or might your parish respond to them?**

SECOND READING » 1 CORINTHIANS 1:1-3

I, Paul, have been called and sent by Jesus, the Messiah, according to God's plan, along with my friend Sosthenes. I send this letter to you in God's church at Corinth, believers cleaned up by Jesus and set apart for a God-filled life. I include in my greeting all who call out to Jesus, wherever they live. He's their Master as well as ours!

May all the gifts and benefits that come from God our Father, and the Master, Jesus Christ, be yours.

Paul begins his letter to the Corinthians with a strong statement of authority: "sent by Jesus, the Messiah, according to God's plan." It's as if he is saying: Dispute *this*. There is much dispute going on in Corinth, which is why Paul is writing. He wants to make sure that his authority is not up for argument.

Authority is one of the many questions Corinth is raising: are they disciples of Paul, their first missionary, or Apollos, their second evangelist? Paul hopes to shatter that false division by reminding them heavy-handedly that they follow Jesus and not any human leader. He uses the name of Jesus four times in the first two sentences of the letter to underscore that: Paul is sent by Jesus, the people are consecrated in Jesus, all call out to Jesus, and every blessing comes through the Father and Jesus. Human authority is a frail claim in light of this truth.

> **How is authority wielded in your circles?**
> **What is the source of that authority?**

GOSPEL » JOHN 1:29-34

The very next day John saw Jesus coming toward him and yelled out, "Here he is, God's Passover Lamb! He forgives the sins of the world! This is the man I've been talking about, 'the One who comes after me but is really ahead of me.' I knew nothing about who he was—only this: that my task has been to get Israel ready to recognize him as the God-Revealer. That is why I came here baptizing with water, giving you a good bath and scrubbing sins from your life so you can get a fresh start with God."

John clinched his witness with this: "I watched the Spirit, like a dove flying down out of the sky, making himself at home in him. I repeat, I know nothing about him except this: The One who authorized me to baptize with water told me, 'The One on whom you see the Spirit come down and stay, this One will baptize with the Holy Spirit.' That's exactly what I saw happen, and I'm telling you, there's no question about it: This is the Son of God."

The lamb is a significant animal in Hebrew tradition. It was one of the most frequently sacrificed animals in ritual. It was the animal slaughtered for Passover, of course, but also for several other feasts, including the Day of Atonement, as well as in daily sacrifices. Because of its premier place as the victim of sacrifice, John calls Jesus by this name in the Gospel.

What does the sacrificial lamb do? Its blood marks the homes of those who will be saved from death in Passover observance. Its death leads to freedom from sin as in the Day of Atonement. The lamb offered to God brings joy to those for whom its blood was shed. If John the Baptist's cry would have been taken to heart by his listeners, no one would have been surprised at the hour of crucifixion. As it was, like the cries of so many prophets, this one went unheeded.

What does it mean to you to receive the Body and Blood of Christ?

WE RESPOND

Pay particular attention to the prayer we recite at Mass: Lamb of God, you take away the sin of the world, have mercy on us. Consider how the mercy of the Lamb commits us to being people of mercy, and find a way this week to show mercy to those who seek it.

"I'm telling you, there's no question about it: This is the Son of God."

THIS TRANSFORMING WORD

THIRD SUNDAY IN ORDINARY TIME

FIRST READING » ISAIAH 8:23—9:3

But there'll be no darkness for those who were in trouble. Earlier he did bring the lands of Zebulun and Naphtali into disrepute, but the time is coming when he'll make that whole area glorious— the road along the Sea, the country past the Jordan, international Galilee.

The people who walked in darkness
    have seen a great light.
For those who lived in a land of deep shadows—
    light! sunbursts of light!
You repopulated the nation,
    you expanded its joy.
Oh, they're so glad in your presence!
    Festival joy!
The joy of a great celebration,
    sharing rich gifts and warm greetings.
The abuse of oppressors and cruelty of tyrants—
    all their whips and cudgels and curses—
Is gone, done away with, a deliverance
    as surprising and sudden as Gideon's old victory over Midian.
The boots of all those invading troops,
    along with their shirts soaked with innocent blood,
Will be piled in a heap and burned,
    a fire that will burn for days!
For a child has been born—for us!
    the gift of a son—for us!
He'll take over
    the running of the world.
His names will be: Amazing Counselor,
    Strong God,
Eternal Father,
    Prince of Wholeness.
His ruling authority will grow,
    and there'll be no limits to the wholeness he brings.
He'll rule from the historic David throne
    over that promised kingdom.
He'll put that kingdom on a firm footing
    and keep it going
With fair dealing and right living,

beginning now and lasting always.
The zeal of God-of-the-Angel-Armies
will do all this.

At a certain point each year, the relentlessness of winter creates a darkness that seems to cloak our hearts. The gloom seems interminable. We hunger for a bit of sun, but it will be a long time coming. When the first day of wavering light finally arrives, it's as if each town and city is reborn. On the buses, in the shops and in the streets, everyone get smiley, friendly, generous. Light opens us all to the possibility of kindness again.

The great light that Isaiah speaks of is the revelation of God's love beyond Israel to the Gentiles. We might think of it as the day when God's love comes to those who don't have a religious bone in their bodies, when materialistic hearts are melted, when people toughened by despair or cynicism learn that love is real and hope is more than a daydream. The great light that comes to those who walk in darkness isn't some paranormal experience. The only way that light can come is if you and I bring it.

> **How do you convincingly convey the light of God's love to others?**

SECOND READING » 1 CORINTHIANS 1:10-13, 17

I have a serious concern to bring up with you, my friends, using the authority of Jesus, our Master. I'll put it as urgently as I can: You must get along with each other. You must learn to be considerate of one another, cultivating a life in common.

I bring this up because some from Chloe's family brought a most disturbing report to my attention—that you're fighting among yourselves! I'll tell you exactly what I was told: You're all picking sides, going around saying, "I'm on Paul's side," or "I'm for Apollos," or "Peter is my man," or "I'm in the Messiah group."

I ask you, "Has the Messiah been chopped up in little pieces so we can each have a relic all our own? Was Paul crucified for you? Was a single one of you baptized in Paul's name?" I was not involved with any of your baptisms—except for Crispus and Gaius—and on getting this report, I'm sure glad I wasn't. At least no one can go around saying he was baptized in my name. (Come to think of it, I also baptized Stephanas's family, but as far as I can recall, that's it.)

God didn't send me out to collect a following for myself, but to preach the Message of what he has done, collecting a following for him. And he didn't send me to do it with a lot of fancy rhetoric of my own, lest the powerful action at the center—Christ on the Cross—be trivialized into mere words.

Paul plunges into the Corinthian debate about allegiances. Paul, Apollos, and Peter all have claims on the loyalty of Christians in Corinth, but their baptism, after all, comes in the name of Christ. "Was I crucified for you?" asks Paul in exasperation. His question cuts to the heart of the issue.

THIS TRANSFORMING WORD

Today, the allegiances of Christianity are spread about: some follow the Pope, others Martin Luther, John Wesley, Mary Baker Eddy. It seems clear that Paul would have some cutting phrase to hurl at us in his unwritten Letter to the Bi-Millennial Christians. Does Christ hold our ultimate allegiance, or are we still unsure whose truth we're serving? If authority is an issue in the church today—and I think it continues to be one—the letter to Corinth is a refresher course in setting priorities. It also affirms the need in this millennium to get serious about ecumenism.

**In what ways is your parish involved in ecumenical dialogue or activity?
What can you do to promote unity among people of faith?**

GOSPEL » MATTHEW 4:12-23

When Jesus got word that John had been arrested, he returned to Galilee. He moved from his hometown, Nazareth, to the lakeside village Capernaum, nestled at the base of the Zebulun and Naphtali hills. This move completed Isaiah's sermon:

> *Land of Zebulun, land of Naphtali,*
> *road to the sea, over Jordan,*
> *Galilee, crossroads for the nations.*
> *People sitting out their lives in the dark*
> *saw a huge light;*
> *Sitting in that dark, dark country of death,*
> *they watched the sun come up.*

This Isaiah-prophesied sermon came to life in Galilee the moment Jesus started preaching. He picked up where John left off: "Change your life. God's kingdom is here."

Walking along the beach of Lake Galilee, Jesus saw two brothers: Simon (later called Peter) and Andrew. They were fishing, throwing their nets into the lake. It was their regular work. Jesus said to them, "Come with me. I'll make a new kind of fisherman out of you. I'll show you how to catch men and women instead of perch and bass." They didn't ask questions, but simply dropped their nets and followed.

A short distance down the beach they came upon another pair of brothers, James and John, Zebedee's sons. These two were sitting in a boat with their father, Zebedee, mending their fishnets. Jesus made the same offer to them, and they were just as quick to follow, abandoning boat and father.

From there he went all over Galilee. He used synagogues for meeting places and taught people the truth of God. God's kingdom was his theme—that beginning right now they were under God's government, a good government! He also healed people of their diseases and of the bad effects of their bad lives. Word got around the entire Roman province of Syria. People brought anybody with an ailment, whether mental, emotional, or physical. Jesus healed them, one and all. More and more people came, the momentum gathering. Besides those from Galilee, crowds came from the "Ten Towns" across the lake, others up from Jerusalem and Judea, still others from across the Jordan.

Everything changes for Jesus after John's arrest. He relocates to the seaside town of Capernaum, takes up John's message, and begins to call personal disciples to his side. Before the arrest, Jesus was baptized and underwent a time of trial in the desert; but we hear nothing of his ministry until John is taken. The silencing of the voice crying in the wilderness means it's time for Jesus to "increase," as John once put it. Jesus always knows the hour, and acts on it.

Matthew is keen on tracing the prophecy-and-fulfillment in Jesus' actions. He attributes Jesus' move from Nazareth to Galilee to the prophecy of light coming to the Gentiles. Well, "heathen Galilee" wasn't quite Gentile territory, but it bordered on it. Matthew is always willing to strain a detail in order to make a point: everything Jesus does is foretold in the Hebrew Scriptures. Ultimately, Matthew wants to convince his Jewish audience that Jesus is the revelation they've been waiting for.

How does Jesus cast a light on our contemporary world and dispel the darkness?

WE RESPOND

Make a personal commitment to ecumenism. Resist presuming that other expressions of faith are inferior to your own. If you have friends of other denominations, ask if you can worship with them and invite them to your parish as well. Pray for an increase in fellowship and understanding among Christians.

"I'll show you how to catch men and women instead of perch and bass."

FOURTH SUNDAY IN ORDINARY TIME
.... Those Who Count for Nothing

FIRST READING » ZEPHANIAH 2:3; 3:12-13

Seek God, all you quietly disciplined people
*   who live by God's justice.*
Seek God's right ways. Seek a quiet and disciplined life.
*   Perhaps you'll be hidden on the Day of God's anger.*
"In the end I will turn things around for the people.
*   I'll give them a language undistorted, unpolluted,*
Words to address God in worship
*   and, united, to serve me with their shoulders to the wheel.*
They'll come from beyond the Ethiopian rivers,
*   they'll come praying—*
All my scattered, exiled people
*   will come home with offerings for worship.*
You'll no longer have to be ashamed
*   of all those acts of rebellion.*
I'll have gotten rid of your arrogant leaders.
*   No more pious strutting on my holy hill!*
I'll leave a core of people among you
*   who are poor in spirit—*
What's left of Israel that's really Israel.
*   They'll make their home in God.*
This core holy people
*   will not do wrong.*
They won't lie,
*   won't use words to flatter or seduce.*
Content with who they are and where they are,
*   unanxious, they'll live at peace."*

This prophet writes in a generation of religious and social degradation. Idols are back in fashion, as Israel creates alliances with its enemies. The first part of Zephaniah's message warns of punishment and destruction to come. But the second part concerns the fate of a faithful few, a "core holy people," who will be preserved on the day when the world comes apart. (The music of the *Dies Irae* or Day of Wrath finds its source in Zephaniah.)

On the Day of Wrath, the humble survive. This idea finds its parallel in the beatitude that the meek shall inherit the earth. When we think of the humble, we tend to imagine a rather wimpy, self-effacing bunch that Darwin would have weeded out long ago. But true humility is the self-recognition that comes when we are still and know who God is. The human spirit isn't crushed in acknowledging its Maker. Rather, when we know who God is, we also know who we are: made in that wonderful image and likeness.

Name the humble in your midst.
Describe how their words, actions,
or demeanor exhibit real humility.

SECOND READING » 1 CORINTHIANS 1:26-31

Take a good look, friends, at who you were when you got called into this life. I don't see many of "the brightest and the best" among you, not many influential, not many from high-society families. Isn't it obvious that God deliberately chose men and women that the culture overlooks and exploits and abuses, chose these "nobodies" to expose the hollow pretensions of the "somebodies"? That makes it quite clear that none of you can get by with blowing your own horn before God. Everything that we have—right thinking and right living, a clean slate and a fresh start—comes from God by way of Jesus Christ. That's why we have the saying, "If you're going to blow a horn, blow a trumpet for God."

The Christian community at Corinth had brief success among the synagogue crowd, but took more lasting root among the low-lifes in this rollicking seaport town. Corinth had everything most ports had, which means plenty of opportunities to misbehave. Corinthian Christians were scraped up from among its fallen citizenry, as Paul describes them: not wise, not influential, not well-born. He goes on to back-handedly insult them by saying God prefers absurd, weak, low-born and despised people like themselves, those who count for nothing in the world. (Kinda makes you want to say: hey, Paul, go easy on these people, will you? This is supposed to be a letter of encouragement.)

Paul's point, of course, is that God chooses the nobodies so that even the some-bodies get the punchline: God is the source of wisdom, grace, and redemption. It has nothing to do with the merits of the individual. Those who count for nothing can boast in the Lord, and watch the wisdom and strength of this world come to shame.

How do you feel about being counted
among the absurd, weak, and despised
who are chosen by God?

GOSPEL » MATTHEW 5:1-12

When Jesus saw his ministry drawing huge crowds, he climbed a hillside. Those who were apprenticed to him, the committed, climbed with him. Arriving at a quiet place, he sat down and taught his climbing companions. This is what he said:

"You're blessed when you're at the end of your rope. With less of you there is more of God and his rule.

"You're blessed when you feel you've lost what is most dear to you. Only then

can you be embraced by the One most dear to you.

"You're blessed when you're content with just who you are—no more, no less. That's the moment you find yourselves proud owners of everything that can't be bought.

"You're blessed when you've worked up a good appetite for God. He's food and drink in the best meal you'll ever eat.

"You're blessed when you care. At the moment of being 'care-full,' you find yourselves cared for.

"You're blessed when you get your inside world—your mind and heart—put right. Then you can see God in the outside world.

"You're blessed when you can show people how to cooperate instead of compete or fight. That's when you discover who you really are, and your place in God's family.

"You're blessed when your commitment to God provokes persecution. The persecution drives you even deeper into God's kingdom.

"Not only that—count yourselves blessed every time people put you down or throw you out or speak lies about you to discredit me. What it means is that the truth is too close for comfort and they are uncomfortable. You can be glad when that happens—give a cheer, even!—for though they don't like it, I do! And all heaven applauds. And know that you are in good company. My prophets and witnesses have always gotten into this kind of trouble.

Of all the good news in the gospels, the Beatitudes are perhaps the best news of all. That is, it's good news for the poor, sorrowing, lowly, hungry, merciful, faithful, peaceful, persecuted and insulted among us. Those of us on the other side of the equation—we might call ourselves "those who count for *something*" in the eyes of the world—may find them more troubling.

Jesus isn't recommending that we all get hungry or get persecuted. Suffering isn't the point. But those of us who imagine we count for *something* in this world had better make friends with those who don't count at all, since they inherit the earth and the kingdom. We had better stand with the voiceless and powerless, we had better champion their cause and be their comfort. Because if we don't use our every advantage to their advantage, how are we going to face the Lord who called the lowly his blessed ones?

> **Count the advantages you have in worldly standards.**
> **How do you put them at the service of the disadvantaged?**

WE RESPOND

Do you have companionship to share with the lonely? Do you have comfort to share with the sorrowful? Do you have goods to share with the poor? Do you have time to share with the neglected? Put your advantage at the disposal of the disadvantaged.

FIFTH SUNDAY OF ORDINARY TIME

FIRST READING » ISAIAH 58:7-10

"This is the kind of fast day I'm after:
to break the chains of injustice,
get rid of exploitation in the workplace,
free the oppressed,
cancel debts.
What I'm interested in seeing you do is:
sharing your food with the hungry,
inviting the homeless poor into your homes,
putting clothes on the shivering ill-clad,
being available to your own families.
Do this and the lights will turn on,
and your lives will turn around at once.
Your righteousness will pave your way.
The God of glory will secure your passage.
Then when you pray, God will answer.
You'll call out for help and I'll say, 'Here I am.'
"If you get rid of unfair practices,
quit blaming victims,
quit gossiping about other people's sins,
If you are generous with the hungry
and start giving yourselves to the down-and-out,
Your lives will begin to glow in the darkness,
your shadowed lives will be bathed in sunlight.
I will always show you where to go.
I'll give you a full life in the emptiest of places—
firm muscles, strong bones.
You'll be like a well-watered garden,
a gurgling spring that never runs dry.
You'll use the old rubble of past lives to build anew,
rebuild the foundations from out of your past.
You'll be known as those who can fix anything,
restore old ruins, rebuild and renovate,
make the community livable again.

"Why does God allow little children to starve?" someone asked not too long ago, referring to the chronic famine in East Africa. Why indeed. One would think with all the power at the disposal of the Almighty, enough food could be produced to feed hungry little kids.

But think about it: Does God allow the starving? Hasn't God been telling us from the beginning to feed them? Why do we blame God for something that's been left in our hands? Didn't God put the world in human hands to manage? And doesn't God give gifts in abundance, enough for everybody? We should better ask why it is, given the abundance of resources available to this world, that WE allow the children to starve.

The Kingdom of God, Jesus tells us, is a reality in conflict with worldly reality. It's where the blind see, the lame walk and the deaf hear; the virgin is the mother, the dead live and the light shines in darkness. The only way to enter the kingdom is by following Jesus. Feed the hungry, clothe the naked, give shelter to the homeless, be a blessing to the poor, a comfort to the sorrowing. Then the light will dawn, the prayer is answered, the healing will come.

In what ways do the humble and lowly reveal God to you?

SECOND READING » 1 CORINTHIANS 2:1-5

You'll remember, friends, that when I first came to you to let you in on God's master stroke, I didn't try to impress you with polished speeches and the latest philosophy. I deliberately kept it plain and simple: first Jesus and who he is; then Jesus and what he did—Jesus crucified.

I was unsure of how to go about this, and felt totally inadequate—I was scared to death, if you want the truth of it—and so nothing I said could have impressed you or anyone else. But the Message came through anyway. God's Spirit and God's power did it, which made it clear that your life of faith is a response to God's power, not to some fancy mental or emotional footwork by me or anyone else.

The Kingdom of God is at hand. It's everywhere, in our midst. It surrounds us and is within us. The problem is that it's not apparent to our senses. Look though we may, we can't see it. Listen carefully, we still can't hear it. Only in faith do we embrace it and experience it as real.

Paul discovered the kingdom all in an hour. The story is recounted in the Acts of the Apostles, chapter nine, and twice more in Acts 22:3-16 and 26:2-18. Saul (his Hebrew name before he adopted Paul, the Greek version) was a man of power and vision. He always knew what to do and was about the business of doing it when he was thrown to the ground and struck blind in an encounter with Jesus. Everything that was ever of value to him became "like rags" he said. From that moment on his life took a dramatic turn. No longer would he persecute the New Way; rather, he would promote it and defend it.

To turn 180 degrees is the meaning of the Greek word we translate as "repentance." To repent is to turn around, to reverse our perspective. This is why Paul, a man of book-learning and fancy speech, came to the Corinthians leaving all those skills behind. He came in humility, proclaiming death and resurrection. His sole testimony was his transformed life.

> **Think of your life as giving testimony, like Paul's.**
> **To what does your lifestyle testify?**

GOSPEL » MATTHEW 5:13-16

"Let me tell you why you are here. You're here to be salt-seasoning that brings out the God-flavors of this earth. If you lose your saltiness, how will people taste godliness? You've lost your usefulness and will end up in the garbage.

"Here's another way to put it: You're here to be light, bringing out the God-colors in the world. God is not a secret to be kept. We're going public with this, as public as a city on a hill. If I make you light-bearers, you don't think I'm going to hide you under a bucket, do you? I'm putting you on a light stand. Now that I've put you there on a hilltop, on a light stand—shine! Keep open house; be generous with your lives. By opening up to others, you'll prompt people to open up with God, this generous Father in heaven.

Salt is not a great mystery. Salt is salt, as basic as it is common. I'll bet there's a shaker close at hand right now. Salt does one thing: it adds flavor. Taste almost any food and you know right away: it needs more, has too much, or is just right.

The job of Christians is to be salt for the world. Our lives should make a difference. The Church's witness is our commitment to live according to kingdom values and not worldly ones. The time, money, and talent in our control should be used to maintain a simple lifestyle, so the surplus can be used to care for those in need. Sprinkled into the world, this kingdom witness flavors the whole generation. The worst we can do is to be sprinkled into the world and change nothing. If no one around you would guess you're a Christian, this is a problem.

The light of goodness comes into the world in the same way. The world is a dark place because of sin. How often we point it out and complain about it (and how the media celebrates it!) Our energy would be better spent generating light through acts of mercy and forgiveness. The light of Christ has come into the world, but it's up to you and me to be the lamps of witness.

> **What are the best ways to utilize your time, your talents**
> **and your money for the sake of the kingdom?**

WE RESPOND

Practice being a lamp today. When you see the darkness of poverty and despair, bring the light of hope through the right use of your resources. Where there is the darkness of sin and personal offense, be a light of forgiveness and reconciliation.

THIS TRANSFORMING WORD

SIXTH SUNDAY IN ORDINARY TIME

.... We Are Given What We Choose

FIRST READING » SIRACH 15:15-20

If you follow God's life-maps, they'll take care of you; if you keep the faith, you'll live God's life. He puts water and fire at your disposal; do with it what you want. The choices are life and death, good and bad—pick one and you'll have it. God's wisdom is great; his strength, massive; his surveillance, continuous and extensive. God has his eye on those who respect him; he knows who does what; he commands that no one carouse; he's given no one a license to sin.

Much wisdom is gleaned from a backward glance at the history of God's people. Written less than 200 years before Jesus, the book of Sirach is the fruit of long reflection on Israel's response to God. The writer has pierced the mystery later reiterated by Christians: "God is love, and whoever lives in love, lives in God" (1 John 5:16).

But love must be a free choice or it's not love at all. We can't love where there is no option. "Love me or else" doesn't work, though many relationships have been propelled by this fuel. In order to be true mirrors to divine love, we must desire to abandon ourselves to love's perfect mystery. If you've ever been madly, deeply in love, no one needs to tell you what this should look like. Abandonment to God is a liberation from fear and worldly restraint. Love makes us free enough to be goofy, to be impractical, even to make fools of ourselves for love's sake.

Sirach views life as a series of choices in which we select what leads to God, or to destruction. But how do we know which is which? Sirach points to God's laws as the guide. God's commandments tell us clearly which choices are fire and which are water, which are death and which are life. Armed with this knowledge, we choose.

What are some good examples of the "fire and water" or "life and death" choices that are placed before you each day?

SECOND READING » 1 CORINTHIANS 2:6-10

We, of course, have plenty of wisdom to pass on to you once you get your feet on firm spiritual ground, but it's not popular wisdom, the fashionable wisdom of high-priced experts that will be out-of-date in a year or so. God's wisdom is something mysterious that goes deep into the interior of his purposes. You don't find it lying around on the surface. It's not the latest message, but more like the oldest—what God determined as the way to bring out his best in us, long before we ever arrived on the scene. The experts of our day haven't a clue about what this eternal plan is. If they had, they wouldn't have killed the Master of the God-designed life on a cross. That's why we have this Scripture text:
No one's ever seen or heard anything like this,
Never so much as imagined anything quite like it—
What God has arranged for those who love him.

But you've seen and heard it because God by his Spirit has brought it all out into the open before you.

The Spirit, not content to flit around on the surface, dives into the depths of God, and brings out what God planned all along. Who ever knows what you're thinking and planning except you yourself? The same with God—except that he not only knows what he's thinking, but he lets us in on it. God offers a full report on the gifts of life and salvation that he is giving us. We don't have to rely on the world's guesses and opinions. We didn't learn this by reading books or going to school; we learned it from God, who taught us person-to-person through Jesus, and we're passing it on to you in the same firsthand, personal way.

Once again Paul writes of the "hidden" nature of God's ways. The experts don't see it. You don't get to be on top without embracing worldly values, which are blinders to cosmic wisdom. The world and everything in it is passing away. This is not a great religious revelation. Science recognizes that one day our planet will dissolve into an expanding sun as the simple physics of stars runs its course. But don't worry about that right now. In the much shorter run, the money we have in the bank will devalue. Our cars will wear out and rust away. Our bodies will grow old and die, despite all efforts to keep them looking good. Those invested in this world and practicing its wisdom are riding a train to destruction, for the world is always becoming history.

But the kingdom is now and it endures forever. Those who live by this faith embrace its values and live by another kind of wisdom. In the end, the wise and the foolish will change seats.

> **Name the things that are passing away in your life.
> What kingdom things are being offered for you to embrace?**

GOSPEL » MATTHEW 5:17-37

"Don't suppose for a minute that I have come to demolish the Scriptures—either God's Law or the Prophets. I'm not here to demolish but to complete. I am going to put it all together, pull it all together in a vast panorama. God's Law is more real and lasting than the stars in the sky and the ground at your feet. Long after stars burn out and earth wears out, God's Law will be alive and working.

"Trivialize even the smallest item in God's Law and you will only have trivialized yourself. But take it seriously, show the way for others, and you will find honor in the kingdom. Unless you do far better than the Pharisees in the matters of right living, you won't know the first thing about entering the kingdom.

"You're familiar with the command to the ancients, 'Do not murder.' I'm telling you that anyone who is so much as angry with a brother or sister is guilty of murder. Carelessly call a brother 'idiot!' and you just might find yourself hauled into court. Thoughtlessly yell 'stupid!' at a sister and you are on the brink of hellfire. The simple moral fact is that words kill.

"This is how I want you to conduct yourself in these matters. If you enter your place of worship and, about to make an offering, you suddenly remember a grudge a friend has against you, abandon your offering, leave immediately, go to this friend and make things right. Then and only then, come back and work things out with God.

"Or say you're out on the street and an old enemy accosts you. Don't lose a minute. Make the first move; make things right with him. After all, if you leave the first move to him, knowing his track record, you're likely to end up in court, maybe even jail. If that happens, you won't get out without a stiff fine.

"You know the next commandment pretty well, too: 'Don't go to bed with another's spouse.' But don't think you've preserved your virtue simply by staying out of bed. Your heart can be corrupted by lust even quicker than your body. Those leering looks you think nobody notices—they also corrupt.

"Let's not pretend this is easier than it really is. If you want to live a morally pure life, here's what you have to do: You have to blind your right eye the moment you catch it in a lustful leer. You have to choose to live one-eyed or else be dumped on a moral trash pile. And you have to chop off your right hand the moment you notice it raised threateningly. Better a bloody stump than your entire being discarded for good in the dump.

"Remember the Scripture that says, 'Whoever divorces his wife, let him do it legally, giving her divorce papers and her legal rights'? Too many of you are using that as a cover for selfishness and whim, pretending to be righteous just because you are 'legal.' Please, no more pretending. If you divorce your wife, you're responsible for making her an adulteress (unless she has already made herself that by sexual promiscuity). And if you marry such a divorced adulteress, you're automatically an adulterer yourself. You can't use legal cover to mask a moral failure.

"And don't say anything you don't mean. This counsel is embedded deep in our traditions. You only make things worse when you lay down a smoke screen of pious talk, saying, 'I'll pray for you,' and never doing it, or saying, 'God be with you,' and not meaning it. You don't make your words true by embellishing them with religious lace. In making your speech sound more religious, it becomes less true. Just say 'yes' and 'no.' When you manipulate words to get your own way, you go wrong.

For 2000 years we've been living in the final chapter of an amazing story. Before it ends, Jesus wants us to get positioned for what's next even as we live in the undeniable context of what's now.

For instance, we're tempted to feel pretty good if we don't kill or commit adultery. Not bad, eh Lord? The religious folk of Jesus' time said the same thing because they led morally correct lives according to the law. Don't kid yourself, Jesus advises. Claiming righteousness now puts us in a bad position for the dawning kingdom. The truth is we're ALL sinners in need of forgiveness. "Who needs a doctor: the healthy or the sick?" Jesus asks later in Matthew, "I'm after mercy, not religion" (9:12-13).

In light of this, it's better to settle our differences than to maintain conflicts. Reconciliation is key: that's why it's a sacrament! It's a visible sign of the inward reality of the kingdom. But to claim it, we have to practice it. Only by living in forgiveness do we experience it.

> **In what ways do you tend to see yourself as a pretty good person?**
> **How does "self-righteousness" teach you**
> **about the deeper reality of sin we all live with?**

WE RESPOND

Make conscious choices today. See the difference between what's passing and what's important. In the light of the forgiveness given to you, choose to be forgiving.

"I'm not here to demolish but to complete.
I am going to put it all together,
pull it all together in a vast panorama."

SEVENTH SUNDAY IN ORDINARY TIME

FIRST READING: LEVITICUS 19:1¬-2, 17-18

God spoke to Moses: "Speak to the congregation of Israel. Tell them, Be holy because I, God, your God, am holy.

"Don't secretly hate your neighbor. If you have something against him, get it out into the open; otherwise you are an accomplice in his guilt.

"Don't seek revenge or carry a grudge against any of your people.

"Love your neighbor as yourself. I am God."

Back in the banner-crazy 1960s, this quote from Leviticus would have made a stellar hanging to contemplate in church. A nice long thin one, every few words on a discreet line separated by its own punctuation mark. *Be holy.* It's a command that implies YOU be holy: pure and consecrated, anointed, set apart with the divine seal. *Because I*—this is why you must be holy, because you are connected to me. GOD: most powerful Being in the universe, pulling rank here. *Your God.* Yes, the most powerful Being is also in unique relationship with you and chooses to be so. *Am holy.* And here's the punch line. Our holiness is not just arbitrarily pleasing to God. It's required of us because we're made in the divine image. So be holy, be God-like, not because God is a stickler for things like that, but because when two love each other, they merge and become one in a way that makes them indistinguishable and inseparable. A lot of theology in a long thin banner of just nine words.

Which of the sections of this saying affects you the most and why?

SECOND READING » 1 CORINTHIANS 3:16–23

You realize, don't you, that you are the temple of God, and God himself is present in you? No one will get by with vandalizing God's temple, you can be sure of that. God's temple is sacred—and you, remember, are the temple.

Don't fool yourself. Don't think that you can be wise merely by being up-to-date with the times. Be God's fool—that's the path to true wisdom. What the world calls smart, God calls stupid. It's written in Scripture,
He exposes the chicanery of the chic.
The Master sees through the smoke screens
of the know-it-alls.
I don't want to hear any of you bragging about yourself or anyone else. Everything is already yours as a gift—Paul, Apollos, Peter, the world, life, death, the present, the future—all of it is yours, and you are privileged to be in union with Christ, who is in union with God.

Here's another amazing sentence of Scripture that collapses up into itself like a telescope trained on eternity. Everything is already yours, Saint Paul says. "Everything" is a pretty big word, and he stuffs into that word the biggest things he can find: the authority of the greatest leaders of the early church. The whole world. Life and death. Even time. *All* of this is in your hands, Paul says. And if that kind of responsibility scares you, then rest in the assurance that you're in the hands of Christ simultaneously. And he, as our faith teaches us, is in the hands of God.

These nesting realities mean all is well. They also say all is *united*: there's no east or west, no Church of Paul vs. Church of Peter, no bad-earth-here-but-good-heaven-someplace-else. The spirit of God chooses to dwell in us, in flesh and blood. The reign of God is a reality that Jesus insists is right outside the door, pressing for admittance at all times. As outrageous as it sounds, we are tabernacles of the sacred. Everything fits into God in the end.

When have you discovered sacred presence in another person?

GOSPEL » MATTHEW 5:38–48

"Here's another old saying that deserves a second look: 'Eye for eye, tooth for tooth.' Is that going to get us anywhere? Here's what I propose: 'Don't hit back at all.' If someone strikes you, stand there and take it. If someone drags you into court and sues for the shirt off your back, giftwrap your best coat and make a present of it. And if someone takes unfair advantage of you, use the occasion to practice the servant life. No more tit-for-tat stuff. Live generously.

"You're familiar with the old written law, 'Love your friend,' and its unwritten companion, 'Hate your enemy.' I'm challenging that. I'm telling you to love your enemies. Let them bring out the best in you, not the worst. When someone gives you a hard time, respond with the energies of prayer, for then you are working out of your true selves, your God-created selves. This is what God does. He gives his best—the sun to warm and the rain to nourish—to everyone, regardless: the good and bad, the nice and nasty. If all you do is love the lovable, do you expect a bonus? Anybody can do that. If you simply say hello to those who greet you, do you expect a medal? Any run-of-the-mill sinner does that.

"In a word, what I'm saying is, Grow up. You're kingdom subjects. Now live like it. Live out your God-created identity. Live generously and graciously toward others, the way God lives toward you."

Full disclosure: I have never done this, offered myself to an enemy for a second go-round. The very idea of turning the other cheek is totally appalling. When Jesus says offer no resistance to one who is evil, I say: Lord, you've got to be kidding. Of course I'm going to resist evil. I'm going to run from the near occasion of the bad guys the moment I see them on the horizon. Jesus wants me to surrender my coat along with my shirt, and work twice as long for someone who's already taking advantage of me. The capstone of the whole teaching is the most ludicrous: love your enemy. Is Jesus pulling our leg?

It's obvious from reading the gospels that Jesus has a sense of humor. But he doesn't simply clown around. Jesus says all of these preposterous things to bring us along to the bottom line on this way of thinking: Be perfect, as God is perfect. Because God does turn the other cheek, doesn't resist us even when we're evil, gives and gives, and loves us who are enemies to the divine will. Maybe we won't do these things. But thank heaven God will.

How willing are you to creep up to the territory of God's perfection?

WE RESPOND

Clean up a mess you didn't make. Turn out a light somebody else left on. Ask a blessing on someone you don't like. Put up with someone who won't stop talking. Practice holiness.

"When someone gives you a hard time,
respond with the energies of prayer,
for then you are working out of your true selves,
your God-created selves."

EIGHTH SUNDAY IN ORDINARY TIME

FIRST READING » ISAIAH 49:14–15

But Zion said, "I don't get it. God has left me.
My Master has forgotten I even exist."
"Can a mother forget the infant at her breast,
walk away from the baby she bore?
But even if mothers forget,
I'd never forget you—never.
Look, I've written your names on the backs of my hands.
The walls you're rebuilding are never out of my sight.
Your builders are faster than your wreckers.
The demolition crews are gone for good.
Look up, look around, look well!
See them all gathering, coming to you?
As sure as I am the living God"—God's Decree—
"you're going to put them on like so much jewelry,
you're going to use them to dress up like a bride."

Say the word "mother," and many people get a warm feeling inside. But you'll also meet people for whom the word conjures up bitter memories of disapproval, neglect, or worse. Not all mamas are created equal. The prophet Isaiah seems to appreciate this. While he presumes the average mother feels a tug of tender feelings for her children that transcends every circumstance, he adds that even if a woman does ignore that bond, God won't forget the ties that bind us to our Maker. God is the best and most faithful Mama around.

Most Christians think of God as "Our Father" or Abba-Dad. God as prize-winning Mama is less familiar but just as biblically established. In Deuteronomy chapter 32, God is the eagle who pushes her young from the nest for their first flight away from home. In Luke 13, Jesus mourns Jerusalem as a hen who longs to gather her chicks protectively under her wings. The writer of Psalm 131 understands God as a maternal lap into which we can crawl and be totally at peace. "Our Mother" is also in heaven!

> **What are the qualities you associate with Mom**
> **and how do they differ from those of Dad?**

SECOND READING » 1 CORINTHIANS 4:1–5

Don't imagine us leaders to be something we aren't. We are servants of Christ, not his masters. We are guides into God's most sublime secrets, not security guards posted to protect them. The requirements for a good guide are reliability and accurate knowledge. It matters very little to me what you think of me, even less where I rank in popular opinion. I don't even rank myself. Comparisons in these matters are pointless. I'm not aware of anything that would disqualify me from being a good guide for you, but that doesn't mean much. The Master makes that judgment.

So don't get ahead of the Master and jump to conclusions with your judgments before all the evidence is in. When he comes, he will bring out in the open and place in evidence all kinds of things we never even dreamed of—inner motives and purposes and prayers. Only then will any one of us get to hear the "Well done!" of God.

We are guides to secrets, keepers of divine mystery. "Mystery" is another word with great evocative appeal. As a professional thinker, I like mysteries because in the presence of one, my work is done. I don't have to parse them out or comprehend them. I approach mystery like art: with simple, humble appreciation for what it is. I can stand before it in awe, or kneel down in wonder. Mystery makes us bigger than we are, opening up worlds not normally available to us.

When dealing with ordinary facts and figures, we seek to master them. In the face of most events, the goal is to control, contain, or harness them. In the presence of a mystery, we admit there's nothing we can do to absorb this thing. We are ourselves absorbed and, if we dismiss pride and arrogance, we're happy to be so. As people of faith, we are keepers of divine mysteries: tabernacles holding the most precious indwelling of all. How wonderful to be here!

How do I respond when knowingly in the presence of a sacred mystery?

GOSPEL » MATTHEW 6:24–34

"You can't worship two gods at once. Loving one god, you'll end up hating the other. Adoration of one feeds contempt for the other. You can't worship God and Money both.

"If you decide for God, living a life of God-worship, it follows that you don't fuss about what's on the table at mealtimes or whether the clothes in your closet are in fashion. There is far more to your life than the food you put in your stomach, more to your outer appearance than the clothes you hang on your body. Look at the birds, free and unfettered, not tied down to a job description, careless in the care of God. And you count far more to him than birds.

"Has anyone by fussing in front of the mirror ever gotten taller by so much as an inch? All this time and money wasted on fashion—do you think it makes that much difference? Instead of looking at the fashions, walk out into the fields and look at the wildflowers. They never primp or shop, but have you ever seen color and design quite like it? The ten best-dressed men and women in the country look shabby alongside them.

"If God gives such attention to the appearance of wildflowers—most of which are never even seen—don't you think he'll attend to you, take pride in you, do *his best for you? What I'm trying to do here is to get you to relax, to not be so preoccupied with getting, so you can respond to God's giving. People who don't know God and the way he works fuss over these things, but you know both God and how he works. Steep your life in God-reality, God-initiative, God-provisions. Don't worry about missing out. You'll find all your everyday human concerns will be met.*

"Give your entire attention to what God is doing right now, and don't get worked up about what may or may not happen tomorrow. God will help you deal with whatever hard things come up when the time comes.

As a blue ribbon, world-class worrier, I try my best to serve God and mammon. I've always been true to the Arab proverb: *Trust in God, but tie your camel.* I believe God will take care of me and always has. I also suspect that I've got to be a good steward of my resources. So I say my prayers AND fret about price tags. I believe God is in the details—and so are the demons, if I'm not watchful.

Is this wrong? Does trusting in God really mean living mindless of tomorrow? If I fall off a financial cliff, will angels catch me? The gospel temptation stories imply that such devil-may-care abandon is not of divine origin. At the same time, Jesus says focusing all our energy on chasing after our daily bread leads us to forget that it is given to us, not just earned. At the bottom line of existence, we do have to choose between God and mammon. It may come down to this: untying the camel and letting it go.

> **How many "camels" do you have on a leash that prevent you from trusting in God?**

WE RESPOND

When a worry comes up today, say to yourself, "God will take care of it." Then, let it go. Remember God cares for you more than a mother for her child.

"Don't get worked up about what may or may not happen tomorrow."

TWELFTH SUNDAY IN ORDINARY TIME

FIRST READING » JEREMIAH 20:10-13

You pushed me into this, God, and I let you do it.
*   You were too much for me.*
And now I'm a public joke.
*   They all poke fun at me.*
Every time I open my mouth
*   I'm shouting, "Murder!" or "Rape!"*
And all I get for my God-warnings
*   are insults and contempt.*
But if I say, "Forget it!
*   No more God-Messages from me!"*
The words are fire in my belly,
*   a burning in my bones.*
I'm worn out trying to hold it in.
*   I can't do it any longer!*
Then I hear whispering behind my back:
*   "There goes old 'Danger-Everywhere.' Shut him up! Report him!"*
Old friends watch, hoping I'll fall flat on my face:
*   "One misstep and we'll have him. We'll get rid of him for good!"*
But God, a most fierce warrior, is at my side.
*   Those who are after me will be sent sprawling—*
Slapstick buffoons falling all over themselves,
*   a spectacle of humiliation no one will ever forget.*
Oh, God-of-the-Angel-Armies, no one fools you.
*   You see through everyone, everything.*
I want to see you pay them back for what they've done.
*   I rest my case with you.*
Sing to God! All praise to God!
*   He saves the weak from the grip of the wicked.*

Jeremiah's writings have an immediacy and passion that catches us by surprise.
We don't expect a biblical prophet to sound so human, to be so confessional. Jeremiah is wounded by the betrayal of friends. He sounds a little paranoid, but as the saying goes, "just because you're paranoid doesn't mean they're NOT out to get you." In Jeremiah's case, he had good reason to be suspicious. And when he prays for vengeance, our fellowship with him is confirmed. Why, this prophet sounds no better than we are!

What distinguishes Jeremiah from us on our bad days is that he's not caught in his bitterness, paranoia, and impulse to violence. Jeremiah laments longer and better than anyone in the Bible, but he takes it all to prayer, not to the pub. He presents his naked heart to God, with all of its warts and frustrations, its less than pious urges. Jeremiah's prayer is startling because it isn't phony: he doesn't flatter God but tells it like it is. He asks for his heart's desire without sanitizing it. His enemies might whisper their evil desires in the shadows, but Jeremiah reveals his heart to the light of God's truth.

How honest are you in prayer?
Do you withhold the unattractive part of your heart from God?

SECOND READING » ROMANS 5:12-15

You know the story of how Adam landed us in the dilemma we're in—first sin, then death, and no one exempt from either sin or death. That sin disturbed relations with God in everything and everyone, but the extent of the disturbance was not clear until God spelled it out in detail to Moses. So death, this huge abyss separating us from God, dominated the landscape from Adam to Moses. Even those who didn't sin precisely as Adam did by disobeying a specific command of God still had to experience this termination of life, this separation from God. But Adam, who got us into this, also points ahead to the One who will get us out of it.

Yet the rescuing gift is not exactly parallel to the death-dealing sin. If one man's sin put crowds of people at the dead-end abyss of separation from God, just think what God's gift poured through one man, Jesus Christ, will do! There's no comparison between that death-dealing sin and this generous, life-giving gift. The verdict on that one sin was the death sentence; the verdict on the many sins that followed was this wonderful life sentence. If death got the upper hand through one man's wrongdoing, can you imagine the breathtaking recovery life makes, sovereign life, in those who grasp with both hands this wildly extravagant life-gift, this grand setting-everything-right, that the one man Jesus Christ provides?

Sin comes in through a small door. A moment of vanity, a selfish choice, a decision to withhold compassion—it takes hardly any energy to welcome sin into the world. We can sin five times before breakfast without breaking a sweat. Sin is so easy. The failure to love is second nature to our mortality.

But our first nature is to love, because we were made for love by Love itself. Our original nature has been clouded by original sin, as the church understands it, and so humanity goes about in a fog of defective inclinations, sinning without noticing, without thinking, without remorse. Another door had to open to challenge those inclinations. It too was a humble door, made of wood, admitting a person loving enough to say no to sin once and for all. That door is open right now. Jesus holds that door open and invites us to come through it. Sin gives us endless excuses to say no, but love makes us yearn to say yes.

Consider the sort of temptation that calls most invitingly to you.
How does it reflect a failure to love?

THIS TRANSFORMING WORD

GOSPEL: MATTHEW 10:26-33

"Don't be intimidated. Eventually everything is going to be out in the open, and everyone will know how things really are. So don't hesitate to go public now.

"Don't be bluffed into silence by the threats of bullies. There's nothing they can do to your soul, your core being. Save your fear for God, who holds your entire life—body and soul—in his hands.

"What's the price of a pet canary? Some loose change, right? And God cares what happens to it even more than you do. He pays even greater attention to you, down to the last detail—even numbering the hairs on your head! So don't be intimidated by all this bully talk. You're worth more than a million canaries.

"Stand up for me against world opinion and I'll stand up for you before my Father in heaven. If you turn tail and run, do you think I'll cover for you?

Jesus says to fear no one; but I run out of fingers counting the people and situations that cause fear and anxiety in my life. I want to believe with the certainty of Paul, but more often I find myself keeping company with Jeremiah, worried to a frazzle. Is it that I doubt God is going to get me out of the latest scrape I'm in? (Yes.) Is it that God has given me reason to doubt that I will be rescued? (No.) So what's the problem?

The problem is me, not God. God keeps track of the hairs on my head and the fate of every sparrow, but I'm keeping the log of everything that can and does go wrong with frail mortality. People go broke. People get sick. People die. These things are often more compelling to me than God's dominion over creation. Jesus reminds us that the body is not as important as the soul, but I have grown very fond of the body and have spent a lifetime preserving it. Still, I crawl up on the rooftop of hope every once in a while and warble faintly about what I've heard and believe, despite all uncertainty, to be true. When I speak this truth, its certainty grows in me. When I act on this truth, I'm brought into the light.

> **Describe the last occasion you had to speak or act in faith.**
> **How did this witness make your faith stronger?**

WE RESPOND

Pray this week like Jeremiah, bringing the lovely and unlovely parts of your heart to God.

THIRTEENTH SUNDAY IN ORDINARY TIME

FIRST READING » 2 KINGS 4:8-11, 14-16A

One day Elisha passed through Shunem. A leading lady of the town talked him into stopping for a meal. And then it became his custom: Whenever he passed through, he stopped by for a meal.

"I'm certain," said the woman to her husband, "that this man who stops by with us all the time is a holy man of God. Why don't we add on a small room upstairs and furnish it with a bed and desk, chair and lamp, so that when he comes by he can stay with us?"

And so it happened that the next time Elisha came by he went to the room and lay down for a nap.

Elisha conferred with Gehazi: "There's got to be something we can do for her. But what?"

Gehazi said, "Well, she has no son, and her husband is an old man."

"Call her in," said Elisha. He called her and she stood at the open door.

Elisha said to her, "This time next year you're going to be nursing an infant son."

Certain passages in the books of Samuel and Kings, some scholars suggest, were written by a woman. The details are such that only a woman might think to include them. The story of the influential Shunammite woman is like that. Sure, it's patterned after other biblical miracle birth stories: the couple who can't conceive suddenly can, by the grace of God. But listen to the way the story unfolds. The woman, not her husband, is described as a person of influence. She issues the dinner invitation to the prophet, and she comes up with plan to set up a permanent guest room. She doesn't ask her husband for permission, but simply informs him of her decision. He, meanwhile, says nothing. The prophet, when he declares the divine reward, addresses only the woman. What a strange event, in that time and culture!

The most curious details are in the furnishing of the prophet's room: a bed, a table, a chair, a lamp. These details are not strictly necessary to the progress of the story. Including them betrays a hostess' checklist, an attention to the comfort of her guest. The cozy little rooftop room demonstrates how one woman prepared a place for God's word to dwell in her house. It was so important to her, she thought it out to the last detail.

> **How do you prepare a place in your life**
> **for the word of God to dwell with you?**

SECOND READING » ROMANS 6:3-4, 8-11

So what do we do? Keep on sinning so God can keep on forgiving? I should hope not! If we've left the country where sin is sovereign, how can we still live in our old house there? Or didn't you realize we packed up and left there for good? That is what happened in baptism. When we went under the water, we left the old country of sin behind; when we came up out of the water, we entered into the new country of grace—a new life in a new land!

That's what baptism into the life of Jesus means. When we are lowered into the water, it is like the burial of Jesus; when we are raised up out of the water, it is like the resurrection of Jesus. Each of us is raised into a light-filled world by our Father so that we can see where we're going in our new grace-sovereign country.

Could it be any clearer? Our old way of life was nailed to the cross with Christ, a decisive end to that sin-miserable life—no longer at sin's every beck and call! What we believe is this: If we get included in Christ's sin-conquering death, we also get included in his life-saving resurrection. We know that when Jesus was raised from the dead it was a signal of the end of death-as-the-end. Never again will death have the last word. When Jesus died, he took sin down with him, but alive he brings God down to us. From now on, think of it this way: Sin speaks a dead language that means nothing to you; God speaks your mother tongue, and you hang on every word. You are dead to sin and alive to God. That's what Jesus did.

One of the great things about being Catholic is that we do death very well. Our rituals around death, from the sacraments attending the dying to the final burial, are wonderfully affirming of all that we believe: the purposefulness of life, the divine companionship within suffering, and the confirmation that death is not the victor over our journey. Often I emerge from a funeral saying to myself: *Thank God for the church.* Through each ritual, death seems less like the enemy, more like a doorstep into a sacred place.

It is difficult to welcome death. When participating in the suffering of those we love, even while recognizing that a return to the life they knew is no longer an option, we cannot wish for death. It's contrary to a living being to seek it. Yet life contains many deaths, some unavoidable, some deliberately chosen. Baptism is the sign of our deliberate surrender of a life gnawed by sin to a new life glorified by grace. This chosen death is a precursor to the one we face in the dying of others and will some-day experience more personally. Death can be a friend, uniting us with a greater, fuller life than this one.

How prepared are you for death?
What does death teach you about the meaning of your life?

GOSPEL » MATTHEW 10:37-42

"Don't think I've come to make life cozy. I've come to cut—make a sharp knife-cut between son and father, daughter and mother, bride and mother-in-law—cut through these cozy domestic arrangements and free you for God. Well-meaning family members can be your worst enemies. If you prefer father or mother over me, you don't deserve me. If you prefer son or daughter over me, you don't deserve me.

"If you don't go all the way with me, through thick and thin, you don't deserve me. If your first concern is to look after yourself, you'll never find yourself. But if you forget about yourself and look to me, you'll find both yourself and me.

"We are intimately linked in this harvest work. Anyone who accepts what you do, accepts me, the One who sent you. Anyone who accepts what I do accepts my Father, who sent me. Accepting a messenger of God is as good as being God's messenger. Accepting someone's help is as good as giving someone help. This is a large work I've called you into, but don't be overwhelmed by it. It's best to start small. Give a cool cup of water to someone who is thirsty, for instance. The smallest act of giving or receiving makes you a true apprentice. You won't lose out on a thing."

Something needs to be said about the flip side of receiving a prophet into your home. Yes, you may receive a prophet's reward. But you also have to listen to the prophet and the prophecy. This may be why prophets aren't swamped with invitations when they come to town.

When Jesus came to town, sinners and religious folks alike vied for his presence in their homes—at first. But Jesus had a way of criticizing his hosts, even berating the manner in which he was received by them, that made a second invitation unlikely. Only those willing to take his words to heart and repent were glad that Jesus came under their roof.

Prophecy is by its nature a challenge to the way things are. If we don't want to change, then prophets will always seem like threatening characters. They don't come to affirm us, but to invite us to come closer to the will of God. Receive a prophet if you dare, but be prepared to do more than rearrange the furniture of your world.

> **Have you ever received a prophetic person into your life?**
> **How did he/she challenge you?**

WE RESPOND

Find the corner of your life where the irritability factor is high. Chances are this is the very place where prophecy is trying to speak. Listen to the challenge being offered to you, and reply.

FOURTEENTH SUNDAY IN ORDINARY TIME

FIRST READING » ZECHARIAH 9:9-10

"Shout and cheer, Daughter Zion!
  Raise the roof, Daughter Jerusalem!
Your king is coming!
  a good king who makes all things right,
  a humble king riding a donkey,
  a mere colt of a donkey.
I've had it with war—no more chariots in Ephraim,
  no more war horses in Jerusalem,
  no more swords and spears, bows and arrows.
He will offer peace to the nations,
  a peaceful rule worldwide,
  from the four winds to the seven seas.

It's been a long time since most of us have ridden a donkey. I rode a mule once at the Grand Canyon, and remember the strong-smelling humility of that occasion. What's obvious about any trip you've taken recently—on an animal, bike, car, or city bus—is that you can't take much with you. Traveling means leaving a lot of stuff behind. Often we fill a suitcase for a weekend visit and then have to struggle to close the zipper. What are we carrying that makes these bags so full?

I examined a packed bag recently to discover the following: clothes chosen to represent me accurately in different settings, items for hygiene, articles against boredom, sundries to remedy a variety of fears. Pills for headaches I might have; credit cards for emergencies that might arise; addresses in case I'm seized with a need to reach out to high school classmates. So much stuff!

Yet the king of kings arrives on an ass. No entourage in tow, no stowaway items in overhead bins. The awaited one comes with nothing to represent him but himself. One aspect of his meekness is that he doesn't bring a big show, or even a large steed. And with nothing more than his own authority, his dominion is established from sea to sea.

> **Take a mental inventory of your stuff: house, car, closets, storage.**
> **How much of it is necessary?**
> **How much of your life is invested in sustaining it?**

SECOND READING » ROMANS 8:9, 11-13

But if God himself has taken up residence in your life, you can hardly be thinking more of yourself than of him. Anyone, of course, who has not welcomed this invisible but clearly present God, the Spirit of Christ, won't know what we're talking about. But for you who welcome him, in whom he dwells—even though you still experience all the limitations of sin—you yourself experience life on God's terms. It stands to reason, doesn't it, that if the alive-and-present God who raised Jesus from the dead moves into your life, he'll do the same thing in you that he did in Jesus, bringing you alive to himself? When God lives and breathes in you (and he does, as surely as he did in Jesus), you are delivered from that dead life. With his Spirit living in you, your body will be as alive as Christ's!

But if God himself has taken up residence in your life, you can hardly be thinking more of yourself than of him. Anyone, of course, who has not welcomed this invisible but clearly present God, the Spirit of Christ, won't know what we're talking about. But for you who welcome him, in whom he dwells—even though you still experience all the limitations of sin—you yourself experience life on God's terms. It stands to reason, doesn't it, that if the alive-and-present God who raised Jesus from the dead moves into your life, he'll do the same thing in you that he did in Jesus, bringing you alive to himself? When God lives and breathes in you (and he does, as surely as he did in Jesus), you are delivered from that dead life. With his Spirit living in you, your body will be as alive as Christ's!

So don't you see that we don't owe this old do-it-yourself life one red cent. There's nothing in it for us, nothing at all. The best thing to do is give it a decent burial and get on with your new life. God's Spirit beckons. There are things to do and places to go!

No one has to convince us that flesh is doomed. The older we get, the more often friend's names make the obituaries. How many classmates have had heart attacks, cancers, become disabled—not to mention our own creeping infirmities? In high school we thought we'd live forever, our bodies would always be strong, and pain would be banished with an aspirin. There comes a saturation point in our lives when we know, frankly and personally, that none of this is true.

"Flesh is grass," the psalmist says. It blooms one day, withers the next. This isn't a formula for despair, but a clear-eyed look at mortality. The response of a believer is to cultivate the life that doesn't fade, the life of the spirit that can grow stronger even as bodies grow weaker, that outlives failing organs and eyesight, and outlasts beauty and success. Our world is set up to support a life which is passing—cultural values are absurdly geared to prop up what's surely to be lost. Only the life of the spirit remains; it is a mistake to neglect it.

> **How much of your time is spent in maintaining your physical life?**
> **How much is spent in spiritual growth?**

GOSPEL » MATTHEW 11:25-30

Abruptly Jesus broke into prayer: "Thank you, Father, Lord of heaven and earth. You've concealed your ways from sophisticates and know-it-alls, but spelled them out clearly to ordinary people. Yes, Father, that's the way you like to work."

Jesus resumed talking to the people, but now tenderly. "The Father has given me all these things to do and say. This is a unique Father-Son operation, coming out of Father and Son intimacies and knowledge. No one knows the Son the way the Father does, nor the Father the way the Son does. But I'm not keeping it to myself; I'm ready to go over it line by line with anyone willing to listen.

"Are you tired? Worn out? Burned out on religion? Come to me. Get away with me and you'll recover your life. I'll show you how to take a real rest. Walk with me and work with me—watch how I do it. Learn the unforced rhythms of grace. I won't lay anything heavy or ill-fitting on you. Keep company with me and you'll learn to live freely and lightly."

Consider the last time you struggled with a too-heavy suitcase, or had to pack and move your possessions to another address. Compare that with the yoke of Christ: the burden of love we carry in our hearts. Which experience is better, more life-giving, more real?

The yoke of Christ is the mandate to love, even when it means sacrifice, even if it involves suffering. It's not the silly, romantic love that shows up in all the movies, but the day-to-day love of parents for children, the plodding fidelity of spouses, the single-hearted devotion of artists for their craft, the constancy of friends who support us even when the news is bad. It's a mirror of the love God has for us, and when we're faithful in love, we open a window to that greater love for those around us to experience.

Love is a burden; but it's a lovely one to bear. Anyone who has loved, in sickness and in health, for richer for poorer, knows that some burdens are a privilege to carry. If our love is tied up in the things of this world, we'll be dragging that overstuffed suitcase around and wondering why we ache so. If our hearts are free to love others, Christ will carry that love to places we haven't dreamed of.

> How do you spend your love, on people or things?
> Are the burdens you carry difficult , or easy?

WE RESPOND

Make a decision to simplify. Be drastic! Give away one-third of what owns you: books, clothes, CDs, money, or some other item that's collected around you. Contemplate what the new space in your life means, and what it's for.

FIFTEENTH SUNDAY IN ORDINARY TIME

FIRST READING » ISAIAH 55:10-11

"I don't think the way you think.
*   The way you work isn't the way I work."*
*   God's Decree.*
"For as the sky soars high above earth,
*   so the way I work surpasses the way you work,*
*   and the way I think is beyond the way you think.*
Just as rain and snow descend from the skies
*   and don't go back until they've watered the earth,*
Doing their work of making things grow and blossom,
*   producing seed for farmers and food for the hungry,*
So will the words that come out of my mouth
*   not come back empty-handed.*
They'll do the work I sent them to do,
*   they'll complete the assignment I gave them.*

God's word accomplishes what it sets out to do. Compare this effectiveness to all the idle talk we hear. People daydream about things they never intend to do. People make promises they won't keep. People boast and wish and plan a lot, and it all comes to nothing.

But God's word created the world and everything in it. God's word, in the person of Jesus, bought the world back from death and gives the fulfillment of life. God's word, planted in hearts like a seed, produces a harvest that neither time nor hardship can destroy. It's a fruitful word. God's effective will is behind it.

Our words, cheap and plentiful, often lack the will behind them to follow through. And so marriages fail, children are conceived and unwanted, projects are begun and abandoned, help is promised and undelivered. "God's will" is a phrase often used as a catch-all for things that go wrong in our lives. It's shorthand for "Blame God." The essence of Holy Will is the dynamism between what God says and does. God's will HAPPENS. We can count on it.

> **How good is your word?**
> **Do you finish what you start?**
> **Is your will as good as your word?**

SECOND READING » ROMANS 8:18-23

That's why I don't think there's any comparison between the present hard times and the coming good times. The created world itself can hardly wait for what's coming next. Everything in creation is being more or less held back. God reins it in until both creation and all the creatures are ready and can be released at the same moment into the glorious times ahead. Meanwhile, the joyful anticipation deepens.

All around us we observe a pregnant creation. The difficult times of pain throughout the world are simply birth pangs. But it's not only around us; it's within us. The Spirit of God is arousing us within. We're also feeling the birth pangs. These sterile and barren bodies of ours are yearning for full deliverance. That is why waiting does not diminish us, any more than waiting diminishes a pregnant mother. We are enlarged in the waiting. We, of course, don't see what is enlarging us. But the longer we wait, the larger we become, and the more joyful our expectancy.

Science reveals the interrelatedness of living things. "The Great Chain of Being" or "Circle of Life" describes how every living thing, whether sentient or simple, plays a role in the maintenance of creation. Environmentalists are understandably fearful when human decisions threaten whole species as if they're expendable. If every living thing has its place, erasing a species affects the whole order in some way.

Recognizing the interrelatedness of creation in a theological sense, Paul talks about how all of creation labors under the effects of sin and hopes to share in the liberation that's on its way. Does creation suffer from sin? We only have to consider how greed and thoughtlessness pollute our planet to answer that. Can living things hope to be redeemed from sin? We can point out how heroic efforts at conservation and restoration heal rivers and forests that were nearly lost.

Paul advances an argument to consider in our relationship to the whole earth. If sin leads to the corruption of ALL life, not just human life, then the eternity that awaits redeemed humanity might also include a redemption of all of God's creatures. When a child asks if there is an animal heaven, it isn't so easy from Paul's view to say no.

How is your stewardship of creation?
Do you care for, neglect, or harm creation by your lifestyle?

GOSPEL » MATTHEW 13:1-23

At about that same time Jesus left the house and sat on the beach. In no time at all a crowd gathered along the shoreline, forcing him to get into a boat. Using the boat as a pulpit, he addressed his congregation, telling stories.

"What do you make of this? A farmer planted seed. As he scattered the seed, some of it fell on the road, and birds ate it. Some fell in the gravel; it sprouted quickly but didn't put down roots, so when the sun came up it withered just as quickly. Some fell in the weeds; as it came up, it was strangled by the weeds. Some fell on good earth, and produced a harvest beyond his wildest dreams.

"Are you listening to this? Really listening?"

The disciples came up and asked, "Why do you tell stories?"

He replied, "You've been given insight into God's kingdom. You know how it works. Not everybody has this gift, this insight; it hasn't been given to them. Whenever someone has a ready heart for this, the insights and understandings flow freely. But if there is no readiness, any trace of receptivity soon disappears. That's why I tell stories: to create readiness, to nudge the people toward receptive insight. In their present state they can stare till doomsday and not see it, listen till they're blue in the face and not get it. I don't want Isaiah's forecast repeated all over again:

> Your ears are open but you don't hear a thing.
> Your eyes are awake but you don't see a thing.
> The people are blockheads!
> They stick their fingers in their ears
> > so they won't have to listen;
> They screw their eyes shut
> > so they won't have to look,
> > so they won't have to deal with me face-to-face
> > and let me heal them.

"But you have God-blessed eyes—eyes that see! And God-blessed ears—ears that hear! A lot of people, prophets and humble believers among them, would have given anything to see what you are seeing, to hear what you are hearing, but never had the chance.

"Study this story of the farmer planting seed. When anyone hears news of the kingdom and doesn't take it in, it just remains on the surface, and so the Evil One comes along and plucks it right out of that person's heart. This is the seed the farmer scatters on the road.

"The seed cast in the gravel—this is the person who hears and instantly responds with enthusiasm. But there is no soil of character, and so when the emotions wear off and some difficulty arrives, there is nothing to show for it.

"The seed cast in the weeds is the person who hears the kingdom news, but weeds of worry and illusions about getting more and wanting everything under the sun strangle what was heard, and nothing comes of it.

"The seed cast on good earth is the person who hears and takes in the News, and then produces a harvest beyond his wildest dreams."

My Dad's hearing is starting to fail. My vision has gotten to the point where I need two kinds of glass in my glasses. Our senses have a built-in obsolescence that we ignore till they balk and we find out there's no warranty.

Seeing and hearing are gifts not to be taken for granted, but understanding with the heart is greater still. Jesus never blames a blind man for his blindness, nor a deaf person for not responding. But he does have a lot to say about people who walk wide-eyed into episodes of sin. Jesus is blunt with religious people who refuse to change their hearts. They (we!) enjoy the advantage of having God's word sown like seed in our soil, and yet nothing is cultivated and nothing grows. No plot of ground is responsible for its barrenness if the seed never arrives there. But woe to the ground that's planted and yields dust! Far better to stop going to church and stop calling ourselves Christian, than to adopt the name and go on, deaf and blind to Jesus.

How do you prepare the soil of your life
for the word of God to take root in you?

WE RESPOND

Make a commitment to God's word. Get a readable Bible—it may not be the big leather one in the living room. Spend ten minutes a day, on one passage or even one verse. Make a commitment reasonable enough to see it through.

"That's why I tell stories:
to create readiness,
to nudge the people
toward receptive insight."

SIXTEENTH SUNDAY IN ORDINARY TIME
.... Might and Mercy

FIRST READING: WISDOM 12:13, 16-19

Lord, there's no other God but you, and no one takes care of everybody the way you do. Your record is unimpeachable, so who would impeach you?

Your strength is the beginning of your justice; as we know, you're the God of all, but you act sparingly with each and every one.

You show your resolve by not overreacting when your jurisdiction is challenged; you don't blow your top every time your existence is denied. On the contrary, your judge with clemency; you govern with indulgence, even though you can dump us anytime you want! Your conduct on the judicial bench has taught your people that justice must always be kind; your conduct as a parent has given your children hope in forgiveness.

They don't call this book Wisdom for nothing. In a few short verses, we get an understanding of what's wrong with the popular definitions of words like *justice, mercy, power.* Justice isn't simply paying the price for wrongdoing. Divine justice includes the notion of clemency, even kindness. Divine justice is more preventative than punitive. If we had more gentle justice up front, we wouldn't need the punitive kind.

In the same way, power is redefined in its relationship to mercy. What power do we see, in politics or marriages or on the playground, that yields to this idea? God's strength is the source of God's justice, the writer tells us. God's ability to do ANYTHING makes it possible for God to choose gentleness. Only the strong can opt to be gentle; the weak are simply weak. True power yields to kindness just as true justice yields to mercy. How different our families and communities and governments would be if wisdom were our guide.

> **How are you just? Where do you show mercy?**
> **Over whom do you wield power?**

SECOND READING » ROMANS 8:26-27

Meanwhile, the moment we get tired in the waiting, God's Spirit is right alongside helping us along. If we don't know how or what to pray, it doesn't matter. He does our praying in and for us, making prayer out of our wordless sighs, our aching groans. He knows us far better than we know ourselves, knows our pregnant condition, and keeps us present before God. That's why we can be so sure that every detail in our lives of love for God is worked into something good.

Power means many things: physical strength, moral authority, economic superiority, or personal charisma. We may have power over others, or over the elements of a particular situation. Power is morally ambiguous. It can be used for good, or wreak terrible harm.

The power of the Holy Spirit seems very mysterious to us. Does it make miraculous things happen? Sometimes. Does it heal the sick? It can. What else does it do? Mostly it transforms us into channels of God's grace. If we invite God's Spirit to reside in us, things happen to us and around us beyond our power to create or control. We may become compassionate where we're normally irritated, or tireless rather than burned out. We find our hearts lightened, bitterness lifted, patience extended, love renewed and deepened. We find healing where the wounds used to be. We find hope where others see darkness, courage when others are afraid. The power of God's Spirit transforms its vessel first, then moves outward into the world. God's power is subject to nothing, yet chooses to act in harmony with our freedom. If we say no to this power, we say no for ourselves and for the world.

How do you cooperate with the power of the Holy Spirit?
How do you deny it?

GOSPEL » MATTHEW 13:24-43

He told another story. "God's kingdom is like a farmer who planted good seed in his field. That night, while his hired men were asleep, his enemy sowed thistles all through the wheat and slipped away before dawn. When the first green shoots appeared and the grain began to form, the thistles showed up, too.

"The farmhands came to the farmer and said, 'Master, that was clean seed you planted, wasn't it? Where did these thistles come from?'

"He answered, 'Some enemy did this.'

"The farmhands asked, 'Should we weed out the thistles?'

"He said, 'No, if you weed the thistles, you'll pull up the wheat, too. Let them grow together until harvest time. Then I'll instruct the harvesters to pull up the thistles and tie them in bundles for the fire, then gather the wheat and put it in the barn.'"

Another story. "God's kingdom is like a pine nut that a farmer plants. It is quite small as seeds go, but in the course of years it grows into a huge pine tree, and eagles build nests in it."

Another story. "God's kingdom is like yeast that a woman works into the dough for dozens of loaves of barley bread—and waits while the dough rises."

All Jesus did that day was tell stories—a long storytelling afternoon. His storytelling fulfilled the prophecy:

I will open my mouth and tell stories;
I will bring out into the open
    things hidden since the world's first day.

Jesus dismissed the congregation and went into the house. His disciples came in and said, "Explain to us that story of the thistles in the field."

So he explained. "The farmer who sows the pure seed is the Son of Man. The field is the world, the pure seeds are subjects of the kingdom, the thistles are subjects of the Devil, and the enemy who sows them is the Devil. The harvest is the end of the age, the curtain of history. The harvest hands are angels.

"The picture of thistles pulled up and burned is a scene from the final act. The Son of Man will send his angels, weed out the thistles from his kingdom, pitch them in the trash, and be done with them. They are going to complain to high heaven, but nobody is going to listen. At the same time, ripe, holy lives will mature and adorn the kingdom of their Father.

"Are you listening to this? Really listening?"

Just as power is used for good or harm, not all seeds are created equal. Jesus tells a story of good seed and bad, and how they grow up together in the harvest of the world. We experience this reality in the contents of our own hearts. We have wonderful, generous impulses; and also cruel, petty thoughts. We may be heroic in our love one day, and selfish the next. We forgive and withhold forgiveness. Our fields are waist-high in grain and thistles.

No wonder that good and bad grow up together in families; parishes are a mixture of charity and snobbery; politics is full of high-minded ideals and crude scandal. If we're surprised when nice people do things that are not nice, we have to look no further than this parable for the reason. Reasons are not excuses, of course. Jesus says even a tiny seed of good can create immense goodness. A bit of yeast makes the whole dough rise. The existence of evil is no reason to view it as inevitable. If I find within myself both good and evil, I have a responsibility to grow the grain and invite the Spirit to uproot the thistle in me.

> **Make a list of some "grain" and "thistle" growing in your heart.**
> **How do you cultivate one and defeat the other?**

WE RESPOND

Try "preventative" over "punitive" justice. Give people a break: forgive and show mercy before it's deserved. Be kind when kindness isn't returned. Try patience instead of irritation. Plant a good seed in every encounter.

"Are you listening to this? Really listening?"

SEVENTEENTH SUNDAY IN ORDINARY TIME

FIRST READING » 1 KINGS 3:5, 7-12

The king went to Gibeon, the most prestigious of the local shrines, to worship. He sacrificed a thousand Whole-Burnt-Offerings on that altar. That night, there in Gibeon, God appeared to Solomon in a dream: God said, "What can I give you? Ask."

"And now here I am: God, my God, you have made me, your servant, ruler of the kingdom in place of David my father. I'm too young for this, a mere child! I don't know the ropes, hardly know the 'ins' and 'outs' of this job. And here I am, set down in the middle of the people you've chosen, a great people—far too many to ever count.

"Here's what I want: Give me a God-listening heart so I can lead your people well, discerning the difference between good and evil. For who on their own is capable of leading your glorious people?"

God, the Master, was delighted with Solomon's response. And God said to him, "Because you have asked for this and haven't grasped after a long life, or riches, or the doom of your enemies, but you have asked for the ability to lead and govern well, I'll give you what you've asked for—I'm giving you a wise and mature heart. There's never been one like you before; and there'll be no one after. As a bonus, I'm giving you both the wealth and glory you didn't ask for—there's not a king anywhere who will come up to your mark. And if you stay on course, keeping your eye on the life-map and the God-signs as your father David did, I'll also give you a long life."

Has there ever been a king with a prayer like Solomon's? It makes you wonder what government might be like if every elected official who claims to be a church member actually prayed for the wisdom to be a good leader. If only those in power wanted to be wise more than they wanted wealth, opportunity, and re-election. Instead, the electorate remains disillusioned because our leaders act like greedy children.

Solomon didn't face an electorate, having been born to his office. Yet he knew the folks outside his palace walls wanted the same things people have always wanted: security, prosperity, a measure of peace. He also recognized that he was not God, and mortals can't always deliver on a grand scale. So he chose to submit to God. He asked for wisdom, which is asking to see the world as God sees. The kingdom of God starts here, in the heart of every person who seeks wisdom before all else.

Who is the wisest person you know personally?
How does that person use the power available to him or her?

SECOND READING » ROMANS 8:28-30

Meanwhile, the moment we get tired in the waiting, God's Spirit is right alongside helping us along. If we don't know how or what to pray, it doesn't matter. He does our praying in and for us, making prayer out of our wordless sighs, our aching groans. He knows us far better than we know ourselves, knows our pregnant condition, and keeps us present before God. That's why we can be so sure that every detail in our lives of love for God is worked into something good.

God knew what he was doing from the very beginning. He decided from the outset to shape the lives of those who love him along the same lines as the life of his Son. The Son stands first in the line of humanity he restored. We see the original and intended shape of our lives there in him. After God made that decision of what his children should be like, he followed it up by calling people by name. After he called them by name, he set them on a solid basis with himself. And then, after getting them established, he stayed with them to the end, gloriously completing what he had begun.

A woman happily married for eighteen years suddenly loses her husband to an aggressive cancer. An able-bodied man wakes up from an accident paralyzed. A child is born mentally impaired. All things work for good for those who love God?

People come to the church asking these kinds of questions. They aren't looking for empty pieties or good theology. When Paul asserts that ALL things work for good, we naturally insert our own dilemmas. Does my unemployment serve God? What about my loneliness at being overlooked for companionship, or my money trouble, or my ruined health or reputation? My heartfelt response, when listening to these questions or living within some of them: What ELSE are you going to do with this sorrow? What ELSE can we do with loss, illness, disappointment, and need, but surrender it to the business of God's kingdom? God promises to use everything, to redeem what is lost, to glorify every wound. If we don't allow God to bring good out of the depths of what seems vicious and wrong, the evil will only beget more evil. Grief will lead to bitterness, fear to desperate acts, loneliness to depression. Only God can bring good out of anything.

> **What dilemma in your life awaits God's ability**
> **to bring good out of any situation?**

GOSPEL » MATTHEW 13:44-52

"God's kingdom is like a treasure hidden in a field for years and then accidentally found by a trespasser. The finder is ecstatic—what a find!—and proceeds to sell everything he owns to raise money and buy that field.

"Or, God's kingdom is like a jewel merchant on the hunt for excellent pearls. Finding one that is flawless, he immediately sells everything and buys it.

"Or, God's kingdom is like a fishnet cast into the sea, catching all kinds of

fish. When it is full, it is hauled onto the beach. The good fish are picked out and put in a tub; those unfit to eat are thrown away. That's how it will be when the curtain comes down on history. The angels will come and cull the bad fish and throw them in the garbage. There will be a lot of desperate complaining, but it won't do any good."

Jesus asked, "Are you starting to get a handle on all this?"

They answered, "Yes."

He said, "Then you see how every student well-trained in God's kingdom is like the owner of a general store who can put his hands on anything you need, old or new, exactly when you need it."

The last few weeks we've been treated with kingdom stories. Some are casual, like the woman kneading dough or the sower going out to plant a field. Some are loaded with suppressed excitement: the merchant finding the pearl, or the discovery of treasure in an unmarked field. What kind of kingdom can be glimpsed from a net cast lightly into the sea, emerging with the day's catch AND a year's worth of junk?

What's clear is that the kingdom of God isn't a simple idea. It's not the usual religious jaunt from a life of good works to a heavenly reward. The kingdom is known through fidelity to small tasks, yet holds enormous surprises and can lead to high spiritual gambles. We may be willing to put a pinch of piety into the dough and watch the bread rise. But not all of us will sell everything, even to purchase the brightest pearl on earth. Gamble, with our nest egg? This is America!

In fact, every kingdom story has its own risk factor. Not every loaf will rise, not every field sown will produce a yield. The dragnet of human experience pulls up what's useful to spiritual growth and also more garbage to haul around. We're choosing, in every minute, how much we will sacrifice, how much to risk.

> **Which of the kingdom stories in the last two Sundays' gospels speaks to your life right now?**

WE RESPOND

Bake a loaf of bread. Plant a seed. Go fishing. Invest in something really important. But whatever you do, consider how your actions teach you about God's kingdom and how it comes into the world through you.

EIGHTEENTH SUNDAY IN ORDINARY TIME

FIRST READING » ISAIAH 55:1-3

"Hey there! All who are thirsty,
come to the water!
Are you penniless?
Come anyway—buy and eat!
Come, buy your drinks, buy wine and milk.
Buy without money—everything's free!
Why do you spend your money on junk food,
your hard-earned cash on cotton candy?
Listen to me, listen well: Eat only the best,
fill yourself with only the finest.
Pay attention, come close now,
listen carefully to my life-giving, life-nourishing words.
I'm making a lasting covenant commitment with you,
the same that I made with David: sure, solid, enduring love.
I set him up as a witness to the nations,
made him a prince and leader of the nations,
And now I'm doing it to you:
You'll summon nations you've never heard of,
and nations who've never heard of you
will come running to you
Because of me, your God,
because The Holy of Israel has honored you."

I'm not much of a shopper. It's a task I'd happily delegate. But I have to admit there are times when I wander downtown vaguely and buy something I neither need nor, on second thought, really want. My motivation: unhappiness. When I'm unhappy, I buy things.

Buying things never makes you happier, of course. But it's an American solution to all kinds of problems. Material consumption is just another way of trying to feed a hunger. Despite the fact that it doesn't work, we keep trying it anyway. The media all around keeps telling us what fun looks like and what we need to own, wear, or drive to get there. How could the entire culture be wrong?

It could. Despite the enticing promises, no one can sell us happiness off the rack. Prophets have always insisted that our real hunger is for union with God. If we settle for less, less is what we'll get.

> **Look around the rooms of your house, or search your pockets.**
> **How many things can you find that you don't need?**

SECOND READING » ROMANS 8:35, 37-39

So, what do you think? With God on our side like this, how can we lose? If God didn't hesitate to put everything on the line for us, embracing our condition and exposing himself to the worst by sending his own Son, is there anything else he wouldn't gladly and freely do for us? And who would dare tangle with God by messing with one of God's chosen? Who would dare even to point a finger? The One who died for us—who was raised to life for us!—is in the presence of God at this very moment sticking up for us. Do you think anyone is going to be able to drive a wedge between us and Christ's love for us? There is no way! Not trouble, not hard times, not hatred, not hunger, not homelessness, not bullying threats, not backstabbing, not even the worst sins listed in Scripture:

> *They kill us in cold blood because they hate you.*
> *We're sitting ducks; they pick us off one by one.*

None of this fazes us because Jesus loves us. I'm absolutely convinced that nothing—nothing living or dead, angelic or demonic, today or tomorrow, high or low, thinkable or unthinkable—absolutely nothing can get between us and God's love because of the way that Jesus our Master has embraced us.

A friend once read this passage aloud and replied, "What will separate me from Christ: trouble? Yep. Hard times? You bet. Hunger, homelessness, bullying...yes, all of the above." In our more honest moments, we might say the same. Faith is as easy to maintain as a potted plant on the windowsill—until the time of challenge comes. But how many of us really intend to be "crucified with Christ," as Paul writes elsewhere? At the first sign of trouble, we might well take cover like Peter and behave as if we don't know the man.

We hope to be faithful, now and at the hour of our death; but those are precisely the two hardest times to BE faithful. Neither death nor life will be able to separate us from God, Paul insists, yet we feel uncertain. It might help to consider that Paul isn't commenting on our fidelity, but on Christ's. It is Christ's steadfastness we're counting on. While we have good reason to mistrust our dedication, we need not doubt his.

> **Under what circumstances might your faith be shaken?**
> **Envision Christ being faithful even as you are in doubt.**

GOSPEL » MATTHEW 14:13-21

When Jesus got the news, he slipped away by boat to an out-of-the-way place by himself. But unsuccessfully—someone saw him and the word got around. Soon a lot of people from the nearby villages walked around the lake to where he was. When he saw them coming, he was overcome with pity and healed their sick.

Toward evening the disciples approached him. "We're out in the country and it's getting late. Dismiss the people so they can go to the villages and get some supper."

But Jesus said, "There is no need to dismiss them. You give them supper."
"All we have are five loaves of bread and two fish," they said.

Jesus said, "Bring them here." Then he had the people sit on the grass. He took the five loaves and two fish, lifted his face to heaven in prayer, blessed, broke, and gave the bread to the disciples. The disciples then gave the food to the congregation. They all ate their fill. They gathered twelve baskets of leftovers. About five thousand were fed.

Jesus never met a crowd he couldn't satisfy. If they were ignorant, he taught them. If they were sinners, he forgave them. If they brought their sick, he healed them. If they were hungry, he fed them. No one who yearned and brought their yearning to him went unanswered, not even the women and the children.

But Jesus didn't come to found a school, hospital, counseling practice, or bakery. He comes to bring abundant life to people who've gotten used to the half-life of a world in which evil has free rein. The hungry child can only experience God through bread. Jesus brings life to the world to match its need. Neither the finality of death nor the harshness of life can overcome the gift he offers. That's why the miracle of feeding a crowd of five thousand, as grand as it is, is dwarfed by the generations of people who've been fed by Jesus since.

> **What form would Jesus take,
> in order to come into your life
> and fill your need today?**

WE RESPOND

Help someone to experience the abundant life of Christ. Tutor someone who wants to learn. Comfort someone in sickness or distress. Forgive a person who's wronged you. Feed the hungry.

*"There is no need to dismiss them.
You give them supper."*

NINETEENTH SUNDAY IN ORDINARY TIME

FIRST READING » 1 KINGS 19:9A, 11-13A

He got up, ate and drank his fill, and set out. Nourished by that meal, he walked forty days and nights, all the way to the mountain of God, to Horeb. When he got there, he crawled into a cave and went to sleep.

Then the word of God came to him: "So Elijah, what are you doing here?"

Then he was told, "Go, stand on the mountain at attention before God. God will pass by."

A hurricane wind ripped through the mountains and shattered the rocks before God, but God wasn't to be found in the wind; after the wind an earthquake, but God wasn't in the earthquake; and after the earthquake fire, but God wasn't in the fire; and after the fire a gentle and quiet whisper.

When Elijah heard the quiet voice, he muffled his face with his great cloak, went to the mouth of the cave, and stood there. A quiet voice asked, "So Elijah, now tell me, what are you doing here?" Elijah said it again, "I've been working my heart out for God, the God-of-the-Angel-Armies, because the people of Israel have abandoned your covenant, destroyed your places of worship, and murdered your prophets. I'm the only one left, and now they're trying to kill me."

Many of us harbor romantic notions of the God quest involving grand and heroic gestures. We think one must become celibate, live among lepers, or hand over one's body to be burned to have an encounter with the divine. Perhaps we've read a few too many glamorized accounts of the saints. At the least, we'd appreciate a roll of thunder to announce God's entrance into our history.

Elijah the prophet was no stranger to *theophanies*, those grand announcements of God's presence and power in the world. But he was also aware that God could be found in stillness and arrive in silence. God speaks in the unfolding of a flower. We can encounter God by doing small, ordinary things—what Therese of Lisieux called "the little way" to holiness. Our daily fidelities along the way of love can reveal God's face as mightily as wind and fire. God speaks to us each day in ways that escape our notice.

What is God saying to you through the ordinary events of your life?

SECOND READING » ROMANS 9:1-5

At the same time, you need to know that I carry with me at all times a huge sorrow. It's an enormous pain deep within me, and I'm never free of it. I'm not exaggerating—Christ and the Holy Spirit are my witnesses. It's the Israelites... If there were any way I could be cursed by the Messiah so they could be blessed by him, I'd do it in a minute. They're my family. I grew up with them. They had everything going for them—family, glory, covenants, revelation, worship, promises, to say nothing of being the race that produced the Messiah, the Christ, who is God over everything, always. Oh, yes!

Paul's grief that his fellow Israelites did not accept the revelation of Jesus was profound. He would rather accept condemnation himself if it could mean their salvation. But of course, no one can accept salvation for another. It has to be a personal choice. Parents can have their children baptized, enroll them in parochial school—but these actions cannot guarantee a life of faith will follow. One can drag a spouse to church for years, but this is not the same as making a personal commitment. Faith is, necessarily, an individual assent.

The Israelites had it all, by Paul's reckoning: a history studded with the activity of God. Still they remained free to ignore God's personal investment in them by rejecting the fulfillment of divine promises that Jesus embodied. We too can look back at our personal history and find the blessings of God at every turn. But we're free to make our way apart from God if we choose. The call to discipleship is not a draft. Only a free assent to love will do.

Compare a free act with an obligation. Which word best describes your faith?

GOSPEL » MATTHEW 14:22-33

As soon as the meal was finished, he insisted that the disciples get in the boat and go on ahead to the other side while he dismissed the people. With the crowd dispersed, he climbed the mountain so he could be by himself and pray. He stayed there alone, late into the night.

Meanwhile, the boat was far out to sea when the wind came up against them and they were battered by the waves. At about four o'clock in the morning, Jesus came toward them walking on the water. They were scared out of their wits. "A ghost!" they said, crying out in terror.

But Jesus was quick to comfort them. "Courage, it's me. Don't be afraid."

Peter, suddenly bold, said, "Master, if it's really you, call me to come to you on the water."

He said, "Come ahead."

Jumping out of the boat, Peter walked on the water to Jesus. But when he looked down at the waves churning beneath his feet, he lost his nerve and started to sink. He cried, "Master, save me!"

Jesus didn't hesitate. He reached down and grabbed his hand. Then he said, "Faint-heart, what got into you?"

The two of them climbed into the boat, and the wind died down. The disciples in the boat, having watched the whole thing, worshiped Jesus, saying, "This is it! You are God's Son for sure!"

Peter was a fisherman. He was long accustomed to the sea and its moods, and surely this was not the first stormy night he'd spent on the water. Peter knew how to compensate for wind and waves in choppy weather. He also knew there was a point beyond which negotiation with a tempest was impossible. But Peter had no experience at all with a ghost, or a man, walking on the waves. Like the others in the boat, he was afraid. But unlike the others, he was willing to negotiate with this new situation. Peter decided to take a walk on the wild side.

A fisherman who stays with his boat knows how to ride a wave. But with wind at his back and water under his feet, all Peter had for support was the steady view of his Lord. As his consciousness of the peril grew, his confidence in the Lord shrank. Many of us too have lost our faith in time of crisis. Our trust in God is steady within the boat, and up for grabs when life is less predictable. Peter scores points for risking a walk on the wild side, which the rest of the disciples were unwilling to do. An untested faith is worse than the "little faith" Peter showed. God can always plant a mustard seed.

> **When has your faith been tested by stormy events?**
> **How did your faith endure?**

WE RESPOND

Walk in faith, even if it means getting out of the safe boat you've been sailing lately. Take a risk: give charitably beyond what's comfortable. Tell the truth even if it costs you. Pray through your doubts.

"Courage, it's me. Don't be afraid."

FIRST READING » ISAIAH 56:1, 6-7

God's Message:
"Guard my common good:
Do what's right and do it in the right way,
For salvation is just around the corner,
my setting-things-right is about to go into action.
How blessed are you who enter into these things,
you men and women who embrace them,
Who keep Sabbath and don't defile it,
who watch your step and don't do anything evil!
Make sure no outsider who now follows God
ever has occasion to say, 'God put me in second-class.
I don't really belong.'
And make sure no physically mutilated person
is ever made to think, 'I'm damaged goods.
I don't really belong.'"

"And as for the outsiders who now follow me,
working for me, loving my name,
and wanting to be my servants—
All who keep Sabbath and don't defile it,
holding fast to my covenant—
I'll bring them to my holy mountain
and give them joy in my house of prayer.
They'll be welcome to worship the same as the 'insiders,'
to bring burnt offerings and sacrifices to my altar.
Oh yes, my house of worship
will be known as a house of prayer for all people."
The Decree of the Master, God himself,
who gathers in the exiles of Israel:
"I will gather others also,
gather them in with those already gathered."

I've got a pal who is practically my twin. Maybe you have a friend like this: we think alike, finish each other's sentences, have heart-to-hearts about politics, religion, values, you name it. No matter what the topic is, we're on the same page. Well, except for those rare times when we disagree. Then it's like somebody threw a firecracker into the conversation! We're so used to finding agreement, we scarcely recognize each other in disagreement.

For the friends of God, arguments about religious belief are like that firecracker.

People who declare allegiance to the Holy are suddenly at each other's throats in a way that is quite a bit less than holy. When those who believe in God are at war, they become unrecognizable as believers. In the prophecies of Isaiah, God promises over and over to call all nations together in worship and friendship. We may not know how to get along, but we better learn fast. And those of us who profess belief in God already ought to have a steeper learning curve.

How do you feel about "sharing God" with people of other religious traditions? How do you reconcile God's peaceful vision with our conflicted world?

SECOND READING » ROMANS 11:13–15, 29–32

But I don't want to go on about them. It's you, the outsiders, that I'm concerned with now. Because my personal assignment is focused on the so-called outsiders, I make as much of this as I can when I'm among my Israelite kin, the so-called insiders, hoping they'll realize what they're missing and want to get in on what God is doing. If their falling out initiated this worldwide coming together, their recovery is going to set off something even better: mass homecoming! If the first thing the Jews did, even though it was wrong for them, turned out for your good, just think what's going to happen when they get it right!

I want to lay all this out on the table as clearly as I can, friends. This is complicated. It would be easy to misinterpret what's going on and arrogantly assume that you're royalty and they're just rabble, out on their ears for good. But that's not it at all. This hardness on the part of insider Israel toward God is temporary. Its effect is to open things up to all the outsiders so that we end up with a full house. Before it's all over, there will be a complete Israel. As it is written,

> *A champion will stride down from the mountain of Zion;*
>   *he'll clean house in Jacob.*
> *And this is my commitment to my people:*
>   *removal of their sins.*

From your point of view as you hear and embrace the good news of the Message, it looks like the Jews are God's enemies. But looked at from the long-range perspective of God's overall purpose, they remain God's oldest friends. God's gifts and God's call are under full warranty—never canceled, never rescinded.

There was a time not so long ago when you were on the outs with God. But then the Jews slammed the door on him and things opened up for you. Now they are on the outs. But with the door held wide open for you, they have a way back in. In one way or another, God makes sure that we all experience what it means to be outside so that he can personally open the door and welcome us back in.

God's call was once compared to the invitation of a king who opened his banquet to folks from the highways and byways. God wants everybody at the party! The typical human approach is to be selective and critical, but Jesus repeats often that the kingdom is sown in every kind of soil, giving all of us a chance to receive it.

So the call goes out to Jews and Gentiles... and, we can imagine today, to followers of Islam and Buddha and the Almighty Dollar. The call goes out to nice people and nasty ones. It's meant for the person we least care for, and the one dearest to our hearts. God invites the baptized as well as those scared to death of the water of the church. God throws a big net, hoping to catch everyone.

And Paul says God doesn't take back the invitation once it goes out. You can't lose it by being bad—not even by being very bad. You don't get uninvited for not coming to Mass on Sunday, even for years. You can't lose it for marrying the wrong person or for not being the child your parents wanted you to be. God holds out an invitation to the party to you, today.

> **Does your parish hold out God's invitation to everybody freely,**
> **or does it seem to restrict its welcome?**
> **How can you show the generous welcome of God**
> **to those who feel outside of it?**

GOSPEL » MATTHEW 15:21-28

From there Jesus took a trip to Tyre and Sidon. They had hardly arrived when a Canaanite woman came down from the hills and pleaded, "Mercy, Master, Son of David! My daughter is cruelly afflicted by an evil spirit."

Jesus ignored her. The disciples came and complained, "Now she's bothering us. Would you please take care of her? She's driving us crazy."

Jesus refused, telling them, "I've got my hands full dealing with the lost sheep of Israel."

Then the woman came back to Jesus, went to her knees, and begged. "Master, help me."

He said, "It's not right to take bread out of children's mouths and throw it to dogs."

She was quick: "You're right, Master, but beggar dogs do get scraps from the master's table."

Jesus gave in. "Oh, woman, your faith is something else. What you want is what you get!" Right then her daughter became well.

Even dogs have hope! This is what the woman says to Jesus, when she asks him to heal her tormented daughter. She classifies her family with the dogs, knowing the average Israelite would describe a Canaanite that way. Jesus is astounded by her faith, and gives her the desire of her heart.

Some scholars claim Jesus was testing the woman by not responding to her request right away. Others say Jesus learned from her that his mission was larger than Israel. This seems strange to those of us who were taught that Jesus had the mind of God from the time Mary first laid him in the straw. But if Jesus is also fully human, he'd have to grow in wisdom and grace, as Luke says Jesus did.

This woman summoned up the courage to tell Jesus how to run his own ministry! The best of the prophets and saints showed this kind of spirit, sparring with God over matters of importance to them. Who knows what could happen if more people prayed with such confidence? Who knows how many of us could wrestle with God like Abraham, Jacob, Hannah, and the Canaanite woman—and win?

Do you think God's mind can be changed?
Do you think there are things about which "God's mind is made up"?
Name some things that might fall in either category.

WE RESPOND

Show some chutzpah! Resolve to pray for the things that are most important to you–peace in the world, an answer to hunger–or a job or a better relationship with your spouse. Pray unceasingly, as Paul says, or sing your prayer, as Augustine recommends. But pray most of all unfailingly.

"Oh, woman, your faith is something else.
What you want is what you get!"

TWENTY-FIRST SUNDAY IN ORDINARY TIME
....A Peg in a Sure Spot

FIRST READING » ISAIAH 22:19-23

The Master, God-of-the-Angel-Armies, spoke: "Come. Go to this steward, Shebna, who is in charge of all the king's affairs, and tell him: What's going on here? You're an outsider here and yet you act like you own the place, make a big, fancy tomb for yourself where everyone can see it, making sure everyone will think you're important. God is about to sack you, to throw you to the dogs. He'll grab you by the hair, swing you round and round dizzyingly, and then let you go, sailing through the air like a ball, until you're out of sight. Where you'll land, nobody knows. And there you'll die, and all the stuff you've collected heaped on your grave. You've disgraced your master's house! You're fired—and good riddance!

"On that Day I'll replace Shebna. I will call my servant Eliakim son of Hilkiah. I'll dress him in your robe. I'll put your belt on him. I'll give him your authority. He'll be a father-leader to Jerusalem and the government of Judah. I'll give him the key of the Davidic heritage. He'll have the run of the place—open any door and keep it open, lock any door and keep it locked. I'll pound him like a nail into a solid wall. He'll secure the Davidic tradition. Everything will hang on him—not only the fate of Davidic descendants but also the detailed daily operations of the house, including cups and cutlery.

A prophet's enemy has this oracle leveled at him: his tenure has come to an end. In place of him, God intends to raise up a more faithful servant, and honor him with great authority. So ends verse 23. But if you look up vs. 24-25, you find out that the next fellow will be brought down as well. He was a peg in a sure spot, a nail in the wall, but a nail can only bear so much weight.

This is a story as old as the Bible: God chooses someone for a special purpose, like Abraham, Moses, David. And that nail driven into the wall of history is not as certain as the divine hand that hammered it in. Human beings are imperfect by definition, and every one of God's special friends is a bit of a traitor, here and there. Every time God swings a hammer, the aim is sure but the nail is untrustworthy. Maybe that's why the final nail to be driven by the divine hammer is into God's own flesh. The cross is the surest spot in all of creation and time.

**If God fixed you to a particular mission,
what would it take to detach you from that spot?**

SECOND READING » ROMANS 11:33-36

Have you ever come on anything quite like this extravagant generosity of God, this deep, deep wisdom? It's way over our heads. We'll never figure it out. Is there anyone around who can explain God?

Anyone smart enough to tell him what to do?
Anyone who has done him such a huge favor
that God has to ask his advice?
Everything comes from him;
Everything happens through him;
Everything ends up in him.
Always glory! Always praise!
Yes. Yes. Yes.

Paul is an interesting thinker. First he spends the greater part of a chapter configuring the precise relationship between Jews and Gentiles in the plan of salvation. After doing all the theology, however, he acknowledges that God's ways are wonderful and unknowable. This is the sort of humility most of us practice: first, we want to get it all figured out. Once we've got it down to our satisfaction, we're willing to bow before the Mystery.

The unknown is uncomfortable. We don't like mystery and ambiguity, so we crowd our minds with facts and try to solve puzzles. We'd like to fix GOD in a sure spot, because it's the "unknowability" of God's ways that's most unnerving. People like me go into theology for the same reason: we get to be professional second-guessers of God's intentions. But even professional God-talkers must bow before the Mystery sooner or later. Love so vast cannot be explained, only surrendered to. And be at peace: love is the safest place there is.

Where in your life do you make room for Mystery?

GOSPEL » MATTHEW 16:13-20

When Jesus arrived in the villages of Caesarea Philippi, he asked his disciples, "What are people saying about who the Son of Man is?"

They replied, "Some think he is John the Baptizer, some say Elijah, some Jeremiah or one of the other prophets."

He pressed them, "And how about you? Who do you say I am?"

Simon Peter said, "You're the Christ, the Messiah, the Son of the living God."

Jesus came back, "God bless you, Simon, son of Jonah! You didn't get that answer out of books or from teachers. My Father in heaven, God himself, let you in on this secret of who I really am. And now I'm going to tell you who you are, really are. You are Peter, a rock. This is the rock on which I will put together my church, a church so expansive with energy that not even the gates of hell will be able to keep it out.

"And that's not all. You will have complete and free access to God's kingdom, keys to open any and every door: no more barriers between heaven and earth, earth and heaven. A yes on earth is yes in heaven. A no on earth is no in heaven."

He swore the disciples to secrecy. He made them promise they would tell no one that he was the Messiah.

One day soon, Peter will deny he ever knew Jesus. But at this moment, he's chosen to be the foundation upon which the future church will rest. Peter, in a sure spot? He was a nail driven into spackle! Is Jesus being ironic when he calls him a rock? In just a few more verses (see vs. 23), Jesus will call Peter the devil.

Jesus is Lord—but also a realist. Human nature is soft, like the flesh that contains it, and there truly is no better choice among the Twelve than Peter. From this impulsive, unschooled, self-preserving fisherman, God will raise up the rafters of a church that will see twenty centuries and more. Not because Peter is great, but because God is. Not much can be built on flesh, as frail and uncertain as human beings are. But through the Spirit which gives the church its breath, the reign of God keeps on coming, on earth as it is in heaven.

> **What part of your Christian commitment is like rock?**
> **What part is flesh?**

WE RESPOND

Spend time with God the Mystery. Without words, prayer aids, or the usual props, sit in silence and let God's "unknowability" find you. Seek to be known, and not to know.

"And now I'm going to tell you who you are, really are. You are Peter, a rock."

TWENTY-SECOND SUNDAY IN ORDINARY TIME

FIRST READING » JEREMIAH 20:7-9

You pushed me into this, God, and I let you do it.
*   You were too much for me.*
And now I'm a public joke.
*   They all poke fun at me.*
Every time I open my mouth
*   I'm shouting, "Murder!" or "Rape!"*
And all I get for my God-warnings
*   are insults and contempt.*
But if I say, "Forget it!
*   No more God-Messages from me!"*
The words are fire in my belly,
*   a burning in my bones.*
I'm worn out trying to hold it in.
*   I can't do it any longer!*
Then I hear whispering behind my back:
*   "There goes old 'Danger-Everywhere.' Shut him up! Report him!"*
Old friends watch, hoping I'll fall flat on my face:
*   "One misstep and we'll have him. We'll get rid of him for good!"*

Jeremiah's outrage at his circumstance is understandable. God chose him to be a prophet; and then, when the going gets tough, God's support is nowhere in evidence. Jeremiah feels betrayed and abused.

We've all cried Jeremiah's cry during the dark hours of our lives. When illness comes, or failure or loss or loneliness, we wonder what good it does us to be the friends of God. Teresa of Avila shook her fist at the sky on a stormy night when her carriage was stalled in the mud. "It's no wonder You have so few friends!" she shouted at God, "If this is how You treat them!" Being the friends of God, we might presume, puts us in line for special favors, if not preferential treatment. But the rain falls on the just and the unjust. If we expect kickbacks from God in return for our loyalty, we will certainly feel as duped as the prophet did. Even Jesus does not insist that the cup of suffering pass him by, and no one had an "in" with the Father like he does.

Under what circumstances have you felt duped by God?

SECOND READING » ROMANS 12:1-2

So here's what I want you to do, God helping you: Take your everyday, ordinary life—your sleeping, eating, going-to-work, and walking-around life—and place it before God as an offering. Embracing what God does for you is the best thing you can do for him. Don't become so well-adjusted to your culture that you fit into it without even thinking. Instead, fix your attention on God. You'll be changed from the inside out. Readily recognize what he wants from you, and quickly respond to it. Unlike the culture around you, always dragging you down to its level of immaturity, God brings the best out of you, develops well-formed maturity in you.

"Rend your hearts, not your garments." We hear these words from Joel's prophecy read at the start of Lent. The idea is not to make changes in our lives which are just for show, but to change our way of being and behaving. In Romans, Paul invites us to the same kind of genuine transformation. Don't adjust to this culture; don't buy into its values and goals. Instead, renew yourself; or as a popular ad campaign says, "Think different."

Granted, it's not easy. When every media message is prompting us to get a bigger house, a better car, more technological toys, how can we break free of the brainwashing and want LESS? My friend Mary says Christians are called to "downward mobility" in an upwardly mobile world. We're invited to get smaller, poorer, more humble, as the rest of the culture strives for more visibility, wealth, and prestige. Talk about thinking differently! But what a marvelous sign of our faith, if we can accomplish this downward spiral with joy and grace.

> **Are you moving up or down in worldly wealth?**
> **Can you surrender power in this world with a cheerful heart?**

GOSPEL » MATTHEW 16:21-27

Then Jesus made it clear to his disciples that it was now necessary for him to go to Jerusalem, submit to an ordeal of suffering at the hands of the religious leaders, be killed, and then on the third day be raised up alive. Peter took him in hand, protesting, "Impossible, Master! That can never be!"

But Jesus didn't swerve. "Peter, get out of my way. Satan, get lost. You have no idea how God works."

Then Jesus went to work on his disciples. "Anyone who intends to come with me has to let me lead. You're not in the driver's seat; I am. Don't run from suffering; embrace it. Follow me and I'll show you how. Self-help is no help at all. Self-sacrifice is the way, my way, to finding yourself, your true self. What kind of deal is it to get everything you want but lose yourself? What could you ever trade your soul for?

"Don't be in such a hurry to go into business for yourself. Before you know it the Son of Man will arrive with all the splendor of his Father, accompanied by an army of angels. You'll get everything you have coming to you, a personal gift. This isn't pie in the sky by and by. Some of you standing here are going to see it take place, see the Son of Man in kingdom glory."

Peter must have felt duped by God when Jesus rebuked him. What did he say that was so bad? When Jesus foretold of his future suffering and death, Peter took what he considered an appropriate defensive stand. Not you, Lord! Never!

Only moments earlier, he had called Jesus the Messiah. Peter's understanding of that term meant conquering hero, not suffering servant of God's will. Peter liked to imagine victory achieved without a scratch. Victory gained at the cost of ultimate sacrifice was no victory in his mind. If Peter was duped, it was his own preconceptions about God and religion that betrayed him. Gaining the world at the price of the soul was no bargain. But losing everything for the sake of God's victory is the one purchase we all want to consider.

For what are you willing to suffer
(i.e., love, money, justice, peace, the truth)?
How much are you willing to suffer for these things?

WE RESPOND

Avoid being deceived by worldly values. Spend a week refusing to read billboards and magazine ads, watching commercials, even noting brand labels. Turn your back on the consumer message and exercise your freedom.

"Self-help is no help at all.
Self-sacrifice is the way, my way,
to finding yourself, your true self."

TWENTY-THIRD SUNDAY IN ORDINARY TIME

FIRST READING » EZEKIEL 33:7-9

"You, son of man, are the watchman. I've made you a watchman for Israel. The minute you hear a message from me, warn them. If I say to the wicked, 'Wicked man, wicked woman, you're on the fast track to death!' and you don't speak up and warn the wicked to change their ways, the wicked will die unwarned in their sins and I'll hold you responsible for their bloodshed. But if you warn the wicked to change their ways and they don't do it, they'll die in their sins well-warned and at least you will have saved your own life.

Are you a special agent of God? Think carefully before you answer. On the old civil service test, this question was asked to weed out potentially dangerous personalities who might "go postal" someday on the job. If you answered Yes to this question, you would never get a job with the civil service.

But perhaps we ARE special agents of God, all of us who have been baptized and marked with a special character of grace. We have a mission—not a mission impossible, but certainly not easy—which is to convince an old and cynical world that love is still the most powerful force of all. We have a message: that justice pays more than crime, truth is more exciting than the lies we tell and believe, and death is the biggest deceiver of all.

Like Ezekiel, we have to be willing to call Evil by its right name and to prophesy against it. (Discernment is important here: we can't afford to testify to our own prejudices.) God will hold us accountable for all we know and don't bear witness to. As special agents, we aren't on the payroll for nothing. We have a job to do.

How do you serve, in a unique way, the mission of the church?

SECOND READING » ROMANS 13:8-10

Don't run up debts, except for the huge debt of love you owe each other. When you love others, you complete what the law has been after all along. The law code—don't sleep with another person's spouse, don't take someone's life, don't take what isn't yours, don't always be wanting what you don't have, and any other "don't" you can think of—finally adds up to this: Love other people as well as you do yourself. You can't go wrong when you love others. When you add up everything in the law code, the sum total is love.

For a culture that talks about love all the time, we don't see the real thing much in evidence. We see marriages contracted and annulled. We see parents neglecting and in some cases abandoning their children. We see a lot of portrayals of sexual conquest and the use of persons as means to an end. We ask for love and are sold romantic fantasy. No wonder upcoming generations are skeptical. Love is hardly more than a bumper sticker at the start of the twenty-first century.

Love, according to Paul's thumbnail definition, does no evil. All of the self-gratifying, open-ended associations that pass for relationships these days do not fall within the bounds of love, since they generate great harm for vulnerable people, especially children. Love is an extraordinary achievement that animates our humanity and makes our likeness to God transparent. When people experience genuine love, they feel brushed by the divine. If love is a rare event in our world, it's because we trade the risk of love for the poor rags of sentiment.

> **When have you experienced being loved in its fullest sense?**
> **When have you loved this way?**

GOSPEL » MATTHEW 18:15-20

"If a fellow believer hurts you, go and tell him—work it out between the two of you. If he listens, you've made a friend. If he won't listen, take one or two others along so that the presence of witnesses will keep things honest, and try again. If he still won't listen, tell the church. If he won't listen to the church, you'll have to start over from scratch, confront him with the need for repentance, and offer again God's forgiving love.

"Take this most seriously: A yes on earth is yes in heaven; a no on earth is no in heaven. What you say to one another is eternal. I mean this. When two of you get together on anything at all on earth and make a prayer of it, my Father in heaven goes into action. And when two or three of you are together because of me, you can be sure that I'll be there."

If we are special agents of God, then we serve as agents of grace for one another. I am, in a real sense, at your service, as you are at mine. Together, we invite the kingdom of God into our midst. It's not the sort of commission one can achieve alone.

Of all that we do together to promote God's reign, the hardest may be our gentle mutual correction. Unlike yourself, I'm sure, I dislike being told I'm wrong. When I respond in anger and treat someone unfairly, I want to be justified, not reproved. But some of my friends love me enough to tell me when I'm way off base and need to examine my motives. Sometimes it's enough to hear it from one person. Sometimes, I need to hear it from every direction before I'm ready to change. I value this honesty in my life, because I can't always punch my own way out of ignorance. My friends know how dearly I want to hear yes in heaven, so they're willing to say no to me in the here and now.

> **Have you ever corrected someone you love when they're in error?**
> **How do you respond to such correction?**

WE RESPOND

Spend a week mindful that you're God's special agent of grace for others. Wear a cross or display a Bible phrase on your desk to act as your badge of commission. Let love be the goal of your words and actions.

TWENTY-FOURTH SUNDAY IN ORDINARY TIME

FIRST READING » SIRACH 27:30—28:9

Make a wicked judgment and it'll return to haunt you; you won't know where it came from. Illusion and impropriety belong to the proud; vengeance lies in wait for them like a lion. Take pleasure when the just fail and you'll be caught by the same trap. Anger and furor are both detestable, yet the sinner holds on to them for dear life.

If you seek revenge upon another, you'll get your comeuppance from the Lord; the Lord already has you on the Revenge Watch List. Forgive your neighbors on the near side when they sin against you; in return, your neighbors on the far side will do the same. Should anyone harbor anger against another and expect to be forgiven? If you don't show mercy toward another, should the Lord still show mercy to you? Can human beings keep their anger on high and still expect forgiveness from the Lord?

Plan for the end times; quit stirring things up. Remember death and dying; don't forget the life-maps of the Lord. With these in mind, don't rile your neighbor and you'll do the smart thing with the Most High.

A friend of mine describes herself as a rage-oholic. She's addicted to the condition of being angry. She blames everyone around her for what goes wrong in her life. Though her father is no longer living and her mother is 2000 miles away, she can't stop being angry with them. Such anger continues to make her life miserable.

Not all of us carry our wrath to this extreme. But we know what bearing anger, even for a few hours, can do to our disposition, not to mention our judgment. If the sinner hugs rage, as Sirach says, then it's also true that anger embraces us back. We form an alliance with our rage, the way an alcoholic talks to his drink for solace. It's tough to let go of a companion who seems to be the one who sympathizes with our position. Still, anger is a false friend, seen in hindsight for the monster it is. Once our hearts are lifted free of it, we're amazed at the imprisoning grasp that once held us. What seemed like an embrace was really a stranglehold.

We wouldn't be human, of course, if we didn't feel anger now and then. But anger is a guest who should be given a quick chance to visit and speak his peace, not granted permission to unpack her bags and find a home in us.

What makes you angry?
How long do you hold on to anger, and it to you?

SECOND READING » ROMANS 14:7-9

What's important in all this is that if you keep a holy day, keep it for God's sake; if you eat meat, eat it to the glory of God and thank God for prime rib; if you're a vegetarian, eat vegetables to the glory of God and thank God for broccoli. None of us are permitted to insist on our own way in these matters. It's God we are answerable to—all the way from life to death and everything in between—not each other. That's why Jesus lived and died and then lived again: so that he could be our Master across the entire range of life and death, and free us from the petty tyrannies of each other.

While caring for a friend with a terminal illness, I had space to reflect on my own relationship to death. When he received the anointing of the sick in the hospital, my friend offered a prayer for peace of mind to accept his situation. But afterwards he confided to me, "What I really wanted to pray for is another chance to have breakfast at my favorite diner!"

I replied, "We'll have that breakfast, guaranteed—though it may be at the banquet hall of heaven. But the food is probably better there anyway."

In life and death, we are the Lord's. My friend survived long enough to have breakfast at that diner, but I'm equally sure we'll share another breakfast sometime in the future. As human beings, life or death makes a great deal of difference to us. But as people of faith, we can be confident about celestial breakfasts too. Sometimes I can smell the feast from here. At other times my grief outweighs my senses. But not my hope. I've witnessed too many holy deaths not to believe in what they saw. Life and death make a difference now, but that difference is temporary. Christ is Lord over both.

> **Consider an experience you've had
> in which you confronted the possibility of death.
> What did you learn about your readiness to die?**

GOSPEL » MATTHEW 18:21-35

At that point Peter got up the nerve to ask, "Master, how many times do I forgive a brother or sister who hurts me? Seven?"

Jesus replied, "Seven! Hardly. Try seventy times seven.

"The kingdom of God is like a king who decided to square accounts with his servants. As he got under way, one servant was brought before him who had run up a debt of a hundred thousand dollars. He couldn't pay up, so the king ordered the man, along with his wife, children, and goods, to be auctioned off at the slave market.

"The poor wretch threw himself at the king's feet and begged, 'Give me a chance and I'll pay it all back.' Touched by his plea, the king let him off, erasing the debt.

"The servant was no sooner out of the room when he came upon one of his fellow servants who owed him ten dollars. He seized him by the throat and demanded, 'Pay up. Now!'

"The poor wretch threw himself down and begged, 'Give me a chance and I'll pay it all back.' But he wouldn't do it. He had him arrested and put in jail

until the debt was paid. When the other servants saw this going on, they were outraged and brought a detailed report to the king.

"The king summoned the man and said, 'You evil servant! I forgave your entire debt when you begged me for mercy. Shouldn't you be compelled to be merciful to your fellow servant who asked for mercy?' The king was furious and put the screws to the man until he paid back his entire debt. And that's exactly what my Father in heaven is going to do to each one of you who doesn't forgive unconditionally anyone who asks for mercy."

If ever someone was locked in the embrace of sin, it's the servant in this parable about mercy. Though compassion is shown to him, he's incapable of returning it. Watch the way he treats his fellow servant! His unforgiveness imprisons him in the same way.

The spirit of unforgiveness lurks in Peter's question about "how much" forgiveness is required. What he's really asking is: When can I reasonably refuse to forgive those who offend me? Surely there's a limit to how much forgiveness is strictly necessary.

Jesus won't play this game. Jesus paints God as a king willing to forgive an outrageous sum owed him, not because it's necessary—a king has no obligation to forgive anything—but for compassion's sake. Peter, in the guise of the first servant, sees his anger against his brother as actually justifiable. In the world of gospel parable, that attitude is destined for destruction. Holding others bound to their sin poisons our love. Our unforgiveness reveals how far short we fall of the mercy God shows to us. When I'm in opposition to a sister or brother, I know it's for my sake, as much as for theirs, that I find my way to forgiveness. To the extent that I choke my neighbor with my wrath, that's how far the embrace of sin has choked the love out of me.

Whom do you find hardest to forgive?
What makes it hard, and what price do you pay for unforgiveness?

WE RESPOND

As Scripture says, "Do not give the devil a chance to work on you." Resolve not to allow unforgiveness a breeding ground in your heart. Confess it and reconcile with your offender as quickly as possible.

TWENTY-FIFTH SUNDAY IN ORDINARY TIME

FIRST READING » ISAIAH 55:6-9

Seek God while he's here to be found,
pray to him while he's close at hand.
Let the wicked abandon their way of life
and the evil their way of thinking.
Let them come back to God, who is merciful,
come back to our God, who is lavish with forgiveness.
"I don't think the way you think.
The way you work isn't the way I work."
God's Decree.
"For as the sky soars high above earth,
so the way I work surpasses the way you work,
and the way I think is beyond the way you think.
Just as rain and snow descend from the skies
and don't go back until they've watered the earth,
Doing their work of making things grow and blossom,
producing seed for farmers and food for the hungry,
So will the words that come out of my mouth
not come back empty-handed.
They'll do the work I sent them to do,
they'll complete the assignment I gave them.

"Smells like grace," a friend says to me, whenever a situation arises that can't be dismissed as mere coincidence. Knowing the "smell" of grace is vital to Christian discernment. Being able to separate God's will from our fears and prejudices is a mark of spiritual maturity. In the beginning, it's helpful to have a spiritual director or trusted friend sniff out avenues of grace in our circumstance. But learning the smell of grace for yourself is a valuable tool of discipleship.

God draws near in every hour, showering us with blessings too numerous to count. Most of these gifts of presence and caring are silent and unacknowledged, like those lovers bestow on each other. Seeking God is as simple as practicing gratitude for these gifts as they come. Our prayer life blooms when prayer isn't relegated to special times and formulas, but infuses the day as we thank God for the bright sun, the warm meal, the good companion, the beauty of an unexpected flower. We seek God in church, but also in the letter from an old friend or the soft chair that receives us after an exertion. When we learn to call out while God is near, we discover how near God is at all times, and how much is done for our delight.

What are the elements of a situation in which grace is present?

SECOND READING » PHILIPPIANS 1:20C-24, 27A

So how am I to respond? I've decided that I really don't care about their motives, whether mixed, bad, or indifferent. Every time one of them opens his mouth, Christ is proclaimed, so I just cheer them on!

And I'm going to keep that celebration going because I know how it's going to turn out. Through your faithful prayers and the generous response of the Spirit of Jesus Christ, everything he wants to do in and through me will be done. I can hardly wait to continue on my course. I don't expect to be embarrassed in the least. On the contrary, everything happening to me in this jail only serves to make Christ more accurately known, regardless of whether I live or die. They didn't shut me up; they gave me a pulpit! Alive, I'm Christ's messenger; dead, I'm his bounty. Life versus even more life! I can't lose.

As long as I'm alive in this body, there is good work for me to do. If I had to choose right now, I hardly know which I'd choose. Hard choice! The desire to break camp here and be with Christ is powerful. Some days I can think of nothing better. But most days, because of what you are going through, I am sure that it's better for me to stick it out here. So I plan to be around awhile, companion to you as your growth and joy in this life of trusting God continues. You can start looking forward to a great reunion when I come visit you again. We'll be praising Christ, enjoying each other.

Meanwhile, live in such a way that you are a credit to the Message of Christ. Let nothing in your conduct hang on whether I come or not. Your conduct must be the same whether I show up to see things for myself or hear of it from a distance. Stand united, singular in vision, contending for people's trust in the Message, the good news, not flinching or dodging in the slightest before the opposition. Your courage and unity will show them what they're up against: defeat for them, victory for you—and both because of God. There's far more to this life than trusting in Christ. There's also suffering for him. And the suffering is as much a gift as the trusting. You're involved in the same kind of struggle you saw me go through, on which you are now getting an updated report in this letter.

How we envy Paul's ability to speak these words! He is pleased to live as Christ's messenger, and pleased to die and be with Christ. He's torn between two great goods, and finds the choice between life and death a win-win situation.

Most of us are quite a bit more attached to life than the possibility of death. Only when our lives are emptied of purpose and filled with pain are we attracted to death as our last hope for peace. Imagine the freedom of being able to stand between life and death and receive either one gratefully! In his love for Christ, Paul lived in that freedom and died in it.

This, then, is our goal: not the American dream, the house, the car, the thin body—but a love for Christ so strong that it liberates us from every other need. Our goal is a life so energetically free that we can love, move, sacrifice or be present as the need to serve arises. The call to a liberated heart is the call to Christ. For those like Paul who answer it fully, there are no limitations and nothing to fear.

How free are you? To what are you bound?

GOSPEL » MATTHEW 20:1-16A

"God's kingdom is like an estate manager who went out early in the morning to hire workers for his vineyard. They agreed on a wage of a dollar a day, and went to work.

"Later, about nine o'clock, the manager saw some other men hanging around the town square unemployed. He told them to go to work in his vineyard and he would pay them a fair wage. They went.

"He did the same thing at noon, and again at three o'clock. At five o'clock he went back and found still others standing around. He said, 'Why are you standing around all day doing nothing?'

"They said, 'Because no one hired us.'

"He told them to go to work in his vineyard.

"When the day's work was over, the owner of the vineyard instructed his foreman, 'Call the workers in and pay them their wages. Start with the last hired and go on to the first.'

"Those hired at five o'clock came up and were each given a dollar. When those who were hired first saw that, they assumed they would get far more. But they got the same, each of them one dollar. Taking the dollar, they groused angrily to the manager, 'These last workers put in only one easy hour, and you just made them equal to us, who slaved all day under a scorching sun.'

"He replied to the one speaking for the rest, 'Friend, I haven't been unfair. We agreed on the wage of a dollar, didn't we? So take it and go. I decided to give to the one who came last the same as you. Can't I do what I want with my own money? Are you going to get stingy because I am generous?'

"Here it is again, the Great Reversal: many of the first ending up last, and the last first."

RCIA Catholics often report that they feel somehow inferior to cradle Catholics. Having come to the church as adults, they don't share the parochial-school history and inculturated Catholic memories that veteran members of the church have. In the same way, younger people in the church feel left out of the pre-Vatican II storehouse of comparisons that the post-conciliar crowd is always using as a reference point. Latecomers in any arena can feel that their presence or commitment is less authentic. They don't have the battle scars to compete for acceptance.

Jesus doesn't hire by the years or the scars, happily, but by the heart. Having heard Mass in Latin doesn't make one more genuinely Catholic, and wearing a plaid uniform for eight years is not a certificate of authentic faith. Punching the clock doesn't make us disciples, but rather answering the call. The vineyard needs laborers. The only laborers who count are the ones whose hearts are for hire, and not just their time.

How long have you been a member of the church? How much of that time have you been authentically invested in a life of faith?

WE RESPOND

Enter a period of discernment about your call to follow Jesus. Go on a weekend retreat. Seek spiritual direction. Form a support group of friends who share your faith. Listen intently for the direction you're being invited to go.

"Here it is again, the Great Reversal: many of the first ending up last, and the last first."

.... Is God Fair?

FIRST READING » EZEKIEL 18:25-28

"Do I hear you saying, 'That's not fair! God's not fair!'?

"Listen, Israel. I'm not fair? You're the ones who aren't fair! If a good person turns away from his good life and takes up sinning, he'll die for it. He'll die for his own sin. Likewise, if a bad person turns away from his bad life and starts living a good life, a fair life, he will save his life. Because he faces up to all the wrongs he's committed and puts them behind him, he will live, really live. He won't die.

I've searched the Bible backwards and forwards, and have yet to find a verse in which one of the friends of God gets cancer and dies. Or has an accident on the road which ends her life. Or becomes disabled by stroke and lives on under perilous and sad conditions. But we've personally known many friends of God who've endured these events, and we wonder why.

The Bible often presents a fundamentalist view of fortune: God's friends find good things multiplied in their lives, and God's enemies suffer plagues and disasters. Except of course for people like Job and Jesus. Job is, by God's own admission, a thoroughly good person. Yet nothing but sorrow comes to him. Job loses his children, his possessions, and his health, and is abandoned by his wife in the midst of his suffering. His friends are cheerless and accusing. But in the long run, goodness is restored to him. And of course Jesus is the best person ever to walk the earth, yet he faces the agony and ignominy of the cross. In the end, restoration and glorification are his.

What this means for the friends of God is that suffering may not be avoidable, yet none is irredeemable. This consolation may seem faint as Job's skin festers, or as Jesus sweats blood in the garden. But both believed in a redemption they could not see, and are lifted up.

When has suffering caused you to doubt God?

SECOND READING » PHILIPPIANS 2:1-11

If you've gotten anything at all out of following Christ, if his love has made any difference in your life, if being in a community of the Spirit means anything to you, if you have a heart, if you care— then do me a favor: Agree with each other, love each other, be deep-spirited friends. Don't push your way to the front; don't sweet-talk your way to the top. Put yourself aside, and help others get ahead. Don't be obsessed with getting your own advantage. Forget yourselves long enough to lend a helping hand.

Think of yourselves the way Christ Jesus thought of himself. He had equal status with God but didn't think so much of himself that he had to cling to the advantages of that status no matter what. Not at all. When the time came, he set aside the privileges of deity and took on the status of a slave, became human! Having become human, he stayed human. It was an incredibly humbling process. He didn't claim special privileges. Instead, he lived a selfless, obedient life and then died a selfless, obedient death—and the worst kind of death at that—a crucifixion.

Because of that obedience, God lifted him high and honored him far beyond anyone or anything, ever, so that all created beings in heaven and on earth— even those long ago dead and buried—will bow in worship before this Jesus Christ, and call out in praise that he is the Master of all, to the glorious honor of God the Father.

The exact nature of Jesus' equality with God is something theologians have debated for twenty centuries. But one thing is not up for debate: the idea that Jesus chooses to relinquish his unique equality out of obedience. God's will is more precious than what Jesus could claim as his right. Jesus could have taken, as rightfully his, everything the devil offers during the temptation in the desert. But he chose much less, so that we might have infinitely more.

Is God fair? Thankfully, the answer is no. God is much, much better than human fairness would allow. God does not answer us with eye-for-an-eye justice, or the whole world would be blind in an hour. God answers sin with forgiveness, and death with new life. God makes the last first and the first last. If God were fair, our cries for mercy would be useless. If God were fair, Jesus wouldn't have been born in a stable or ascended the cross. But because God is better than fair, we have hope of joy that doesn't end, no matter who we've been or what little we've done to earn it. Fairness is a small thing, compared with grace.

Do you treat people fairly, giving as good as you get?
Or do go beyond fairness as God does?

GOSPEL » MATTHEW 21:28-32

"Tell me what you think of this story: A man had two sons. He went up to the first and said, 'Son, go out for the day and work in the vineyard.'

"The son answered, 'I don't want to.' Later on he thought better of it and went.

"The father gave the same command to the second son. He answered, 'Sure, glad to.' But he never went.

"Which of the two sons did what the father asked?"

They said, "The first."

Jesus said, "Yes, and I tell you that crooks and whores are going to precede you into God's kingdom. John came to you showing you the right road. You turned up your noses at him, but the crooks and whores believed him. Even when you saw their changed lives, you didn't care enough to change and believe him.

I have an employee who drives me crazy. He does nothing I ask him to do: is always late, leaves early, takes endless breaks, follows my orders only when it suits him. Most of the time he does just what he wants to do, and is completely ungovernable.

Why don't I fire this guy? Because, although he does nothing I ask him to do, he does everything well. He does what needs to be done, and sometimes more than I would ever expect from anyone. Though I tear my hair out about his blatant disregard for my wishes, I have to admit he's the best I've ever seen. He's like the first son in the parable: he says No but does Yes.

Lots of people say No but do Yes in the reign of God. They don't go to church, baptize their babies, or live by the Book in the way we would like. They don't seem to worship the same God we do, or any God at all. Yet God has a different abacus than ours, and the tally may come out better for them than for faithful churchgoers who live by the Book but have no love in their hearts. Is this fair? Not while we are pushing the beads, perhaps. But God doesn't stoop so low as fairness, and all kinds of unlikely people are making their way toward the Kingdom.

> **Are you more like the first or second son in the parable?**
> **Can you forgive the other son?**

WE RESPOND

Conquer judgmentalism! Whenever the little judge pops up in your mind and condemns a fellow traveler, retire him promptly. And watch out for the way the little judge accuses YOU. Show mercy to all, including yourself.

*"Don't be obsessed with getting
your own advantage.
Forget yourselves long enough
to lend a helping hand."*

TWENTY-SEVENTH SUNDAY IN ORDINARY TIME

FIRST READING » ISAIAH 5:1-7

I'll sing a ballad to the one I love,
    a love ballad about his vineyard:
The one I love had a vineyard,
    a fine, well-placed vineyard.
He hoed the soil and pulled the weeds,
    and planted the very best vines.
He built a lookout, built a winepress,
    a vineyard to be proud of.
He looked for a vintage yield of grapes,
    but for all his pains he got junk grapes.
"Now listen to what I'm telling you,
    you who live in Jerusalem and Judah.
What do you think is going on
    between me and my vineyard?
Can you think of anything I could have done
    to my vineyard that I didn't do?
When I expected good grapes,
    why did I get bitter grapes?
"Well now, let me tell you
    what I'll do to my vineyard:
I'll tear down its fence
    and let it go to ruin.
I'll knock down the gate
    and let it be trampled.
I'll turn it into a patch of weeds, untended, uncared for—
    thistles and thorns will take over.
I'll give orders to the clouds:
    'Don't rain on that vineyard, ever!'"
Do you get it? The vineyard of God-of-the-Angel-Armies
    is the country of Israel.
All the men and women of Judah
    are the garden he was so proud of.
He looked for a crop of justice
    and saw them murdering each other.
He looked for a harvest of righteousness
    and heard only the moans of victims.

Have you ever put a lot of effort into something that didn't pan out? Studied long hours for a test and then failed anyway? Put in weekends at work only to lose the promotion? Spent years at a relationship that did not last? We've all planted a garden or two that promised flowers and produced weeds. Despite our best efforts, our will may be undone by the factors around us.

God knows what that's like. Once upon a time, God planted a garden the likes of which had not been seen before. It could have been perfect, but God decided to go one better than perfect: God made it free. Once freedom entered the garden, creation was at liberty to move with or away from the divine will, and take history along with it. What could have been vintage wine, grew up to be wild grapes.

The outcome for the vineyard in Isaiah's parable is grim. Wild grapes don't serve the vintner's purpose, and God withdraws protection and nurture from such a yield. Every plant has its season to produce; but only a season. Then comes the harvest.

What bitter grapes emerge from your freedom to choose?

SECOND READING » PHILIPPIANS 4:6-9

Don't fret or worry. Instead of worrying, pray. Let petitions and praises shape your worries into prayers, letting God know your concerns. Before you know it, a sense of God's wholeness, everything coming together for good, will come and settle you down. It's wonderful what happens when Christ displaces worry at the center of your life.

Summing it all up, friends, I'd say you'll do best by filling your minds and meditating on things true, noble, reputable, authentic, compelling, gracious—the best, not the worst; the beautiful, not the ugly; things to praise, not things to curse. Put into practice what you learned from me, what you heard and saw and realized. Do that, and God, who makes everything work together, will work you into his most excellent harmonies.

Paul knows some things in this world are false, dishonorable, unjust, and inauthentic—which is why he urges us to choose the opposite consciously. Not only to *do* what is good and gracious, but to fill ourselves up with such things. We're to choose what's worthy of praise and also to concentrate on the praiseworthy. He seems aware that it's so easy, even when choosing the good, to lust after the bad. Paul affirms what Jesus knew: that all sin begins in the mind, and spreads to the rest of us.

Often we're in the midst of doing the right thing, and sighing after the kind of life that permits the opposite choice. We may be responsible, charitable, or sympathetic, yet still contemplating the apparent freedom of those who "go fishing" while we're stuck laboring in the fields of righteousness. Contemplating wrong action is the kissing cousin of bad behavior. The longer it lingers, the closer we are to accepting its invitation.

When has brooding over a wrong action led you to bad behavior?

"Here's another story. Listen closely. There was once a man, a wealthy farmer, who planted a vineyard. He fenced it, dug a winepress, put up a watchtower, then turned it over to the farmhands and went off on a trip. When it was time to harvest the grapes, he sent his servants back to collect his profits.

"The farmhands grabbed the first servant and beat him up. The next one they murdered. They threw stones at the third but he got away. The owner tried again, sending more servants. They got the same treatment. The owner was at the end of his rope. He decided to send his son. 'Surely,' he thought, 'they will respect my son.'

"But when the farmhands saw the son arrive, they rubbed their hands in greed. 'This is the heir! Let's kill him and have it all for ourselves.' They grabbed him, threw him out, and killed him.

"Now, when the owner of the vineyard arrives home from his trip, what do you think he will do to the farmhands?"

"He'll kill them—a rotten bunch, and good riddance," they answered. "Then he'll assign the vineyard to farmhands who will hand over the profits when it's time."

Jesus said, "Right—and you can read it for yourselves in your Bibles:
The stone the masons threw out
    is now the cornerstone.
This is God's work;
we rub our eyes, we can hardly believe it!
"This is the way it is with you. God's kingdom will be taken back from you and handed over to a people who will live out a kingdom life. Whoever stumbles on this Stone gets shattered; whoever the Stone falls on gets smashed."

It sounds like the same story repeated from Isaiah: a vineyard fails to produce a harvest. But this time, it's not the grapes that fail, but the farmhands who work the land. The harvest is available, but the workers won't give it up to the owner. They're willing to go far beyond selfishness. They'll accept bloodshed to hold onto what they see as rightfully theirs.

Isaiah's parable presents sin in a passive light: a failure to produce what's good. Jesus tells a story of sin that's about actively choosing to pervert the good. These two kinds of sin have been called "acts of omission and commission" by the church. They are "what we have done and failed to do," as we confess at Mass. We are responsible for both behaviors: choosing not to do good as much as the deliberate decision for evil. Even in Jesus' time, people boasted of keeping the Ten Commandments, as though that fulfilled their obligation to God. But the absence of active evil is not the same as the presence of love.

Consider "what you have done, and what you have failed to do."
Which weighs on your conscience more?

WE RESPOND

"Cease doing evil. Learn to do good" (Isaiah 1:16-17). Turn down one temptation to uncharity every day, and replace it with a conscious choice to be gracious.

"God's kingdom will be taken back from you
and handed over to a people
who will live out a kingdom life."

TWENTY-EIGHTH SUNDAY IN ORDINARY TIME

FIRST READING » ISAIAH 25:6-10A

But here on this mountain, God-of-the-Angel-Armies
  will throw a feast for all the people of the world,
A feast of the finest foods, a feast with vintage wines,
  a feast of seven courses, a feast lavish with gourmet desserts.
And here on this mountain, God will banish
  the pall of doom hanging over all peoples,
The shadow of doom darkening all nations.
  Yes, he'll banish death forever.
And God will wipe the tears from every face.
  He'll remove every sign of disgrace
From his people, wherever they are.
  Yes! God says so!
Also at that time, people will say,
  "Look at what's happened! This is our God!
We waited for him and he showed up and saved us!
  This God, the one we waited for!
Let's celebrate, sing the joys of his salvation.
  God's hand rests on this mountain!"
As for the Moabites, they'll be treated like refuse,
  waste shoveled into a cesspool.
Thrash away as they will,
  like swimmers trying to stay afloat,
They'll sink in the sewage.
  Their pride will pull them under.
Their famous fortifications will crumble to nothing,
  those mighty walls reduced to dust.

I like to eat. And having lived in a region of the country known for its wineries, I'll take a good, choice wine when it's offered. According to prophecy, when God is the host we can expect rich food and the right wine to be served. And happily for us, when God is the host, the food has no calories and the wine holds no terrors. God would never serve anything that could harm us.

When we find ourselves at God's house at last, the veil of death will be lifted, and every tear will be wiped away. We're looking forward to that part, because we've loved those who've died and cried our share of tears over hurts and failures. We want to be there when the happy shouting starts: "This is the God we've been waiting for!" We want a happy ending to the story of the world, and to our stories too. Our faith promises there will be one, when the hand of the Lord comes to rest on us at last.

SECOND READING » PHILIPPIANS 4:12-14, 19-20

I'm glad in God, far happier than you would ever guess—happy that you're again showing such strong concern for me. Not that you ever quit praying and thinking about me. You just had no chance to show it. Actually, I don't have a sense of needing anything personally. I've learned by now to be quite content whatever my circumstances. I'm just as happy with little as with much, with much as with little. I've found the recipe for being happy whether full or hungry, hands full or hands empty. Whatever I have, wherever I am, I can make it through anything in the One who makes me who I am. I don't mean that your help didn't mean a lot to me—it did. It was a beautiful thing that you came alongside me in my troubles.

And now I have it all—and keep getting more! The gifts you sent with Epaphroditus were more than enough, like a sweet-smelling sacrifice roasting on the altar, filling the air with fragrance, pleasing God no end. You can be sure that God will take care of everything you need, his generosity exceeding even yours in the glory that pours from Jesus. Our God and Father abounds in glory that just pours out into eternity. Yes.

We've all heard the ironic line: "I been rich and I been poor. Rich is better." The person who first said that seems not to have experienced either state meaningfully. If they had, they may have realized that rich and poor are superficial realities, not touching deeply on happiness or peace at all. For the record, I've jostled back and forth between upper poverty and the middle class, and the moral struggles are surprisingly the same. Having or not having plays only a minor role in my development as a person, much less as a disciple. What we have seems less important than what we do with it.

Paul says the secret to living at the top or the bottom is to find strength, not in outward reality, but in the inward truth of Christ. Outward circumstances shift and may fail us, but Jesus is the same yesterday, today and always. Once we know that, we live like Jesus, dining one night with the upper crust and the next with a poor sinner, feeling at home at every table. If Jesus is our strength, every meal is a wedding feast, and every circumstance a cause for thanksgiving.

How much of your contentment is tied to possessions?

GOSPEL » MATTHEW 22:1-14

Jesus responded by telling still more stories. "God's kingdom," he said, "is like a king who threw a wedding banquet for his son. He sent out servants to call in all the invited guests. And they wouldn't come!

"He sent out another round of servants, instructing them to tell the guests,

'Look, everything is on the table, the prime rib is ready for carving. Come to the feast!'

"They only shrugged their shoulders and went off, one to weed his garden, another to work in his shop. The rest, with nothing better to do, beat up on the messengers and then killed them. The king was outraged and sent his soldiers to destroy those thugs and level their city.

"Then he told his servants, 'We have a wedding banquet all prepared but no guests. The ones I invited weren't up to it. Go out into the busiest intersections in town and invite anyone you find to the banquet.' The servants went out on the streets and rounded up everyone they laid eyes on, good and bad, regardless. And so the banquet was on—every place filled.

"When the king entered and looked over the scene, he spotted a man who wasn't properly dressed. He said to him, 'Friend, how dare you come in here looking like that!' The man was speechless. Then the king told his servants, 'Get him out of here—fast. Tie him up and ship him to hell. And make sure he doesn't get back in.'

"That's what I mean when I say, 'Many get invited; only a few make it.'"

This is a strange story: why would invited guests not come to a king's wedding feast? In our time, any celebrity who throws a party can expect everyone to come, the invited along with the uninvited. People want to see and be seen at notable occasions. Certainly, a royal wedding qualifies as a must-see event.

But in this story people do the remarkably inappropriate thing: they snub the king. And when the king practically begs them to come a second time, some of those invited do violence to the messengers. This is such an incredible response, we recognize that Jesus is referring to the response to himself and to prophets who came before him. No one would behave this way to a king, his son, and his servants, Jesus is saying. And yet you behave this way to God, his son, and the prophets.

As listeners to this story, we have a choice. We can be like those invited who don't bother to go, or who retaliate with rage. We can come without preparation. Or we can have something to say for ourselves if caught poorly clad at God's feast. "O God, have mercy on me, a sinner," is a good prayer to have on hand.

Which role do you see yourself playing in the parable of the wedding feast?

WE RESPOND

Dine at God's house this week. Feed the hungry, share a meal with someone who needs you, and don't forget the Eucharist.

.... Tax Time

FIRST READING » ISAIAH 45:1, 4-6

God's Message to his anointed,
    to Cyrus, whom he took by the hand
To give the task of taming the nations,
    of terrifying their kings—
He gave him free rein,
    no restrictions:
"I'll go ahead of you,
    clearing and paving the road.
I'll break down bronze city gates,
    smash padlocks, kick down barred entrances.
I'll lead you to buried treasures,
    secret caches of valuables—
Confirmations that it is, in fact, I, God,
    the God of Israel, who calls you by your name.
It's because of my dear servant Jacob,
    Israel my chosen,
That I've singled you out, called you by name,
    and given you this privileged work.
    And you don't even know me!
I am God, the only God there is.
    Besides me there are no real gods.
I'm the one who armed you for this work,
    though you don't even know me,
So that everyone, from east to west, will know
    that I have no god-rivals.
    I am God, the only God there is.
I form light and create darkness,
    I make harmonies and create discords.
    I, God, do all these things.

What an astonishing idea! God is behind the army of Cyrus, a foreigner and non-believer. God is guiding the hand of someone who never contemplated God at all. God is Lord of more than those who like to be known by the Holy Name. The consequences of this passage are considerable.

We like to think of God as the property of the Roman Catholic Church, or at least of Christianity proper. Maybe, on a generous day, we're willing to admit that the Jewish people have a prior claim to God's story as well. But the Muslims? Or the Unitarians? The Buddhists? The out-and-out atheists? Would God be willing to move in *their* histories as well as ours, use *their* leaders to some greater end? The question Isaiah raises is not simply "Who gets saved?" but "Who gets used in salvation history?" If God is Lord of all, then anyone can be part of the plan, whether they know it or not.

When have you seen a non-believer act in harmony with God's will?

SECOND READING » 1 THESSALONIANS 1:1-5B

I, Paul, together here with Silas and Timothy, send greetings to the church at Thessalonica, Christians assembled by God the Father and by the Master, Jesus Christ. God's amazing grace be with you! God's robust peace!

Every time we think of you, we thank God for you. Day and night you're in our prayers as we call to mind your work of faith, your labor of love, and your patience of hope in following our Master, Jesus Christ, before God our Father. It is clear to us, friends, that God not only loves you very much but also has put his hand on you for something special. When the Message we preached came to you, it wasn't just words. Something happened in you. The Holy Spirit put steel in your convictions.

You paid careful attention to the way we lived among you, and determined to live that way yourselves. In imitating us, you imitated the Master. Although great trouble accompanied the Word, you were able to take great joy from the Holy Spirit! — taking the trouble with the joy, the joy with the trouble.

Religion can never be a matter of words: saying we believe this or that about God, the pope, or life after death. The power of what we believe has to be *lived*. If our faith makes no difference in us, then what we say is a lie. If we believe God is real, Jesus is Lord, and the Spirit of holiness lives in us, then such power would have to be felt, wouldn't it? We would experience it transforming our way of life, and others would see our conviction and be challenged by it.

Saint Paul rejoices in the Thessalonians because they not only accepted the gospel and were baptized, but the Spirit's power moved among them at once. Where do we see this kind of holy power moving in our community? Are people being healed, divisions mended? Does a spirit of hope and peace exist around us? Is there generosity toward the unfortunate, encouragement for the fallen? Is truth spoken where we live? If signs like these are not among us, then the authentic experience of faith is yet to come.

Consider a person you know who lives what he or she believes.
How is the Holy Spirit evident in that person?

GOSPEL » MATTHEW 22:15-21

That's when the Pharisees plotted a way to trap him into saying something damaging. They sent their disciples, with a few of Herod's followers mixed in, to ask, "Teacher, we know you have integrity, teach the way of God accurately, are indifferent to popular opinion, and don't pander to your students. So tell us honestly: Is it right to pay taxes to Caesar or not?"

Jesus knew they were up to no good. He said, "Why are you playing these games with me? Why are you trying to trap me? Do you have a coin? Let me see it." They handed him a silver piece.

"This engraving—who does it look like? And whose name is on it?"

They said, "Caesar."

"Then give Caesar what is his, and give God what is his."

What is a tax? In the best of circumstances, it's a private payment for the public good. It's how individuals contribute to the interests of the community of which they're a part. In the time of the Roman empire, taxation among the occupied provinces was a troubling matter. It could be argued that what went into the pocket of Rome went out of the province for good.

Those who questioned Jesus about taxes, of course, weren't asking for a moral decision. They wanted him to betray himself by being politically incorrect in front of the people. And Jesus, of course, was above politics, framing his answer in larger terms than the Pharisees cared to consider. Those who are obliged to Caesar should certainly make payment in the coin of the realm. But those who are obliged to God— and who isn't?—owe a debt to be paid in the province of the human spirit. It is this larger obligation that should capture our concern.

Do we commit more of our time, energy, and resources to Caesar or to God? What do we currently give to Caesar that belongs to God?

WE RESPOND

Consider making a new tithe to God. Allot a portion of your time to worship, contemplation or spiritual reading. Give a portion of your wealth to the needy. Spend a portion of your energy on a just cause.

"Then give Caesar what is his, and give God what is his."

THIRTIETH SUNDAY IN ORDINARY TIME

FIRST READING » EXODUS 22:20-26

"Anyone who sacrifices to a god other than God alone must be put to death.

"Don't abuse or take advantage of strangers; you, remember, were once strangers in Egypt.

"Don't mistreat widows or orphans. If you do and they cry out to me, you can be sure I'll take them most seriously; I'll show my anger and come raging among you with the sword, and your wives will end up widows and your children orphans.

"If you lend money to my people, to any of the down-and-out among you, don't come down hard on them and gouge them with interest.

"If you take your neighbor's coat as security, give it back before nightfall; it may be your neighbor's only covering—what else does the person have to sleep in? And if I hear the neighbor crying out from the cold, I'll step in—I'm compassionate.

Who is my neighbor? Another way of phrasing that question is: for whom am I responsible? Early on in the story of the Bible, the people of God assume a responsibility beyond the expected relationships to family and tribe. Anyone who dines at the table of an Israelite or receives hospitality in his home is guaranteed the full protection due a member of the household. Table fellowship makes the stranger a friend.

When Jesus tells the story of the good Samaritan, he defines neighbor in the largest possible sense, including the enemy. Jesus also excludes as a neighbor anyone who doesn't accept responsibility natural to tribe and kin.

Today, we shrink-wrap the meaning of neighbor to its narrowest definition. Culturally we limit our responsibilities to the nuclear family at best. At worst, we look out for Number One and cast off parents, children, spouses, and friends. Our unwillingness to be neighbor to many—or any—makes local harmony unlikely, and global peace impossible. However we define the word, God hears the cries of our neighbors in the widest possible terms.

Who is your neighbor? For whom do you share responsibility?

SECOND READING » 1 THESSALONIANS 1:5C-10

Every time we think of you, we thank God for you. Day and night you're in our prayers as we call to mind your work of faith, your labor of love, and your patience of hope in following our Master, Jesus Christ, before God our Father. It is clear to us, friends, that God not only loves you very much but also has put his hand on you for something special. When the Message we preached came to you, it wasn't just words. Something happened in you. The Holy Spirit put steel in your convictions.

You paid careful attention to the way we lived among you, and determined to live that way yourselves. In imitating us, you imitated the Master. Although great trouble accompanied the Word, you were able to take great joy from the Holy Spirit!—taking the trouble with the joy, the joy with the trouble.

Do you know that all over the provinces of both Macedonia and Achaia believers look up to you? The word has gotten around. Your lives are echoing the Master's Word, not only in the provinces but all over the place. The news of your faith in God is out. We don't even have to say anything anymore—you're the message! People come up and tell us how you received us with open arms, how you deserted the dead idols of your old life so you could embrace and serve God, the true God. They marvel at how expectantly you await the arrival of his Son, whom he raised from the dead—Jesus, who rescued us from certain doom.

Paul was understandably proud of the Thessalonians. They embraced the gospel he preached as wholeheartedly as they could, rejecting idolatry, carrying the flame of the Holy Spirit even farther in their own missionary zeal. They showed the kind of total conversion the rest of us may only dream about.

Think back to something that captured your imagination so completely, you became obsessed by the beauty of its message. Children and teenagers most often have this experience: generations fell in love with *Star Trek's* Prime Directive; The Force in the *Star Wars* series; or the benevolent magic of Harry Potter's world. As an avid reader, I surrendered my heart to one story after another, always convinced that the last novel I'd read contained the key to noble living or the meaning of existence. Do we ever come close to feeling that way about the story of God and its thrilling message of fullness of life? When we do, we'll feel the passion of the Thessalonians alive in us.

> **To what do you surrender your passion?**
> **Would you call your response in faith passionate?**

GOSPEL » MATTHEW 22:34-40

When the Pharisees heard how he had bested the Sadducees, they gathered their forces for an assault. One of their religion scholars spoke for them, posing a question they hoped would show him up: "Teacher, which command in God's Law is the most important?"

Jesus said, "'Love the Lord your God with all your passion and prayer and intelligence.' This is the most important, the first on any list. But there is a second to set alongside it: 'Love others as well as you love yourself.' These two commands are pegs; everything in God's Law and the Prophets hangs from them."

Moses drew the bottom line for the people of God when he presented the stone tablets to them at the base of Sinai: *Here are ten things you must, and must not, do.* Love God, honor your parents; don't lie, steal, kill. Most of us know the commandments well enough to know when we break them, without peeking back at Exodus.

To ask — which commandment of God is the greatest? — is a bit like asking for a hierarchy of evil for future reference. The popularity of lists of venial and mortal sins is that they give us guidelines as to how far we can go in sin before we're over our heads. As Robert Orbin says, most of us would like to be delivered from evil—but would like to keep in touch. The great commandment of Jesus doesn't give us that option. Loving God with heart, soul, and mind is a pretty exclusive commitment. When it comes to monogamy, even a little infidelity is too much.

How does your commitment to God measure up against the Ten Commandments? How does it measure against the love command of Jesus?

WE RESPOND

Express your love for God this week in prayer, praise and thanksgiving. Express your love for your neighbor, near and far, in concrete and significant ways.

"These two commands are pegs; everything in God's Law and the Prophets hangs from them."

THIRTY-FIRST SUNDAY IN ORDINARY TIME

FIRST READING » MALACHI 1:14B—2:2B, 8-10

*"A curse on the person who makes a big show of doing something great for me—
an expensive sacrifice, say—and then at the last minute brings in something
puny and worthless! I'm a great king, God-of-the-Angel-Armies, honored far and
wide, and I'll not put up with it!"*

*"And now this indictment, you priests! If you refuse to obediently listen, and
if you refuse to honor me, God-of-the-Angel-Armies, in worship, then I'll put you
under a curse. I'll exchange all your blessings for curses. In fact, the curses are
already at work because you're not serious about honoring me. Yes, and the curse
will extend to your children. I'm going to plaster your faces with rotting garbage,
garbage thrown out from your feasts. That's what you have to look forward to!*

Feeling a little outrage lately? Read the book of Malachi: three short chapters of
prophecy in which the writer blasts just about everybody in the name of the Lord.
Sometimes we get the urge to do the same, but Malachi does it better than anybody.
The prophet starts with an oracle criticizing the religious leaders, but before the laity
can get too comfortable, he switches his audience halfway through and points out
the sins of the populace as well.

Malachi writes anonymously: the name means only "My Messenger," since the
writer claims to speak for God. God's message as he proclaims it is two-fold. The
main theme of his writing is "Repent and be forgiven, or prepare to be destroyed,"
a common refrain in prophecy. But the underlying platform is that God's in charge.
This isn't a random world, where we can get away with murder. This is God's world,
and actions have celestial consequences. Beyond hearing of God's outrage, we get
an affirmation of God's sovereignty. Those who remember the latter will not suffer
the other.

> **How is God "in charge" of your life?**
> **In what ways are you still in charge?**

SECOND READING » 1 THESSALONIANS 2:7B-9, 13

*Even though we had some standing as Christ's apostles, we never threw our
weight around or tried to come across as important, with you or anyone else.
We weren't aloof with you. We took you just as you were. We were never
patronizing, never condescending, but we cared for you the way a mother cares
for her children. We loved you dearly. Not content to just pass on the Message, we
wanted to give you our hearts. And we did.*

*You remember us in those days, friends, working our fingers to the bone,
up half the night, moonlighting so you wouldn't have the burden of supporting
us while we proclaimed God's Message to you. You saw with your own eyes*

how discreet and courteous we were among you, with keen sensitivity to you as fellow believers. And God knows we weren't freeloaders! You experienced it all firsthand. With each of you we were like a father with his child, holding your hand, whispering encouragement, showing you step-by-step how to live well before God, who called us into his own kingdom, into this delightful life.

And now we look back on all this and thank God, an artesian well of thanks! When you got the Message of God we preached, you didn't pass it off as just one more human opinion, but you took it to heart as God's true word to you, which it is, God himself at work in you believers!

I used to teach preaching at a seminary. One of the hardest things to wean students away from was the desire to give a speech instead of a homily. The difference was unclear to them at first: weren't they supposed to give a little talk about the readings? Weren't they supposed to tell people what to do, how to live? Well, that would be fine, of course, if every preacher could be trusted to *know* what to do and how to live. That isn't the preacher's job, in fact. The task of the preacher is to proclaim God's word and break it open so that we all can hear it.

"I made it my aim to preach only Christ and him crucified," Saint Paul once asserted. Paul had been a student of one of the greatest rabbis of his day. He could easily have impressed others with his learning, his careful theology, his eloquent rhetoric. But Paul gave that up in favor of letting the word of God do its thing, allowing the power of God to act. He trusted God's word enough to set it free wherever he went. And no missionary born of woman was ever as successful as Paul.

> How do you make room in your life for the word of God:
> at Mass on Sundays? in private reading? in Bible study?
> in sacred song or some other medium?

GOSPEL » MATTHEW 23:1-12

Now Jesus turned to address his disciples, along with the crowd that had gathered with them. "The religion scholars and Pharisees are competent teachers in God's Law. You won't go wrong in following their teachings on Moses. But be careful about following them. They talk a good line, but they don't live it. They don't take it into their hearts and live it out in their behavior. It's all spit-and-polish veneer.

"Instead of giving you God's Law as food and drink by which you can banquet on God, they package it in bundles of rules, loading you down like pack animals. They seem to take pleasure in watching you stagger under these loads, and wouldn't think of lifting a finger to help. Their lives are perpetual fashion shows, embroidered prayer shawls one day and flowery prayers the next. They love to sit at the head table at church dinners, basking in the most prominent positions, preening in the radiance of public flattery, receiving honorary degrees, and getting called 'Doctor' and 'Reverend.'

"Don't let people do that to you, put you on a pedestal like that. You all have

a single Teacher, and you are all classmates. Don't set people up as experts over your life, letting them tell you what to do. Save that authority for God; let him tell you what to do. No one else should carry the title of 'Father'; you have only one Father, and he's in heaven. And don't let people maneuver you into taking charge of them. There is only one Life-Leader for you and them—Christ.

"Do you want to stand out? Then step down. Be a servant. If you puff yourself up, you'll get the wind knocked out of you. But if you're content to simply be yourself, your life will count for plenty.

Rabbi, father, master. In the time of Jesus, these were terms of respect reserved for people in authority. Jesus was a controversial figure precisely because of his power to command. He seemed to have a natural authority expressed in his words and extraordinary works, whereas the leaders with lofty titles often failed to demonstrate any real signs of leadership. We can safely say this is a modern problem as well. The titles and trappings of leadership do not necessarily identify people with the ability to lead. Someone may be a president, priest, or professor, but authority has to be earned personally and not simply academically or electorally.

We have to be careful in deciding whom to follow and how to lead. We choose the leaders, thinkers, and do-ers who will serve as our moral guides. Some we will outgrow, and some will continue to inform our consciences. In turn, we have authority over others around us—the young, the weak, the voiceless—and we have to use our power for their benefit. The way to make both choices well is to reflect on how Jesus is our ultimate master and teacher. Jesus is anointed with God's authority. All legitimate leadership imitates his example.

What kind of authority does Jesus wield in your life?

WE RESPOND

Reflect on the most difficult situation you face in your life right now, and surrender it into God's hands. Give God the authority to bring about the best outcome for you.

"Do you want to stand out?
Then step down. Be a servant."

THIRTY-SECOND SUNDAY IN ORDINARY TIME

FIRST READING » WISDOM 6:12-16

Lady Wisdom is smartly spoken, impeccably dressed; her door is always open; she's quick to make friends. These last she surprises, addressing them by name; no name tags for her. Those who join the line to meet her don't have long to wait. As the sun rises, there she is, sitting on her porch. You have only to look at her to get the picture; her smile eases tension, lifts depression.

Those who need her the most become her pets.

"Knowledge is power," Ben Franklin once said. In this country, a good education is the key to open the coveted doors to opportunity and financial security. But one thing that doesn't come bundled automatically with knowledge is wisdom. For that, you have to go to the source.

And who or what is the source of wisdom? Hebrew Scriptures tell of Lady Wisdom, God's partner in creation, an active agent of God's desire. What God wants, Wisdom makes clear to those who seek her. And Wisdom doesn't play hide-n-seek; rather, she energetically makes her rounds in the hopes of meeting one who waits for her. Wisdom is our guide on the sacred journey toward harmonizing our lives with God's will.

Knowledge may bring us worldly power and success. But the remarkable peace and purposefulness that belong to the wise can't be bought or studied. Wisdom is God's gift for those who look for her. She waits even now at the gate.

Where do you look for wisdom?

SECOND READING » 1 THESSALONIANS 4:13-18

And regarding the question, friends, that has come up about what happens to those already dead and buried, we don't want you in the dark any longer. First off, you must not carry on over them like people who have nothing to look forward to, as if the grave were the last word. Since Jesus died and broke loose from the grave, God will most certainly bring back to life those who died in Jesus.

And then this: We can tell you with complete confidence—we have the Master's word on it—that when the Master comes again to get us, those of us who are still alive will not get a jump on the dead and leave them behind. In actual fact, they'll be ahead of us. The Master himself will give the command. Archangel thunder! God's trumpet blast! He'll come down from heaven and the dead in Christ will rise—they'll go first. Then the rest of us who are still alive at the time will be caught up with them into the clouds to meet the Master. Oh, we'll be walking on air! And then there will be one huge family reunion with the Master. So reassure one another with these words.

What happens to those who have died? What will happen to us when *we* die? The Old Testament is largely silent on this important matter. Hebrew tradition didn't develop a theology of life after death. Vague hints of an ongoing life with God emerge only in late writings like Wisdom and Maccabees.

The letters of Paul offer us repeated affirmations of resurrected life: "If we die with Christ, we'll live with Christ" (2 Tm 2:11). This is so crucial to Paul's theology that he dares to say faith is meaningless without the promise of resurrection (1 Cor 15:14). This is no academic matter since people we love have died and are dying, and we ourselves face death, sooner or later. To me, eternal life with God isn't an article within the Creed so much as a hope I have for my sister who died at forty, or for a friend whose hand I held while he slipped away. The death of my friend was particularly affecting, because the moment he no longer inhabited his body, all of us in the room were powerfully aware of his presence, full and wonderful, everywhere around us. In the midst of our tears, we began laughing together, sharing his joy at being liberated from a suffering body and delivered into a gracious new reality. This is our faith, and mere words about life after death can't begin to communicate its meaning.

> **Do you believe in resurrection?**
> **What does resurrected life mean to you?**

GOSPEL » MATTHEW 25:1-13

"God's kingdom is like ten young virgins who took oil lamps and went out to greet the bridegroom. Five were silly and five were smart. The silly virgins took lamps, but no extra oil. The smart virgins took jars of oil to feed their lamps. The bridegroom didn't show up when they expected him, and they all fell asleep.

"In the middle of the night someone yelled out, 'He's here! The bride-groom's here! Go out and greet him!'

"The ten virgins got up and got their lamps ready. The silly virgins said to the smart ones, 'Our lamps are going out; lend us some of your oil.'

"They answered, 'There might not be enough to go around; go buy your own.'

"They did, but while they were out buying oil, the bridegroom arrived. When everyone who was there to greet him had gone into the wedding feast, the door was locked.

"Much later, the other virgins, the silly ones, showed up and knocked on the door, saying, 'Master, we're here. Let us in.'

"He answered, 'Do I know you? I don't think I know you.'

"So stay alert. You have no idea when he might arrive."

For several years I worked in downtown San Francisco. It's a lovely city by every standard, but it has one drawback that gives newcomers pause: it's located on an earthquake fault line. When you ask long-term residents how they cope with the idea that at any moment, without warning, their entire world could collapse under their feet, they look at you with the amusement of experience. "You get used to it," they tell you.

Most people who live on fault lines dismiss the odds. They don't have the emergency supplies on hand that local phone books recommend: enough bottled water for several days, flashlights, spare batteries, a transistor radio. To non-residents, this seems like madness. But consider all the things you may not be prepared for. How many people go through life without health insurance? Who prepares for divorce, disability, or unemployment? In some ways, we all go about without oil in our lamps, like the five in the story, playing the odds that we won't come up short.

One way to be prepared for any eventuality is to ground our lives, not in fluctuating circumstances, but in Christ. Though the earth shiver and crack open beneath us someday, we won't be lost if Christ is the bedrock upon which we stand.

> **What is the central truth upon which your life is grounded?**
> **Will that truth support you "come hell or high water"?**

WE RESPOND

Keep vigil for wisdom. Make time for spiritual reading regularly, as well as prayer, solitude, and worship. Get into the habit of discerning God's will as you make decisions regarding relationships and resources.

"So stay alert.
You have no idea when he might arrive."

THIRTY-THIRD SUNDAY IN ORDINARY TIME

....Faithful in Small Matters

FIRST READING » PROVERBS 31:10-13, 19-20, 30-31

A good woman is hard to find,
*   and worth far more than diamonds.*
Her husband trusts her without reserve,
*   and never has reason to regret it.*
Never spiteful, she treats him generously
*   all her life long.*
She shops around for the best yarns and cottons,
*   and enjoys knitting and sewing.*
She's like a trading ship that sails to faraway places
*   and brings back exotic surprises.*
She's up before dawn, preparing breakfast
*   for her family and organizing her day.*
She looks over a field and buys it,
*   then, with money she's put aside, plants a garden.*
First thing in the morning, she dresses for work,
*   rolls up her sleeves, eager to get started.*
She senses the worth of her work,
*   is in no hurry to call it quits for the day.*
She's skilled in the crafts of home and hearth,
*   diligent in homemaking.*
She's quick to assist anyone in need,
*   reaches out to help the poor.*
She doesn't worry about her family when it snows;
*   their winter clothes are all mended and ready to wear.*
She makes her own clothing,
*   and dresses in colorful linens and silks.*
Her husband is greatly respected
*   when he deliberates with the city fathers.*
She designs gowns and sells them,
*   brings the sweaters she knits to the dress shops.*
Her clothes are well-made and elegant,
*   and she always faces tomorrow with a smile.*
When she speaks she has something worthwhile to say,
*   and she always says it kindly.*
She keeps an eye on everyone in her household,
*   and keeps them all busy and productive.*
Her children respect and bless her;

her husband joins in with words of praise:
"Many women have done wonderful things,
*   but you've outclassed them all!"*
Charm can mislead and beauty soon fades.
*   The woman to be admired and praised*
*   is the woman who lives in the Fear-of-God.*
Give her everything she deserves!
*   Festoon her life with praises!*

Praise all the holy women who have inspired us through the years! This includes extraordinary figures like Mary, mother of all who say yes; and Teresa of Avila, Catherine of Siena, and foundresses of religious communities like Catherine McAuley and Clare of Assisi. In our own time, Mother Teresa showed us how to love the dying, Dorothy Day insisted we feed the hungry, and Catherine de Hueck Dougherty founded Friendship House to increase conversation between Christians. Often in this world, we throw up our hands and say nothing can be done. These women were among those who rolled up their sleeves and did something.

We can also point to women whose names are known only to us and God: our mothers and sisters and teachers who revealed compassion and courage in their example. I remember the religious sister who loved me back to life during a troubled adolescence, and the women in my parish who make aid to the needy a priority in their lives. I think of friends who faced the perils of growing up female to become women of graciousness and good humor. The value of these women, as the writer of Proverbs seems to know, is beyond pearls, and their worth can't be measured by the style of their hair or the prettiness of their clothes. Society has long admired the appearance of a woman and not her substance. God grant that we know better.

> **Who are the holy women who have inspired you**
> **and how did their example affect you?**

SECOND READING » 1 THESSALONIANS 5:1-6

I don't think, friends, that I need to deal with the question of when all this is going to happen. You know as well as I that the day of the Master's coming can't be posted on our calendars. He won't call ahead and make an appointment any more than a burglar would. About the time everybody's walking around complacently, congratulating each other—"We've sure got it made! Now we can take it easy!"—suddenly everything will fall apart. It's going to come as suddenly and inescapably as birth pangs to a pregnant woman.

But friends, you're not in the dark, so how could you be taken off guard by any of this? You're sons of Light, daughters of Day. We live under wide open skies and know where we stand. So let's not sleepwalk through life like those others. Let's keep our eyes open and be smart. People sleep at night and get drunk at night. But not us! Since we're creatures of Day, let's act like it. Walk out into the daylight sober, dressed up in faith, love, and the hope of salvation.

Peace and security. The older I get, the more I prefer these two things to most else that life can offer. A spirit untroubled by anger and unforgiveness is a great gift, but it has to be cultivated everyday to pluck out the weeds of discord that can sprout up any hour. Security too is a fragile prize, its stillness disturbed by small fears and doubts like a finger touching the surface of a pond.

As creatures of Day, we know our peace and security don't rely on the circumstances of the present hour, but in the eternal realm. Children of Day remain vigilant for God's hour: any hour in which God calls us into service. Living in the light means being aware that the veil separating heaven and earth is made of illusions of our own self-sufficiency. Angels pass between heaven and earth at all times; we have only to acknowledge the messenger to receive the message. Sometimes we pretend heaven is far away and God is hidden, just to absolve ourselves for not paying attention. If we choose light, the illumination of God's nearness may blind us to the faint treasures of this world for good.

> Think of a time when you felt peaceful and secure.
> What contributed to those feelings?

GOSPEL » MATTHEW 25:14-30

"It's also like a man going off on an extended trip. He called his servants together and delegated responsibilities. To one he gave five thousand dollars, to another two thousand, to a third one thousand, depending on their abilities. Then he left. Right off, the first servant went to work and doubled his master's investment. The second did the same. But the man with the single thousand dug a hole and carefully buried his master's money.

"After a long absence, the master of those three servants came back and settled up with them. The one given five thousand dollars showed him how he had doubled his investment. His master commended him: 'Good work! You did your job well. From now on be my partner.'

"The servant with the two thousand showed how he also had doubled his master's investment. His master commended him: 'Good work! You did your job well. From now on be my partner.'

"The servant given one thousand said, 'Master, I know you have high standards and hate careless ways, that you demand the best and make no allowances for error. I was afraid I might disappoint you, so I found a good hiding place and secured your money. Here it is, safe and sound down to the last cent.'

"The master was furious. 'That's a terrible way to live! It's criminal to live cautiously like that! If you knew I was after the best, why did you do less than the least? The least you could have done would have been to invest the sum with the bankers, where at least I would have gotten a little interest.

"'Take the thousand and give it to the one who risked the most. And get rid of this "play-it-safe" who won't go out on a limb. Throw him out into utter darkness."

I was talking to a group of small children about the gifts God had given them. One girl seemed unconvinced. Her older sister, she told me with dewy-eyed admiration, had all the talent in the family: intelligence, athletic ability, and creativity. She herself, however, had none.

On the contrary, I assured her, she had many gifts of her own. She had a generous love for her sister, a pleasant personality, a warm smile, and a way of making people happy to talk with her. These were talents from God, too, and I urged her to name other things she was good at that were less obvious than these.

Some weeks later I was at home, having a bad spell of writer's block, and began to feel frustrated with the blank computer screen. Going to the mailbox to retrieve my letters, I noticed one printed in pencil. It was from the little girl I had spoken with, and inside the envelope was a crayon drawing with these simple words penciled alongside: *You have talents. God created you to use your talents. NAME THEM.* In a moment, my sense of failure was gone, replaced by a child's wonderful courage. She gave the story of the talents back to me multiplied, and I got back to work exhilarated.

> **What talents have you been given by God,
> and how have you invested them?**

WE RESPOND

Give thanks to a woman who has inspired you with her holy fidelity. If possible, call or write and tell her what her example has meant for you. If not, spend a day appreciating her by emulating her witness.

*"If you knew I was after the best,
   why did you do less than the least?"*

CHRIST THE KING

FIRST READING » EZEKIEL 34:11-12, 15-17

God, the Master, says: From now on, I myself am the shepherd. I'm going looking for them. As shepherds go after their flocks when they get scattered, I'm going after my sheep. I'll rescue them from all the places they've been scattered to in the storms. I'll bring them back from foreign peoples, gather them from foreign countries, and bring them back to their home country. I'll feed them on the mountains of Israel, along the streams, among their own people. I'll lead them into lush pasture so they can roam the mountain pastures of Israel, graze at leisure, feed in the rich pastures on the mountains of Israel. And I myself will be the shepherd of my sheep. I myself will make sure they get plenty of rest. I'll go after the lost, I'll collect the strays, I'll doctor the injured, I'll build up the weak ones and oversee the strong ones so they're not exploited.

"And as for you, my dear flock, I'm stepping in and judging between one sheep and another, between rams and goats. Aren't you satisfied to feed in good pasture without taking over the whole place? Can't you be satisfied to drink from the clear stream without muddying the water with your feet? Why do the rest of my sheep have to make do with grass that's trampled down and water that's been muddied?"

Does God really love the poor, and hate the rich? Sometimes Scripture sounds that way to us. Jesus compares the relationship of the rich person and God's kingdom to a camel trying to get through a needle's eye. Ezekiel talks about God destroying the sleek and the strong, and binding up the lost, injured and sick.

But if you read all of Ezekiel chapter 34, you see his prophecy concerns those who "pasture themselves" at the expense of those in their care. The disadvantaged are always at the mercy of those with the advantage. God's outrage is not directed at wealth but at those who ignore the essential responsibility that comes with it. Those who "pasture themselves" are parents who build careers while neglecting their children; employers who cheat their workers of a just wage; educators more interested in research than mentoring their students; pastors more concerned with popularity than in guiding their communities to Christ. We all wield power and authority—our "wealth"—somewhere in our lives. Which means someone is looking to us for justice, mercy, or nurturing. Sometimes this means surrendering our dollar bills to the needy, but just as often it means using our authority compassionately and fairly.

**What kinds of power are exercised in your community?
Where is power used fairly, and where is it used to benefit the powerful?**

SECOND READING » 1 CORINTHIANS 15:20-26, 28

If corpses can't be raised, then Christ wasn't, because he was indeed dead. And if Christ weren't raised, then all you're doing is wandering about in the dark, as lost as ever. It's even worse for those who died hoping in Christ and resurrection, because they're already in their graves. If all we get out of Christ is a little inspiration for a few short years, we're a pretty sorry lot. But the truth is that Christ has been raised up, the first in a long legacy of those who are going to leave the cemeteries.

There is a nice symmetry in this: Death initially came by a man, and resurrection from death came by a man. Everybody dies in Adam; everybody comes alive in Christ. But we have to wait our turn: Christ is first, then those with him at his Coming, the grand consummation when, after crushing the opposition, he hands over his kingdom to God the Father. He won't let up until the last enemy is down—and the very last enemy is death! As the psalmist said, "He laid them low, one and all; he walked all over them." When Scripture says that "he walked all over them," it's obvious that he couldn't at the same time be walked on. When everything and everyone is finally under God's rule, the Son will step down, taking his place with everyone else, showing that God's rule is absolutely comprehensive—a perfect ending!

Talk about power! Here's the Christian bottom line: in the end, Christ will subdue every power, both public and personal, and lay creation at God's feet. What will this mean for those who've put their trust in governments, in economies, in their own wits and charisma? All earthly authority will be revealed as irrelevant as it really is. When God is shown to be "absolutely comprehensive," then all the false gods we've diligently worshipped will seem pretty foolish.

So what can we do *now* to prepare for "the perfect ending" ahead? Live as though it were today. God is comprehensively in possession of the world *right now*. When we live in harmony with God's will, we're soon convinced that the day of the Lord is already happening. The more we surrender to it, the more Kingdom Come arrives in our midst. As a priest friend of mine loves to say, "Don't wait until you die to go to heaven." Heaven is pressing against the windows at all times, waiting for an invitation to come in.

> **How much of your life is surrendered to God,**
> **and how much do other forces exercise power over you?**
> **What would it take to make your surrender to God more complete?**

GOSPEL » MATTHEW 25:31-46

"When he finally arrives, blazing in beauty and all his angels with him, the Son of Man will take his place on his glorious throne. Then all the nations will be arranged before him and he will sort the people out, much as a shepherd sorts out sheep and goats, putting sheep to his right and goats to his left.

"Then the King will say to those on his right, 'Enter, you who are blessed by my Father! Take what's coming to you in this kingdom. It's been ready for you since the world's foundation. And here's why:

> I was hungry and you fed me,
> I was thirsty and you gave me a drink,
> I was homeless and you gave me a room,
> I was shivering and you gave me clothes,
> I was sick and you stopped to visit,
> I was in prison and you came to me.'

"Then those 'sheep' are going to say, 'Master, what are you talking about? When did we ever see you hungry and feed you, thirsty and give you a drink? And when did we ever see you sick or in prison and come to you?' Then the King will say, 'I'm telling the solemn truth: Whenever you did one of these things to someone overlooked or ignored, that was me—you did it to me.'

"Then he will turn to the 'goats,' the ones on his left, and say, 'Get out, worthless goats! You're good for nothing but the fires of hell. And why? Because—

> I was hungry and you gave me no meal,
> I was thirsty and you gave me no drink,
> I was homeless and you gave me no bed,
> I was shivering and you gave me no clothes,
> Sick and in prison, and you never visited.'

"Then those 'goats' are going to say, 'Master, what are you talking about? When did we ever see you hungry or thirsty or homeless or shivering or sick or in prison and didn't help?'

"He will answer them, 'I'm telling the solemn truth: Whenever you failed to do one of these things to someone who was being overlooked or ignored, that was me—you failed to do it to me.'

"Then those 'goats' will be herded to their eternal doom, but the 'sheep' to their eternal reward."

The church year ends this week. Our calendar year is not far behind. These endings carry a certain finality about them. We've spent the year studying Matthew's gospel, with its emphasis on God's kingdom. We look forward to the start of a new cycle following Mark, who ponders the identity of Jesus and the meaning of his coming. We're always glad to get to Advent, the happy season of warmth and giving. But before we leap into tomorrow, this church year has one more lesson to teach us.

The liturgical calendar always ends with Christ the King, but the readings for this feast are remarkably different each time. In Matthew's year, Christ's kingship is defined in terms of judgment. A ruler has the power to separate good from evil, lives worthy of reward from those deserving punishment. Rulers establish the rules and enforce them. But in Matthew's judgment scene, the rules turn out to be completely different from what everyone expected. The Son of Man doesn't quiz people about whether they went to church or obeyed the commandments. No one is asked about divorce or sexual purity or saying their prayers. What does concern the king is how the saddest members of society were treated.

If we took the quiz today, how would we do? This is an appropriate reflection for the end of the year. It's also a good time to consider how we might prepare to pass this exam at the mother of all endings.

Ask yourself the questions that appear in the last judgment.
Where do you stand today, with the sheep or the goats?

WE RESPOND

Find a way to answer the needs of the hungry and thirsty, the stranger and the naked, the sick and imprisoned, in the upcoming year. Gifts of generosity, hospitality, and compassion are always in season.

"I'm telling the solemn truth:
Whenever you did one of these things
to someone overlooked or ignored,
that was me—you did it to me."

OTHER FEASTS, SOLEMNITIES AND HOLY DAYS

THE PRESENTATION OF THE LORD (FEBRUARY 2)

.... Sending the Messenger

FIRST READING » MALACHI 3:1-4

"Look! I'm sending my messenger on ahead to clear the way for me. Suddenly, out of the blue, the Leader you've been looking for will enter his Temple—yes, the Messenger of the Covenant, the one you've been waiting for. Look! He's on his way!" A Message from the mouth of God-of-the-Angel-Armies.

But who will be able to stand up to that coming? Who can survive his apearance?

He'll be like white-hot fire from the smelter's furnace. He'll be like the strongest lye soap at the laundry. He'll take his place as a refiner of silver, as a cleanser of dirty clothes. He'll scrub the Levite priests clean, refine them like gold and silver, until they're fit for God, fit to present offerings of righteousness. Then, and only then, will Judah and Jerusalem be fit and pleasing to God, as they used to be in the years long ago.

"Elvis is in the room!" my friend announces when he wants us to rise and greet an honored guest. It always works. We rise for "Elvis." And we'd rise for the likes of Shakespeare, too, as 19th-century essayist Charles Lamb once wrote: "But if Jesus Christ should come in, we would all kneel." In the person of Jesus, the standard of awe reaches a magnitude well beyond celebrity.

The presence of the Holy is an unmistakable experience. Walking into an empty church, we're instinctively hushed by our awareness of the sacred, the palpable sense of generations of prayer and worship, the fullness of the communion of saints, living here and in the kingdom coming. We have that awareness in the presence of nature's wonders, or the hour when hope is realized or love is made real. The prophet describes the encounter with God as a purifying experience, purging away everything that is not "good as gold" within us. No wonder our instinct is to get down on our knees.

> **In what places or circumstances are you aware of the presence of holiness?**
> **How do you respond to that awareness?**

SECOND READING » HEBREWS 2:14-18

Since the children are made of flesh and blood, it's logical that the Savior took on flesh and blood in order to rescue them by his death. By embracing death, taking it into himself, he destroyed the Devil's hold on death and freed all who cower through life, scared to death of death.

It's obvious, of course, that he didn't go to all this trouble for angels. It was for people like us, children of Abraham. That's why he had to enter into every detail of human life. Then, when he came before God as high priest to get rid of the people's sins, he would have already experienced it all himself—all the pain, all the testing—and would be able to help where help was needed.

Jesus is the ultimate messenger of God, higher than angels, more powerful than prophets. Even more precisely, Jesus is the message, the very word God speaks. When Jesus comes, it's not simply a time for reverence. It's a time to listen; and just as important, a time to respond.

Jesus preaches freedom, something folks in this country are particularly passionate about. But Jesus means a higher freedom than the political liberty to shape our own destinies. Jesus offers liberty from the consequences of sin and death—and the road to that freedom runs through a healing, cosmic forgiveness. We live with a natural fear of death and all of its previews: sickness, disability, loss, loneliness. Still we may embrace occasions of sin that bring on this death. Who wants to give up the habits of our favorite sin even while they enslave us?

Which habits of sin captivate you?
What steps can you take to embrace the freedom Jesus offers?

GOSPEL » LUKE 2:22–40

Then when the days stipulated by Moses for purification were complete, they took him up to Jerusalem to offer him to God as commanded in God's Law: "Every male who opens the womb shall be a holy offering to God," and also to sacrifice the "pair of doves or two young pigeons" prescribed in God's Law.
In Jerusalem at the time, there was a man, Simeon by name, a good man, a man who lived in the prayerful expectancy of help for Israel. And the Holy Spirit was on him. The Holy Spirit had shown him that he would see the Messiah of God before he died. Led by the Spirit, he entered the Temple. As the parents of the child Jesus brought him in to carry out the rituals of the Law, Simeon took him into his arms and blessed God:

God, you can now release your servant;
    release me in peace as you promised.
With my own eyes I've seen your salvation;
    it's now out in the open for everyone to see:
A God-revealing light to the non-Jewish nations,
    and of glory for your people Israel.

Jesus' father and mother were speechless with surprise at these words. Simeon went on to bless them, and said to Mary his mother,

This child marks both the failure and

the recovery of many in Israel,
A figure misunderstood and contradicted—
    the pain of a sword-thrust through you—
But the rejection will force honesty,
    as God reveals who they really are.

Anna the prophetess was also there, a daughter of Phanuel from the tribe of Asher. She was by now a very old woman. She had been married seven years and a widow for eighty-four. She never left the Temple area, worshiping night and day with her fastings and prayers. At the very time Simeon was praying, she showed up, broke into an anthem of praise to God, and talked about the child to all who were waiting expectantly for the freeing of Jerusalem.

When they finished everything required by God in the Law, they returned to Galilee and their own town, Nazareth. There the child grew strong in body and wise in spirit. And the grace of God was on him.

Talk about causing a stir! When Mary and Joseph present their child in the Temple as prescribed by religious law, all heaven breaks loose. The holy man Simeon offers a blessing and a prophecy regarding the boy, calling him a light as well as a sign of contradiction. He warns Mary of sadness to come, but declares it necessary for the unmasking of hearts.

Then the prophetess Anna appears. She's a faithful widow of the sort found throughout Scripture (not to mention the history of the church, which once viewed widowhood as a religious vocation.) The love Anna once shared with her husband is now lavished in constant communion with God. She becomes an early apostle of the good news: Redemption has arrived!

Now it's our turn, to bring God's blessing into the world and to announce the time of redemption. As Simeon and Anna both demonstrate, prophecy doesn't start with religious talk. Our lives are the first and most eloquent message we deliver.

Who's been a messenger of good news to you?
How do you bring news of redemption to others?

WE RESPOND

Refine the message your life delivers. Simplify. Get silence. Choose peace. When tempted to judge, forgive.

"With my own eyes I've seen your salvation;
    it's now out in the open for everyone to see."

SAINTS PETER AND PAUL, APOSTLES (JUNE 29)

FIRST READING » ACTS OF THE APOSTLES 12:1-11

That's when King Herod got it into his head to go after some of the church members. He murdered James, John's brother. When he saw how much it raised his popularity ratings with the Jews, he arrested Peter—all this during Passover Week, mind you—and had him thrown in jail, putting four squads of four soldiers each to guard him. He was planning a public lynching after Passover.

All the time that Peter was under heavy guard in the jailhouse, the church prayed for him most strenuously.

Then the time came for Herod to bring him out for the kill. That night, even though shackled to two soldiers, one on either side, Peter slept like a baby. And there were guards at the door keeping their eyes on the place. Herod was taking no chances!

Suddenly there was an angel at his side and light flooding the room. The angel shook Peter and got him up: "Hurry!" The handcuffs fell off his wrists. The angel said, "Get dressed. Put on your shoes." Peter did it. Then, "Grab your coat and let's get out of here." Peter followed him, but didn't believe it was really an angel—he thought he was dreaming.

Past the first guard and then the second, they came to the iron gate that led into the city. It swung open before them on its own, and they were out on the street, free as the breeze. At the first intersection the angel left him, going his own way. That's when Peter realized it was no dream. "I can't believe it—this really happened! The Master sent his angel and rescued me from Herod's vicious little production and the spectacle the Jewish mob was looking forward to."

How dangerous a character was Peter? In Herod's view, he warrants double chains and a heavy guard. Peter wasn't armed, nor did he have a marked history of violence. (He did cut off the ear of the high priest's slave once—though the fellow gets it back.) Lately, Peter's been occupied with healing the sick and preaching the gospel, neither seemingly threatening activities. But the mood of Jerusalem is uneasy. Since the death of Jesus, Stephen has been martyred. Recently King Herod had James slain, the first apostle to be killed. Peter knows his own trial before Herod tomorrow will not go in his favor. Herod, delighted that the death of James made him popular, is very willing to execute another apostle. He isn't counting on the possibility of an angel opening the prison door, and Peter slipping through his fingers. Double chains, in the end, aren't enough to keep the good news from escaping.

> How does the gospel enable us
> to elude the chains that bind us?
> When have you been set free by a liberating word?

SECOND READING » 2 TIMOTHY 4:6-8, 17-18

You take over. I'm about to die, my life an offering on God's altar. This is the only race worth running. I've run hard right to the finish, believed all the way. All that's left now is the shouting—God's applause! Depend on it, he's an honest judge. He'll do right not only by me, but by everyone eager for his coming.

At my preliminary hearing no one stood by me. They all ran like scared rabbits. But it doesn't matter—the Master stood by me and helped me spread the Message loud and clear to those who had never heard it. I was snatched from the jaws of the lion! God's looking after me, keeping me safe in the kingdom of heaven. All praise to him, praise forever! Oh, yes!

No one knows exactly what happened to Paul at the end of his life. Church tradition places his beheading in Rome in the 60s at the hands of the Roman Empire. According to the same tradition, Peter was crucified because he was Jewish, little better than a slave to Roman eyes. But Paul was a Roman citizen as well as a Jew, so he was eligible for the preferred treatment of beheading. The Bible records nothing of their deaths, even though New Testament writers continued to contribute to the story through the end of the first century.

From the letters of Paul we know he, like Peter, spent time in jail. Paul was convinced he would "finish the race" there. But other traditions hold that Paul won his case before Caesar, was set free, and completed his missionary journey to Spain and died there—or in Rome at a later date. Whenever and however he died, we believe Paul knew the ultimate rescue at the hands of the one for whom he had "kept the faith" so long and so well.

> **When have you poured yourself out**
> **for something or someone you believed in?**
> **Who invested that kind of effort in you?**
> **What did you learn from these offerings?**

GOSPEL » MATTHEW 16:13-19

When Jesus arrived in the villages of Caesarea Philippi, he asked his disciples, "What are people saying about who the Son of Man is?"

They replied, "Some think he is John the Baptizer, some say Elijah, some Jeremiah or one of the other prophets."

He pressed them, "And how about you? Who do you say I am?"

Simon Peter said, "You're the Christ, the Messiah, the Son of the living God."

Jesus came back, "God bless you, Simon, son of Jonah! You didn't get that answer out of books or from teachers. My Father in heaven, God himself, let you in on this secret of who I really am. And now I'm going to tell you who you are, really are. You are Peter, a rock. This is the rock on which I will put together my church, a church so expansive with energy that not even the gates of hell will be able to keep it out.

"And that's not all. You will have complete and free access to God's kingdom, keys to open any and every door: no more barriers between heaven and earth, earth and heaven. A yes on earth is yes in heaven. A no on earth is no in heaven."

Peter and Paul were clear about who Jesus was. Well, maybe not always; but they got it right when it mattered most. Peter called Jesus the Son of the Living God: he also said he didn't know him (three horrible times). Paul wrote some of the most beautiful words ever to be said about Jesus. He also spent a period of his life sending to their deaths anyone who said things like that.

The good news is they both got another chance to name Jesus again, which they did and answered correctly. That's why they get a feast day so big it overrides the normal Sunday celebration. How about us? How do we answer the question? Who is Jesus—not theologically now, but in relationship to us: Is he Lord, or obligation? Friend, or foe? Brother, or stranger? Good news, or just religion?

If you met someone who wanted to know who Jesus is, what would you say? Make a list of ten things you think are important to say about Jesus.

WE RESPOND

Honor Saints Peter and Paul by celebrating Christian liberation! Reach out to someone in chains, whether imprisoned or ill, mentally depressed, spiritually oppressed, or economically cornered.

"My Father in heaven, God himself,
let you in on this secret of who I really am."

THE TRANSFIGURATION OF THE LORD (AUGUST 6)

....Wheels of Burning Fire

FIRST READING » DANIEL 7:9-10, 13-14

"As I was watching all this,
"Thrones were set in place
    and The Old One sat down.
His robes were white as snow,
    his hair was white like wool.
His throne was flaming with fire,
    its wheels blazing.
A river of fire
    poured out of the throne.
Thousands upon thousands served him,
    tens of thousands attended him.
The courtroom was called to order,
    and the books were opened.
"I kept watching. The little horn was speaking arrogantly. Then, as I watched, the
monster was killed and its body cremated in a roaring fire. The other animals
lived on for a limited time, but they didn't really do anything, had no power to
rule. My dream continued.
"I saw a human form, a son of man,
    arriving in a whirl of clouds.
He came to The Old One
    and was presented to him.
He was given power to rule—all the glory of royalty.
    Everyone—race, color, and creed—had to serve him.
His rule would be forever, never ending.
    His kingly rule would never be replaced.

Scenes of glory in the Bible are often portrayed in terms similar to these in the prophecies of Daniel. Dazzling clothes, a flaming throne, and a heavenly cast of thousands! Our response can only be—and is intended to be—awe and wonder. The Ancient One is remarkable to behold.

We too encounter scenes of glory from time to time on a more human scale, but they're no less rapturous. Think of the first sight of a newborn baby, so small and yet such a perfectly formed life. Recall the faces of a bride and groom as they turn from the priest and exit the church, glowing with love and promise. Remember your last vacation at the ocean or in the mountains: how vast and beautiful the world seemed from that perspective. Sometimes it's an exquisite cloudscape, or love in the eyes of someone dear, that opens your heart and admits wonder. Maybe you've spent time at a retreat center, and finally had a spiritual breakthrough that clears your vision and shows you the path you've been looking for.

Could it be that all of these things are ways of beholding the glory of the Ancient One? Wherever we are, the wheels of fire are spinning and burning all the while.

When and where have you seen glory?

SECOND READING » 2 PETER 1:16-19

We weren't, you know, just wishing on a star when we laid the facts out before you regarding the powerful return of our Master, Jesus Christ. We were there for the preview! We saw it with our own eyes: Jesus resplendent with light from God the Father as the voice of Majestic Glory spoke: "This is my Son, marked by my love, focus of all my delight." We were there on the holy mountain with him. We heard the voice out of heaven with our very own ears.

We couldn't be more sure of what we saw and heard—God's glory, God's voice. The prophetic Word was confirmed to us. You'll do well to keep focusing on it. It's the one light you have in a dark time as you wait for daybreak and the rising of the Morning Star in your hearts. The main thing to keep in mind here is that no prophecy of Scripture is a matter of private opinion. And why? Because it's not something concocted in the human heart. Prophecy resulted when the Holy Spirit prompted men and women to speak God's Word.

Some people live as if a shadow's been cast over their lives. They labor in sunless places and find no satisfaction in their work. Everything they do seems to be rooted in purposelessness. They cannot find meaning in anything. They have no place to go, no hope of getting there. No matter what they do, they feel lost. But the life of a Christian is never lost.

The writers of the first-century church felt sure they were in possession of a prophetic message, burning like a lamp in a dark place. We are in possession of this same light, which guides us even through the darkest seasons of our lives. Some call it blessed assurance. Some define it as a code of moral values. We can point to grace, Scripture, the sacraments, or the contemplative life, all illuminated by that same light. However you understand it, attend to that light. One day, the morning star will ascend in our hearts, and justice and peace will kiss. Until that time, follow the light.

Where do you encounter the light of faith, and how do you attend to it?

GOSPEL » MARK 9:2-10

Six days later, three of them did see it. Jesus took Peter, James, and John and led them up a high mountain. His appearance changed from the inside out, right before their eyes. His clothes shimmered, glistening white, whiter than any bleach could make them. Elijah, along with Moses, came into view, in deep conversation with Jesus.

Peter interrupted, "Rabbi, this is a great moment! Let's build three memorials—one for you, one for Moses, one for Elijah." He blurted this out without thinking, stunned as they all were by what they were seeing.

Just then a light-radiant cloud enveloped them, and from deep in the cloud, a voice: "This is my Son, marked by my love. Listen to him."

The next minute the disciples were looking around, rubbing their eyes, seeing nothing but Jesus, only Jesus.

Coming down the mountain, Jesus swore them to secrecy. "Don't tell a soul what you saw. After the Son of Man rises from the dead, you're free to talk." They puzzled over that, wondering what on earth "rising from the dead" meant.

The disciples stood in a privileged place. They beheld the unmitigated glory of Christ. Frankly, they were terrified by the sight.

There's a tradition behind the terror. The Bible continually asserts that no one can see the face of God and live. Abraham hid behind a rock when God passed by, and saw the divine only in departure. Most of the people who touched divine things—the Ark of the Covenant, or the utensils of the Temple—were struck dead for their insolence. Glimpses of God are not healthy for sinners. When Isaiah talks about "the fear of the Lord," he isn't kidding.

Moses encountered God "face to face" in Exodus, whatever that means exactly, on Mount Sinai. And for the privilege , his face turned transfiguration-white. Moses also spent the rest of his life with the Israelites around his neck like an albatross. You and I don't want to be Moses.

So when it's the disciples' turn to see divinity revealed, they are pretty shaken. But they survive, and are ordered not to talk about it until more glory comes into the world than anyone can imagine. It's easy to see why they kept their promise.

How can you both love and "fear" God?

WE RESPOND

Pay attention to light in all its forms. Spend time with a candle, a kerosene lamp, a lit fireplace, moonlight, starlight. Contemplate headlights and tail lights on the freeway. What can light teach you?

"This is my Son, marked by my love.
Listen to him."

THE ASSUMPTION OF THE BLESSED VIRGIN MARY (AUGUST 15)

.... Women and Dragons

FIRST READING » REVELATION 11:19A; 12:1-6A, 10A

The doors of God's Temple in Heaven flew open, and the Ark of his Covenant was clearly seen surrounded by flashes of lightning, loud shouts, peals of thunder, an earthquake, and a fierce hailstorm.

A great Sign appeared in Heaven: a Woman dressed all in sunlight, standing on the moon, and crowned with Twelve Stars. She was giving birth to a Child and cried out in the pain of childbirth.

And then another Sign alongside the first: a huge and fiery Dragon! It had seven heads and ten horns, a crown on each of the seven heads. With one flick of its tail it knocked a third of the Stars from the sky and dumped them on earth. The Dragon crouched before the Woman in childbirth, poised to eat up the Child when it came.

The Woman gave birth to a Son who will shepherd all nations with an iron rod. Her Son was seized and placed safely before God on his Throne. The Woman herself escaped to the desert to a place of safety prepared by God, all comforts provided her for 1,260 days.

Women and dragons go together in ancient tales. Women represent the vulnerable aspect of humanity, not to mention its future as keepers of the womb. Dragons represent everything we most fear, the chaotic, destructive forces that threaten our extinction. As long as there are women, there will be dragons.

Fortunately for us, there is also a God who delights in the mother and child, and snatches them up to freedom at the proper time. Salvation history is full of stories of the poor one rescued from destruction by God's own hand. If we're more accustomed to seeing the vulnerable ones sacrificed to evil intentions in our time, perhaps it's because we're less likely to raise our own hands against it. "Survival of the fittest" has become a motto that excuses our responsibility to the weak and the small. If we don't raise our hands against the dragons, we become them. And in the end, when the mother and child give testimony, God will take their word over ours.

> **Who or what are the dragons in our culture?**
> **Whom do they threaten?**

SECOND READING » 1 CORINTHIANS 15:20-27

If corpses can't be raised, then Christ wasn't, because he was indeed dead. And if Christ weren't raised, then all you're doing is wandering about in the dark, as lost as ever. It's even worse for those who died hoping in Christ and resurrection, because they're already in their graves. If all we get out of Christ is a little inspiration for a few short years, we're a pretty sorry lot. But the truth is that Christ has been raised up, the first in a long legacy of those who are going to leave the cemeteries.

There is a nice symmetry in this: Death initially came by a man, and resurrection from death came by a man. Everybody dies in Adam; everybody comes alive in Christ. But we have to wait our turn: Christ is first, then those with him at his Coming, the grand consummation when, after crushing the opposition, he hands over his kingdom to God the Father. He won't let up until the last enemy is down—and the very last enemy is death! As the psalmist said, "He laid them low, one and all; he walked all over them." When Scripture says that "he walked all over them," it's obvious that he couldn't at the same time be walked on. When everything and everyone is finally under God's rule, the Son will step down, taking his place with everyone else, showing that God's rule is absolutely comprehensive—a perfect ending!

The greatest dragon facing us is death. Mortality sets the clock from the moment we're conceived, and not one of us is guaranteed more than the present hour. We cope with the reality of our dying by not really believing in it until the time arrives. We cannot live with this particular dragon in the house. It is too big.

Jesus slew this dragon. Every authority on earth must bend its knee to Jesus, and death is no exception. This is the great promise of our faith. The very source of destruction will be destroyed, and our disbelief in death will be justified at last. In the meantime, we still watch our loved ones fall prey to destructive forces of many kinds. The apparent victory of death lures us under its spell, hoping we'll put more faith in death than in the power of resurrection. This is the greatest mistake we can make. Believing in dragons enhances their authority over us. So, too, belief in Christ.

> **Name some destructive forces operating in your family or community.**
> **How do you resist their power?**

GOSPEL » LUKE 1:39-56

Mary didn't waste a minute. She got up and traveled to a town in Judah in the hill country, straight to Zachariah's house, and greeted Elizabeth. When Elizabeth heard Mary's greeting, the baby in her womb leaped. She was filled with the Holy Spirit, and sang out exuberantly,
You're so blessed among women,
*   and the babe in your womb, also blessed!*
And why am I so blessed that
*   the mother of my Lord visits me?*
The moment the sound of your
*   greeting entered my ears,*
The babe in my womb
*   skipped like a lamb for sheer joy.*

Blessed woman, who believed what God said,
*   believed every word would come true!*
And Mary said,
I'm bursting with God-news;
*   I'm dancing the song of my Savior God.*
God took one good look at me, and look what happened—
*   I'm the most fortunate woman on earth!*
What God has done for me will never be forgotten,
*   the God whose very name is holy, set apart from all others.*
His mercy flows in wave after wave
*   on those who are in awe before him.*
He bared his arm and showed his strength,
*   scattered the bluffing braggarts.*
He knocked tyrants off their high horses,
*   pulled victims out of the mud.*
The starving poor sat down to a banquet;
*   the callous rich were left out in the cold.*
He embraced his chosen child, Israel;
*   he remembered and piled on the mercies, piled them high.*
It's exactly what he promised,
*   beginning with Abraham and right up to now.*
Mary stayed with Elizabeth for three months and then went back to her own
home.

Mary had to slay some dragons, when an angel first pronounced her blessed. She had to conquer fear, then disbelief. She had to overcome the urge to say *No thank you*, when the invitation to disrupt her life for the sake of God's child came her way. She had to slay the doubt that arose in her betrothed husband who nearly divorced her, and the murmuring disapproval of the town. One by one, the dragons came to her at night, intimidating her with second thoughts and questions that could not be answered. Through it all, God protected her and the child from harm.

When Mary meets her cousin she bursts into song, telling the story of how many a monster is slain for those who are God's beloved. God's mercy is greater than our fear, she sings. And Mary rides that belief all the way to heaven, tradition tells us.

The story of Mary's Assumption is not in Scripture, but it is written in our hearts. We believe God dispenses with the borders between life and death for this woman of faith. She is the woman who faced the ultimate dragon, with God as her champion. Snatched from death's power, she lives with the One who calls her blessed. In her story, we hear our own greatest hope.

God has called you blessed.
What doubts must you overcome for this blessing to bear fruit?

THIS TRANSFORMING WORD

WE RESPOND

Jesus overcomes the powers of destruction. Choose a dragon that resides in you, and pray that Jesus will break its power over your life.

God took one good look at me,
and look what happened—
> *I'm the most fortunate woman on earth!*
What God has done for me
will never be forgotten,
> *the God whose very name is holy,*
> *set apart from all others.*

EXALTATION OF THE HOLY CROSS (SEPTEMBER 14)

FIRST READING » NUMBERS 21:4B-9

They set out from Mount Hor along the Red Sea Road, a detour around the land of Edom. The people became irritable and cross as they traveled. They spoke out against God and Moses: "Why did you drag us out of Egypt to die in this godforsaken country? No decent food; no water—we can't stomach this stuff any longer."

So God sent poisonous snakes among the people; they bit them and many in Israel died. The people came to Moses and said, "We sinned when we spoke out against God and you. Pray to God; ask him to take these snakes from us."

Moses prayed for the people.

God said to Moses, "Make a snake and put it on a flagpole: Whoever is bitten and looks at it will live."

So Moses made a snake of fiery copper and put it on top of a flagpole. Anyone bitten by a snake who then looked at the copper snake lived.

Snakes in the camp! And these, the people feared, were sent by God to punish them for complaining. I don't know about you, but when my mother told me to stop whining, she never put snakes in my room to underscore the point. The suspicion that God makes a bad situation worse if we moan about it is something that's hard to shake, however. Guilt is a powerful shaper of theology. When the inner judge tells us we've done wrong, we may be tempted to attribute the consequences we suffer to God.

So God pointed the people back to the snake. God breaks one of the Ten Commandments to do it, too—the one about making images. Look at evil and know what it is, God seems to be saying. Blame the poison on the snake, not on an act of Mine. The ones who looked at the bronze serpent got better. Those who refused to do so, we can imagine, chose the poison over the cure, not trusting in "the God who made them sick" to make them well.

> **When have you been tempted to view God**
> **as the source of evil, suffering, or misfortune?**
> **How can we see God as the source of goodness and our burdens?**

SECOND READING » PHILIPPIANS 2:6-11

Think of yourselves the way Christ Jesus thought of himself. He had equal status with God but didn't think so much of himself that he had to cling to the advantages of that status no matter what. Not at all. When the time came, he set aside the privileges of deity and took on the status of a slave, became human! Having become human, he stayed human. It was an incredibly humbling process. He didn't claim special privileges. Instead, he lived a selfless, obedient life and then died a selfless, obedient death—and the worst kind of death at that—a crucifixion.

Because of that obedience, God lifted him high and honored him far beyond anyone or anything, ever, so that all created beings in heaven and on earth— even those long ago dead and buried—will bow in worship before this Jesus Christ, and call out in praise that he is the Master of all, to the glorious honor of God the Father.

Folks around Jesus viewed suffering and evil as the will of God at work in the world. It's a strange idea when you think about it: why would the God who created everything and called it good, turn around and unleash such anguish into the works? When Jesus sees the world brimming with sorrow, he's moved with pity and seeks to alleviate pain wherever he finds it. He speaks consolation and joy to the hopeless. He even forgives sinners on the spot, without even demanding a full and frank confession! Jesus leaves the privileges of divinity behind to become one of us. But he doesn't leave behind the compassionate heart of God, which aches for humanity all the time.

In healing the world's hurt, Jesus demonstrates clearly that God is not the source of suffering and evil but is eager to remove it from our lives. The cross is proof that God will go to any lengths to turn our sorrow into joy.

> **Which gospel story most powerfully illustrates**
> **for you the compassion of God?**
> **How do you live out that compassion for the sake of others?**

GOSPEL » JOHN 3:13–17

"No one has ever gone up into the presence of God except the One who came down from that Presence, the Son of Man. In the same way that Moses lifted the serpent in the desert so people could have something to see and then believe, it is necessary for the Son of Man to be lifted up—and everyone who looks up to him, trusting and expectant, will gain a real life, eternal life.

"This is how much God loved the world: He gave his Son, his one and only Son. And this is why: so that no one need be destroyed; by believing in him, anyone can have a whole and lasting life. God didn't go to all the trouble of sending his Son merely to point an accusing finger, telling the world how bad it was. He came to help, to put the world right again. Anyone who trusts in him is acquitted; anyone who refuses to trust him has long since been under the death sentence without knowing it. And why? Because of that person's failure to believe in the one-of-a-kind Son of God when introduced to him.

Saved or condemned? That's the question on the minds of many religious believers. For some, it comes down to a choice. Whether that choice is ours or God's depends on your theology. Are some chosen to be saved and others damned despite our best efforts? Do we choose all in a moment to be saved, or is our rescue a lifelong occupation? Do we contribute to our salvation, or is the effort entirely on God's part? Christians of good will disagree on these matters.

But we all agree on one thing: the cross of Jesus demonstrates the great evil in the world, and the great goodness of God. Human decision condemns Jesus to the cross, and heavenly decision lifts him out of his grave. The stark contrast between what people choose and what God chooses is made plain through this same cross. We may mean to destroy, but God means to save. We celebrate the cross today because it exalts God's design triumphing over ours. Jesus surrenders into the hands of sinners, and today we call him Christ our Lord.

How would you understand salvation: as a decision or a participation? Do we share in the work of salvation, or is it something God does for us?

WE RESPOND

Honor the cross today. Meditate before a crucifix in church, pray the Stations, or contemplate artists' renderings of the crucifixion at a museum. You may want to draw, paint, or fashion a cross from other materials for your reflection.

"This is how much God loved the world:
He gave his Son, his one and only Son."

ALL SAINTS DAY (NOVEMBER 1)

.... We Are God's Children Now

FIRST READING » REVELATION 7:2–4, 9-14

Then I saw another Angel rising from where the sun rose, carrying the seal of the Living God. He thundered to the Four Angels assigned the task of hurting earth and sea, "Don't hurt the earth! Don't hurt the sea! Don't so much as hurt a tree until I've sealed the servants of our God on their foreheads!"

I heard the count of those who were sealed: 144,000! They were sealed out of every Tribe of Israel: 12,000 sealed from Judah, 12,000 from Reuben, 12,000 from Gad, 12,000 from Asher, 12,000 from Naphtali, 12,000 from Manasseh, 12,000 from Simeon, 12,000 from Levi, 12,000 from Issachar, 12,000 from Zebulun, 12,000 from Joseph, 12,000 sealed from Benjamin.

I looked again. I saw a huge crowd, too huge to count. Everyone was there— all nations and tribes, all races and languages. And they were standing, dressed in white robes and waving palm branches, standing before the Throne and the Lamb and heartily singing:

> *Salvation to our God on his Throne!*
> *Salvation to the Lamb!*

All who were standing around the Throne—Angels, Elders, Animals—fell on their faces before the Throne and worshiped God, singing:

> *Oh, Yes!*
> *The blessing and glory and wisdom and thanksgiving,*
> *The honor and power and strength,*
> *To our God forever and ever and ever!*
> *Oh, Yes!*

Just then one of the Elders addressed me: "Who are these dressed in white robes, and where did they come from?" Taken aback, I said, "O Sir, I have no idea—but you must know."

Then he told me, "These are those who come from the great tribulation, and they've washed their robes, scrubbed them clean in the blood of the Lamb. That's why they're standing before God's Throne. They serve him day and night in his Temple. The One on the Throne will pitch his tent there for them: no more hunger, no more thirst, no more scorching heat. The Lamb on the Throne will shepherd them, will lead them to spring waters of Life. And God will wipe every last tear from their eyes."

Some of us have selective hearing, as my Mom used to call it. We hear what we want to hear or sometimes what we expect is being said, regardless of the actual message. Whether we tend to hear the confirmation of our fondest wishes or our greatest fears is a matter of habit for most of us. Either way, we may wind up on the far side of the truth.

How many Christians, for example, have taken as gospel truth that 144,000 is the precise number of those who will be saved? It's a satisfying round number for those who like to quantify salvation and limit it to the right sort of people. But in the same passage from Revelations, the next sentence in fact, before the throne of God stands this uncountable multitude who are also happily delivered into God's presence shouting praises. Why do some folks prefer to ignore this merry crowd entirely?

Are you optimistic or pessimistic about the realm of salvation?
How does your perspective color your judgment of others?

SECOND READING » 1 JOHN 3:1–3

What marvelous love the Father has extended to us! Just look at it—we're called children of God! That's who we really are. But that's also why the world doesn't recognize us or take us seriously, because it has no idea who he is or what he's up to.

But friends, that's exactly who we are: children of God. And that's only the beginning. Who knows how we'll end up! What we know is that when Christ is openly revealed, we'll see him—and in seeing him, become like him. All of us who look forward to his Coming stay ready, with the glistening purity of Jesus' life as a model for our own.

When my brother died, we heard this reading as if for the first time at the funeral Mass. Years later at the death of my father, my family chose to use this passage from the First Letter of John again. It has two very wonderful and comforting things to say. One is that all of us gathered here are the children of God, right now. It doesn't matter who's going to church these days and who isn't; who's been keeping all the rules and who's been a bull in the china shop when it comes to living right. The other thing it reminds us is that none of us knows what's yet to be revealed. God's ways are mysterious; God's thoughts are higher than ours. What we hardly dare to hope for is within God's power to bring into being. And whatever we fear the most, God can save us from without breaking a sweat. So hope big!

How big or small is your hope?
How does the size of your hope affect the way you live?

GOSPEL » MATTHEW 5:1–12A

When Jesus saw his ministry drawing huge crowds, he climbed a hillside. Those who were apprenticed to him, the committed, climbed with him. Arriving at a quiet place, he sat down and taught his climbing companions. This is what he said:

"You're blessed when you're at the end of your rope. With less of you there is more of God and his rule.

"You're blessed when you feel you've lost what is most dear to you. Only then

can you be embraced by the One most dear to you.

"You're blessed when you're content with just who you are—no more, no less. That's the moment you find yourselves proud owners of everything that can't be bought.

"You're blessed when you've worked up a good appetite for God. He's food and drink in the best meal you'll ever eat.

"You're blessed when you care. At the moment of being 'care-full,' you find yourselves cared for.

"You're blessed when you get your inside world—your mind and heart—put right. Then you can see God in the outside world.

"You're blessed when you can show people how to cooperate instead of compete or fight. That's when you discover who you really are, and your place in God's family.

"You're blessed when your commitment to God provokes persecution. The persecution drives you even deeper into God's kingdom.

"Not only that—count yourselves blessed every time people put you down or throw you out or speak lies about you to discredit me. What it means is that the truth is too close for comfort and they are uncomfortable. You can be glad when that happens—give a cheer, even!—for though they don't like it, I do! And all heaven applauds. And know that you are in good company. My prophets and witnesses have always gotten into this kind of trouble.

Matthew's Sermon on the Mount is one of the best-loved passages in Christianity. It inhabits the ranks of great world literature, transcending creedal boundaries. If the teachings of Jesus could be shrunk into a dozen verses, these would serve quite well. Everything Jesus taught—and lived— is right here.

So what does this sermon have to say? Those whom the world despises enjoy God's greatest blessings. Note that it doesn't say what we sometimes expect to hear: that "some day" the poor will be blessed. No: they're blessed right now, in their poverty. And the people crying now are blessed. The kids bullied in schoolyards today are blessed. Those treated unjustly are immersed in blessings. This isn't some form of spiritual delayed gratification. The blessings are real and immediate. Righting these wrongs comes later. But the blessings are here now.

How have you been blessed in the precise hour of your greatest suffering?

WE RESPOND

Join the saints in their blessed work of intercession. Commit to being a healing, forgiving, consoling presence to those around you.

ALL SOULS DAY (NOVEMBER 2)

FIRST READING » DANIEL 12:1-3

"'That's when Michael, the great angel-prince, champion of your people, will step in. It will be a time of trouble, the worst trouble the world has ever seen. But your people will be saved from the trouble, every last one found written in the Book. Many who have been long dead and buried will wake up, some to eternal life, others to eternal shame.

"'Men and women who have lived wisely and well will shine brilliantly, like the cloudless, star-strewn night skies. And those who put others on the right path to life will glow like stars forever.

Some say the era of the book is past. The future is online; who needs the printed page? Maybe tomorrow's libraries will be largely replaced by the Internet, the newspaper will be delivered electronically to every home, and the world's forests will be safe at last. After all, the phrase "written in stone" was once a literal description of the printed page. The written form continues to evolve.

But the idea of a book will always remain the same: a documentation, in its own way sacred and final. When I was a kid, looking up a word in the dictionary was the resolution of every argument. What Webster says, goes. For people of faith, the Bible often has the same "last word" vote or veto. Daniel's image of the Book of Life portrays the permanence of God's commitment to us. Once recorded, our names cannot be forgotten, and our fate is assured.

> **Is your family tree written down in a Bible?**
> **Have you ever kept a diary, journal, or blog?**
> **What gets recorded for posterity in your home?**

SECOND READING » ROMANS 6:3-9

So what do we do? Keep on sinning so God can keep on forgiving? I should hope not! If we've left the country where sin is sovereign, how can we still live in our old house there? Or didn't you realize we packed up and left there for good? That is what happened in baptism. When we went under the water, we left the old country of sin behind; when we came up out of the water, we entered into the new country of grace—a new life in a new land!

That's what baptism into the life of Jesus means. When we are lowered into the water, it is like the burial of Jesus; when we are raised up out of the water, it is like the resurrection of Jesus. Each of us is raised into a light-filled world by our Father so that we can see where we're going in our new grace-sovereign country.

Could it be any clearer? Our old way of life was nailed to the cross with Christ, a decisive end to that sin-miserable life—no longer at sin's every beck and call! What we believe is this: If we get included in Christ's sin-conquering death, we also get included in his life-saving resurrection. We know that when Jesus was raised from the dead it was a signal of the end of death-as-the-end. Never again will death have the last word. When Jesus died, he took sin down with him, but alive he brings God down to us. From now on, think of it this way: Sin speaks a dead language that means nothing to you; God speaks your mother tongue, and you hang on every word. You are dead to sin and alive to God. That's what Jesus did.

Most of us don't worry about loved ones who made it to heaven by a wide margin. We may be sure our grandmother is enjoying the presence of God, and the friend who was always close to the church. But doubt sets in as we think about the baby who died unbaptized; the fallen-away Catholic relative; the neighbor who committed suicide. Did they die without Christ? Is there a chance they still might live with him?

The church teaches that some people are certainly in heaven, like those on the rolls of the canonized saints. But the church has never taught that any particular person is in hell or even in purgatory. God's mercy is wide and our knowledge of the soul of another is very uncertain. We can always presume the door to salvation is open. That's why the church teaches us to pray for the dead: there's always room for hope.

> **How do you honor the dead, keep them in holy memory,**
> **and intercede for them in prayer?**

GOSPEL » JOHN 6:37–40

Jesus said, "I am the Bread of Life. The person who aligns with me hungers no more and thirsts no more, ever. I have told you this explicitly because even though you have seen me in action, you don't really believe me. Every person the Father gives me eventually comes running to me. And once that person is with me, I hold on and don't let go. I came down from heaven not to follow my own whim but to accomplish the will of the One who sent me.

"This, in a nutshell, is that will: that everything handed over to me by the Father be completed—not a single detail missed—and at the wrap-up of time I have everything and everyone put together, upright and whole. This is what my Father wants: that anyone who sees the Son and trusts who he is and what he does and then aligns with him will enter real life, eternal life. My part is to put them on their feet alive and whole at the completion of time."

Sometimes we have dreams of those who have died. They may seem happy and at peace, which could be a sign of consolation for us. Or they may seem preoccupied with some task set before them or troubled in some way. This could signify that they're in need of our prayers. In the Bible, dreams are treated as a realm of communication between the realities of spirit and flesh. There's no reason to believe this has changed.

Can we receive news from those who have died? Many people seem to get such messages, in dreams or in signs that have meaning only for them. A bird out of season lights on the bush a deceased husband planted. A stranger uses an odd parting phrase that a friend was famous for. Are these winks from heaven, assurances that even when we lose our dear ones, nothing is really lost?

Do you believe in life after death?
Have you experienced signs of assurance
from those who have died?

WE RESPOND

"Burying the dead" is one of the corporal works of mercy. It includes all the honor we pay to the deceased, including remembering them in the Eucharist, and keeping them in our prayers.

> *"Every person the Father gives me*
> *eventually comes running to me.*
> *And once that person is with me,*
> *I hold on and don't let go."*

THIS TRANSFORMING WORD

THE DEDICATION OF THE LATERAN BASILICA (NOVEMBER 9)

FIRST READING » EZEKIEL 47:1-2, 8-9, 12

Now he brought me back to the entrance to the Temple. I saw water pouring out from under the Temple porch to the east (the Temple faced east). The water poured from the south side of the Temple, south of the altar. He then took me out through the north gate and led me around the outside to the gate complex on the east. The water was gushing from under the south front of the Temple.

He told me, "This water flows east, descends to the Arabah and then into the sea, the sea of stagnant waters. When it empties into those waters, the sea will become fresh. Wherever the river flows, life will flourish—great schools of fish—because the river is turning the salt sea into fresh water. Where the river flows, life abounds. Fishermen will stand shoulder to shoulder along the shore from En-gedi all the way north to En-eglaim, casting their nets. The sea will teem with fish of all kinds, like the fish of the Great Mediterranean.

"But the river itself, on both banks, will grow fruit trees of all kinds. Their leaves won't wither, the fruit won't fail. Every month they'll bear fresh fruit because the river from the Sanctuary flows to them. Their fruit will be for food and their leaves for healing."

Why should we remember the Lateran Basilica, and allow it to displace the ordinary Sunday observance? Was it as important as the Temple of Jerusalem, which Ezekiel had visions about, or the temple "not made by human hands" that would become the church as we know it today?

Officially called the Basilica of the Most Holy Savior and St. John the Baptist at the Lateran, it was first built in the fourth century on the site of a palace owned by the Laterani family. Constantine gave the property to the church, and it was the pope's dwelling for nearly a thousand years. It suffered from earthquakes, barbarian attacks, and fires, and was regularly rebuilt. You can't keep a good building down. Today it is the cathedral of the Bishop of Rome (the pope), and remains a symbol of the church's endurance.

> **What perils have you endured, and what enables you to remain faithful to whom you are called to be?**

SECOND READING » 1 CORINTHIANS 3:9C-11, 16-17

Who do you think Paul is, anyway? Or Apollos, for that matter? Servants, both of us—servants who waited on you as you gradually learned to entrust your lives to our mutual Master. We each carried out our servant assignment. I planted the seed, Apollos watered the plants, but God made you grow. It's not the one who plants or the one who waters who is at the center of this process but God, who makes things grow. Planting and watering are menial servant jobs at minimum wages. What makes them worth doing is the God we are serving. You happen to be God's field in which we are working.

Or, to put it another way, you are God's house. Using the gift God gave me as a good architect, I designed blueprints; Apollos is putting up the walls. Let each carpenter who comes on the job take care to build on the foundation! Remember, there is only one foundation, the one already laid: Jesus Christ. Take particular care in picking out your building materials. Eventually there is going to be an inspection. If you use cheap or inferior materials, you'll be found out. The inspection will be thorough and rigorous. You won't get by with a thing. If your work passes inspection, fine; if it doesn't, your part of the building will be torn out and started over. But you won't be torn out; you'll survive—but just barely.

You realize, don't you, that you are the temple of God, and God himself is present in you? No one will get by with vandalizing God's temple, you can be sure of that. God's temple is sacred—and you, remember, are the temple.

It can be hard to think of ourselves as temples of holiness. So much that is unholy inhabits our lives! We may use hard language or speak of others disrespectfully. We may be careless of our health, getting too little sleep, eating junk, rarely exercising, taking no Sabbath time for play or rest. We may be bigoted or unjust, unforgiving or violent. We may treat the gift of our sexuality as a recreational item, or use our personal power to manipulate others. There are so many ways to be temples of unholiness, and only one way to invite holiness into our lives: to do as God wills.

How do we know the divine will? Living close to Scripture and the sacraments helps us align our path with God's ways. The community of faith helps; so does the practice of virtues. Like most things, we learn by doing. And we have to start somewhere: maybe today.

> **Can you identify aspects of your life**
> **that are aligned with the way of holiness?**
> **In what areas do you still have work to do?**

GOSPEL » JOHN 2:13–22

When the Passover Feast, celebrated each spring by the Jews, was about to take place, Jesus traveled up to Jerusalem. He found the Temple teeming with people selling cattle and sheep and doves. The loan sharks were also there in full strength.

Jesus put together a whip out of strips of leather and chased them out of the Temple, stampeding the sheep and cattle, upending the tables of the loan sharks, spilling coins left and right. He told the dove merchants, "Get your things out of here! Stop turning my Father's house into a shopping mall!" That's when his disciples remembered the Scripture, "Zeal for your house consumes me."

But the Jews were upset. They asked, "What credentials can you present to justify this?" Jesus answered, "Tear down this Temple and in three days I'll put it back together."

They were indignant: "It took forty-six years to build this Temple, and you're going to rebuild it in three days?" But Jesus was talking about his body as the Temple. Later, after he was raised from the dead, his disciples remembered he had said this. They then put two and two together and believed both what was written in Scripture and what Jesus had said.

It's an easy mistake to make: to confuse a building of brick and mortar with the divine dwelling. For some of us, the church remains that place on the corner with the stained glass windows where we meet on Sundays. We forget that church is also, and more accurately, the place "where two or more are gathered" in the name of Jesus, prepared to do what Jesus did.

Look around. Where do you see church in light of this understanding? Is the church where your family lives? Is it in your neighborhood or your workplace? Is it where you transact business or spend your leisure time? If you find it hard to name the places where church really happens, perhaps it's an invitation to get out there and start bringing the church to those places. It only takes "two or more." Count yourself as one.

Who makes church happen for you?
How can you do the same where you go?

WE RESPOND

Celebrate being church! Pay a visit, say a prayer, or light a candle. Bring church to someone you know who hasn't been to that building in a while. Be church for someone who would never dream of entering such a place.

"You realize, don't you,
that you are the temple of God,
and God himself is present in you?"

THE IMMACULATE CONCEPTION
OF THE BLESSED VIRGIN MARY (DECEMBER 8)

FIRST READING » GENESIS 3:9–15, 20

God called to the Man: "Where are you?"

He said, "I heard you in the garden and I was afraid because I was naked. And I hid."

God said, "Who told you you were naked? Did you eat from that tree I told you not to eat from?"

The Man said, "The Woman you gave me as a companion, she gave me fruit from the tree, and, yes, I ate it."

God said to the Woman, "What is this that you've done?"

"The serpent seduced me," she said, "and I ate."

God told the serpent:

"Because you've done this, you're cursed,
cursed beyond all cattle and wild animals,
Cursed to slink on your belly
and eat dirt all your life.
I'm declaring war between you and the Woman,
between your offspring and hers.
He'll wound your head,
you'll wound his heel."

The Man, known as Adam, named his wife Eve because she was the mother of all the living.

The story of humanity starts with No. We see this in two-year-olds, who discover their distinction from their parents as they exercise that wonderful declaration of their autonomy at the top of their lungs: "No!" It appears instinctive in human nature to define our will over-and-against the Powers That Be.

While most of us eventually learn how to pronounce our refusals to authority without piercing eardrums, not all of us master the opposite skill: aligning ourselves with authority in a constructive way. Such folks remain conflicted at a primary level and become sources of conflict everywhere they go: in school and on the playground, in their marriages and toward their employers. They have problems with government of any kind as well as the perceived tyranny of organized religion. If saying No is an important early lesson to learn for the sake of autonomy, learning to say Yes is equally vital for the sake of the common good.

> **What is my attitude toward authority?**
> **How do I discern when Yes is appropriate,**
> **and when it's time to say No with integrity?**

SECOND READING » EPHESIANS 1:3–6, 11–12

How blessed is God! And what a blessing he is! He's the Father of our Master, Jesus Christ, and takes us to the high places of blessing in him. Long before he laid down earth's foundations, he had us in mind, had settled on us as the focus of his love, to be made whole and holy by his love. Long, long ago he decided to adopt us into his family through Jesus Christ. (What pleasure he took in planning this!) He wanted us to enter into the celebration of his lavish gift-giving by the hand of his beloved Son.

It's in Christ that we find out who we are and what we are living for. Long before we first heard of Christ and got our hopes up, he had his eye on us, had designs on us for glorious living, part of the overall purpose he is working out in everything and everyone.

"Finding yourself" is a significant task of adolescence. Not all of us accomplish the job in the season designed for self-discovery, however, and put the work on hold instead. This makes us prone to jump ship mid-stream later, when we find out we're not who we thought we were or were pretending to be. If you want to avoid a midlife crisis, an honest self-appraisal at the earliest opportunity is in order.

The theology of Saint Paul recommends that, if we want to know who we really are, we can only do that "in Christ." The teachings of Jesus liberate the true man and woman within us, free from the facades of culture, class, local norms, and national bluster. In defeating the Prince of Lies, Jesus leads us to authenticity. I no longer have to be what the parents approved, the mentors insisted, or life circumstances made seem inevitable. I get to become the person God created me to discover and grow into. Life "in Christ" is the only thing worthy of the term "real life."

Who am I in "real life"—in Christ?
How is that identity in harmony or in conflict
with what others expect me to be?

GOSPEL » LUKE 1:26–38

In the sixth month of Elizabeth's pregnancy, God sent the angel Gabriel to the Galilean village of Nazareth to a virgin engaged to be married to a man descended from David. His name was Joseph, and the virgin's name, Mary. Upon entering, Gabriel greeted her:

Good morning!
You're beautiful with God's beauty,
Beautiful inside and out!
God be with you.

She was thoroughly shaken, wondering what was behind a greeting like that. But the angel assured her, "Mary, you have nothing to fear. God has a surprise for you: You will become pregnant and give birth to a son and call his name Jesus.

He will be great,
  be called 'Son of the Highest.'
The Lord God will give him
  the throne of his father David;
He will rule Jacob's house forever—
  no end, ever, to his kingdom."

Mary said to the angel, "But how? I've never slept with a man."
The angel answered,

  The Holy Spirit will come upon you,
    the power of the Highest hover over you;
  Therefore, the child you bring to birth
  will be called Holy, Son of God.

"And did you know that your cousin Elizabeth conceived a son, old as she is?
Everyone called her barren, and here she is six months pregnant! Nothing, you
see, is impossible with God."

And Mary said,
  Yes, I see it all now:
    I'm the Lord's maid, ready to serve.
  Let it be with me
    just as you say.

Then the angel left her.

We could all use a greeting like the one Mary gets from Gabriel. "Good morning!
You're beautiful with God's beauty...inside and out!" How could anyone not say Yes
to that?

If it helps you to remember that it's true, write these words down and tape them
to your bathroom mirror. Let them be the divine greeting that invites you to start
your day. If you come to believe these words, they will gradually bloom in you as
your genuine identity: beautiful in God's eyes, wonderful with a beauty that God
personally bequeaths to you. If you come to believe it, as sincerely as Mary did at
home in Nazareth, it will be easier for you to leap up and say Yes to the divine opportunities that grace provides for you. Don't our hearts soften under the gaze of
those who love us best? Don't we surrender more with each encounter to those who
think we're simply wonderful? It's hard to love a cipher. But if you accept that God
created you to be fantastic, doesn't that nudge you a little closer to wanting to live
up to expectations?

> **How do I see myself today,**
> **within the range of "fantastic" to "not so hot"?**
> **Is there a discrepancy between my view of myself**
> **and God's perspective on me?**

THIS TRANSFORMING WORD

WE RESPOND

Original sin may mark us with No, but God's love for us beckons us to Yes. Resolve to say a deliberate Yes to God at least once a day throughout Advent.

Long before we first heard of Christ
and got our hopes up, he had his eye on us,
had designs on us for glorious living,
part of the overall purpose he is working out
in everything and everyone.

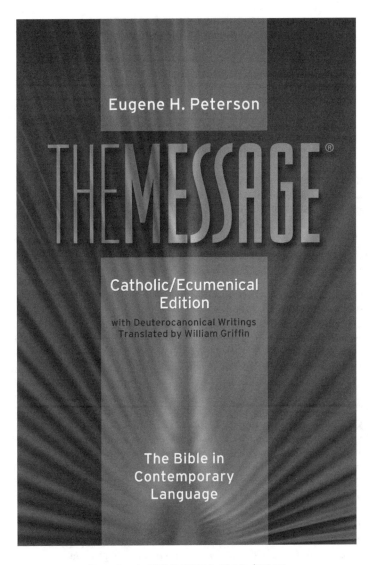

Also by Alice Camille

ISAIAH AND THE KINGDOM OF PEACE
An Illustrated Autobiography for Adults
This unique and stunning "autobiography of the biblical prophet Isaiah captures the intensity, the mysticism, the prophetic faith and wisdom, and the vision of a "kingdom of peace" for those of us living in the twenty-first century. (96 pages, 11 x 14" four color paperback, $19.95)

ANIMALS OF THE BIBLE FROM A TO Z
In this brand-new children's picture book, beautiful artwork from debut artist Sarah Evelyn Showalter depicts 26 animals from the Bible—one for each letter of the alphabet. In the back of the book are chapter-and-verse citations for each letter, where Alice Camille provides "Pages for Grownups" so that parents, grandparents and teachers can explain the significance of each animal. (64 pages, hardcover, $16.95)

INVITATION TO CATHOLICISM
Beliefs + Teachings + Practices
Everyone from inquirers and catechumens to lifelong Catholics will welcome the easy-to-understand, logical explanations found in this clear, concise overview of Catholic beliefs and church teachings. Discussion questions and activities at the end of each chapter make this book ideal for RCIA and adult study groups. (234 pages, paperback, $9.95)

INVITATION TO THE OLD AND NEW TESTAMENTS
A Catholic Approach to the Scriptures
Here are separate award-winning volumes written in language that is both inviting and accessible that help Catholics and others understand the intent and relevance of the Bible for life today. (two 104-page paperbacks, $9.95 each)

THE ROSARY
Mysteries of Joy, Light, Sorrow and Glory
The Rosary contains a series of reflections that explain each mystery and offer practical applications to modern-day life. Camille provides readers with a renewed appreciation of the rosary as a path to love and peace in the new millennium. (112 pages, paperback, $6.95)

Available from booksellers or from ACTA Publications
800-397-2282 • www.actapublications.com